e-flux journal

I0902555

Jalal Toufic

Forthcoming

Second edition

Sternberg Press

Books by Jalal Toufic

What Were You Thinking? (Berliner Künstlerprogramm/DAAD, 2011)

The Portrait of the Pubescent Girl: A Rite of Non-Passage (Forthcoming Books, 2011)

What Is the Sum of Recurrently? (Galeri Nev, 2010)

Graziella: The Corrected Edition (Forthcoming Books, 2009)

The Withdrawal of Tradition Past a Surpassing Disaster (California Institute of the Arts/Roy and Edna Disney/CalArts Theater [REDCAT], 2009; Forthcoming Books, 2009)

Undeserving Lebanon (Forthcoming Books, 2007)

'Āshūrā': This Blood Spilled in My Veins (Forthcoming Books, 2005)

Two or Three Things I'm Dying to Tell You (Post-Apollo Press, 2005)

Undying Love, or Love Dies (Post-Apollo Press, 2002)

Forthcoming (Atelos, 2000)

Over-Sensitivity (Sun & Moon Press, 1996; 2nd ed., Forthcoming Books, 2009)

(Vampires): An Uneasy Essay on the Undead in Film (Station Hill Press, 1993; revised and expanded edition, Post-Apollo Press, 2003)

Distracted (Station Hill Press, 1991; 2nd ed., Tuumba Press, 2003)

Jalal Toufic is a thinker whose influence in the Beirut artistic community over the past two decades has been immense—notwithstanding that, as he put it, many, if not all of his books, most of which were published by Forthcoming Books, "continue to be forthcoming even after their publication." In relation to one of these books, he wondered: "Does not a book titled *Forthcoming* suggest, ostensibly paradoxically, a second edition?" Here's the revised edition of *Forthcoming*, a book first published nearly a decade and a half ago by Atelos press.

—Julieta Aranda, Brian Kuan Wood, Anton Vidokle

In memory of the Nizārī Ḥasan *'alā dhikrihi'l-salām* (on his mention be peace), the Qarmaṭī Abū Ṭāhir Sulaymān al-Jannābī, and the Twelver Shi'ite Abū al-Ḥasan 'Alī b. Muḥammad al-Samarrī

As many as 576,000 Iraqi children may have died since the end of the Persian Gulf War because of economic sanctions imposed by the Security Council, according to two scientists who surveyed the country for the Food and Agriculture Organization.... The results of the survey will appear on Friday in *The Lancet*.

New York Times, December 1, 1995, A6

Each Friday, professors, writers, engineers and students can be found selling off their libraries on its [El Saray Street, Baghdad] sidewalk....

Samir Abu Zaid, a government worker, went one day to sell a favorite book of poems.

"I almost began to cry," he said. "I took my book and ran away."

Los Angeles Times, December 10, 1996

Contents

Avertissement à l'écrivain

Most writers and filmmakers address the social person in us; a small number address the solitary person; but there are others still, rare, who address the one who, for whatever circumstances, is in a state of depersonalization—they accompany someone even when he has deserted himself. Since these instances of depersonalization are rare, and since one often does not wish to be reminded of them, the latter writers and filmmakers, books and films are not popular.

The Threshold of No Return

How not to miss the point—the point of no return? The following symptoms imply that one has neared a threshold to a realm from which one cannot return:

— One feels the urge "to say *who I am*," that "*I am such and such.... Don't mistake me!*" (even when one's "habit, and even more so the pride of" one's "instincts, fundamentally rebels" against doing so [Nietzsche, *Ecce Homo*]); and/or to reiterate and reaffirm one's plans (Alma in Bergman's *Persona*: "I will marry Karl-Henrik and we will have a few children, whom I will raise. That is all determined. It is inside me. There is nothing to worry about"), be they no other than that one day one will return.

— One discovers that one has gone through a lapse of consciousness, if not of being ("Chapter II: Jonathan Harker's Journal [*continued*]. *5 May.*—I must have been asleep, for certainly if I had been fully awake I must have noticed the approach of such a remarkable place"[1]).

— One trips on even ground (Tarkovsky's *The Sacrifice*).

— On the pretext of reacting to the noisy departure or the actual or hallucinated farewell or final warning of those who have just ceased accompanying one (if they are compassionate, they intuitively depart too early and in an arresting manner, "given that at the threshold itself I do not have the chance to deliberate, to make a decision, since I am then and there entranced, thus have no will of my own, and find myself when I come out of the trance already to the other side of the threshold, 'in' the labyrinth, always already 'in' the labyrinth"[2]),[3] one turns one's head backward ostensibly to try to encourage them to accompany one or to bid them farewell or to reiterate one's injunction or entreaty to some, if not all of them to stay behind, but actually to check that one can still turn and, if yes, to reconsider whether to proceed or reckon this turn a leave-taking of turns, of the ability to successfully turn, since thenceforth, owing to over-turns, it is going to be impossible for one to accomplish a turn (the threshold to the realm of over-turns is a point of no return, the limit beyond which turns are over-turned). In Murnau's *Nosferatu*, Harker, who, due to prolonged living with a telepathic wife, hence with someone from whom he was never totally disconnected, had lost the habit of bidding farewell, turned his head backward while crossing the bridge to Nosferatu's castle, ostensibly to look in the direction of the sound made by the two departing Gypsies who had brought him to the Borgo pass but refused to transport him to the other side in their coach. I can easily imagine a remake of *Nosferatu* in which a little (?) farther (?), as far as the protagonist was concerned, he turned on hearing the noisy departure of the coach, yet—as a result of an over-turn—he continued facing in the same direction.

Every Name in History Is I

In memoriam *William S. Burroughs*[4]

To fight the anonymity with which the war enemy is killed even by precision bombing, the soldier has to receive, from their state of being already dead, the calls of the unknown persons who will soon be murdered by him. Such a call is possible in the nonlinear time of undeath. The Jacob Maker of David Blair's *Wax, or the Discovery of Television Among the Bees* (1992) has to receive the call of the two Iraqi tank soldiers at whom he is shortly going to fire a missile during the Gulf War and to whom he is invisible (whether because he is flying a stealth fighter or because the radars of their unit have been blinded). In the state of undeath from which the call is sent, and in the state of death before dying in which it is received, one at times feels: *every name in history is I.*[5] *Every name in history is I* is one way to fight the reduction to anonymity and generality. Jacob Maker's sacrifice does not reside only in dying before dying to access such a call, but also in his becoming oblivious and confused in the realm of the dead as to his initial motives for dying before dying, his gesture getting entangled in the generalized guilt of that state. As long as I, as dead (whether or not before dying physically), have not totally disintegrated into disparate bits of thoughts and affects functioning mostly according to *displacement* and association of sounds, figures, etc., I will try, through the most incredible contortions—which are not felt to be contortions since they are allowed by the nonlinear time and the non-exclusive disjunction reigning in death and dying before (physically) dying—to arrive at a semblance of justice, discovering that I, who will shortly kill, was killed by my anticipated victims: it is because I, as Zoltan Abbasid, was murdered by the (Iraqi) dead taking the form of (Mesopotamian) bees[6] in 1919 that I, Jacob Maker, will take revenge on them in 1991, during the Gulf War, by firing a missile at Iraqi soldiers in a tank, killing them. Vengeance here becomes circular, with the consequence that guilt seems to have been done away with since those concerned are dealing with a series of reactions with no initial action. Yet guilt is neither mitigated nor really dealt with through recourse to this circularity where the constitutive injustice in the realm of the dead—due to the blindness of the vengeance of some of the disparate bits of the minds of the dead—is occulted. Indeed, what most often occurs as a result of the attempt at expunging any trace of guilt through the circularity of mutual wrongdoing is the eruption of an unoriginated guilt ("I was guilty, abominably, intolerably guilty, without cause and without motive"[7]), the formation of a vicious circle of a guilt that "demanded punishment ... [which] consisted, fittingly enough, of being guilty."[8] It is illegitimate and dangerous to generalize from the realm of life to that of undeath or vice versa: if, within limits, life can be just, then can't death as undeath also be just, and, if it can, then shouldn't it be? No, it can't. Although we have to minimize distress, we should not, as long as death as undeath has not been eliminated, have as an ideal to *totally* obliterate perceivable suffering, because that would hide from us the agony of both the dead part of us and the dead. To promote injustice one need not look at nature, with its "survival of the fittest"; one can heed the realm of undeath, with its *survivors* ("He had thought that death would be the end of him. But it was not. Death was the end of the world. To die is to experience the end of the world"[9]), practically all—certainly the practical among them—unfit for that realm of unmotivated, blind, generalized revenge, and then ask: if death is the realm of the blind vengeance of some of the bits of thoughts and affects of the decomposed souls of the dead, why shouldn't life also be unjust, allowing, among other things, for the wholesale slaughter in war? This is the wrong way to reason from undeath to life, for what makes it unjustified to treat me in a substitutive manner is precisely that my specificity as a mortal, that is, as dead while alive, is founded in a basic way on the *every name in history is I* of my death and madness.

Gertrude; or, Love Dies

This play, based on Shakespeare's Hamlet, *was written with Richard Foreman in mind as its director. In case he does direct it, he should play the diegetic role of the theater director. When the play starts, both the theater director and the actor who plays Polonius are already on stage. A tape recorder is visible next to the director.*

ACTOR PLAYING POLONIUS: What are you writing about?

THEATER DIRECTOR: Curtains.

ACTOR PLAYING POLONIUS: How original for a theater director to do that when, like the prompter, curtains are, unfortunately, out!

THEATER DIRECTOR: If by that you mean that I would be instigating some sort of a return of the repressed or some kind of postmodern appropriation, there is nothing original about that. But is the prompter out in theater? Or has he taken other forms, for example, the TAPE in my play *Penguin Touquet*? Also, have you seen Magritte's painting *La Belle Captive* or Lynch's film *Twin Peaks: Fire Walk with Me*? I, a theater director, admire Lynch and Magritte for their curtains.

Fifteen actors enter stage. While fourteen listen to the director's blocking, one, carrying a text of the adaptation, walks, unheeding, straight toward the prompter's box and disappears in it. Shortly, the playwright and an interviewer, carrying each a tape recorder and a microphone, enter stage. For the rest of the play, the playwright and the interviewer occupy the right side of the stage, the others its left side and center. For the most part, the exchanges between the interviewer and the playwright as well as the playwright's asides into his tape recorder take place when the rehearsing actors pause to go over their lines.

THEATER DIRECTOR: Let's resume the rehearsals. We'll redo today the scenes or parts of scenes we had trouble with yesterday.
THE TWO ACTORS PLAYING THE TWO GUARDS AND THE ACTOR PLAYING HORATIO: We saw the spirit of your father.
ACTOR PLAYING HAMLET: Did he fix his eyes upon you?
ACTOR PLAYING HORATIO: No.
ACTRESS PLAYING QUEEN GERTRUDE: I still don't understand why this change in this adaptation from the original "Most constantly" to "No"?
THEATER DIRECTOR: It is because the ghost is overlaid on his whereabouts. Horatio and the two guards misconstrue his averting his gaze as an indication that none of them is the person the late king's ghost is seeking, and thus as an indirect request for someone else: Hamlet. Yet when in the clear air Hamlet stands before the ghost, the latter's gaze is awry with respect to him too. In turn, Hamlet's gaze is askew with regard to the specter even in the absence of the characteristic mist or fog amidst which fictional ghosts appear.
INTERVIEWER (*holding the microphone first to his mouth then in the direction of the playwright*): Do you believe in ghosts?
PLAYWRIGHT: While not an illusion, the ghost of Hamlet's father is the effect of the terminal delusion that a symbolic debt relating to mortality can be settled and thus justice reestablished.
ACTOR PLAYING HAMLET: It is an honest ghost, that let me tell you.

For your desire to know what is between us,
O'ermaster't as you may. And now, good friends,
As you are friends, scholars, and soldiers,
Give me one poor request.

ACTOR PLAYING HORATIO: What is't, my lord?
We will.

ACTOR PLAYING HAMLET: Never make known what you have seen tonight.

THE TWO ACTORS PLAYING HORATIO AND MARCELLUS: My lord, we will not.

ACTOR PLAYING HAMLET: Nay, but swear't.

ACTOR PLAYING HORATIO: In faith, my lord, not I.

ACTOR PLAYING MARCELLUS: Nor I, my lord, in faith.

ACTOR PLAYING HAMLET: Upon my sword.

He holds out his sword.

ACTOR PLAYING MARCELLUS: We have sworn, my lord, already.

ACTOR PLAYING HAMLET: Indeed, upon my sword, indeed.

ACTOR PLAYING THE GHOST (*cries under the stage*):
Swear.

ACTOR PLAYING HAMLET: Ha, ha, boy, sayest thou so? Art thou there, truepenny?
Come on. You hear this fellow in the cellarage.
Consent to swear.

ACTOR PLAYING HORATIO: Propose the oath, my lord.

ACTOR PLAYING HAMLET: Never to speak of this that you have seen ...

PROMPTER: Swear by my sword.

ACTOR PLAYING HAMLET: Swear by my sword.

ACTOR PLAYING THE GHOST (*from under the stage*):
Swear.

They swear.

ACTOR PLAYING HAMLET: *Hic et ubique*? Then we'll shift our ground.
Come hither, gentlemen,
And lay your hands again upon my sword.
Swear by my sword
Never to speak of this that you have heard.
PROMPTER: Swear …
ACTOR PLAYING THE GHOST (*from under the stage*): … by his sword.

They swear.

ACTOR PLAYING HAMLET: Well said, old mole! Canst work i'th'earth so fast?
A worthy pioneer!
PLAYWRIGHT: To listen to a prompter who does not utter the lines only when he senses that the actor has forgotten them, but does so continuously, is to be placed in the structural position of someone who has forgotten the play's lines.
ACTOR PLAYING HAMLET: Why should I listen to the prompter before saying the words "to be, or not to be"? Is this a tribute to Lubitsch's film *To Be or Not to Be*?
THEATER DIRECTOR: In his "to be, or not to be—that is the question," Hamlet forgets what is and is not and neither is nor is not, and as such acts as a messenger between life and death: the ghost. (Is it odd to forget the revenant? Although obsessively enjoining Prince Hamlet to remember, the ghost of King Hamlet is a forgetful creature; any specter who comes back asking for retribution by revealing an ostensibly unknown historical injustice is forgetful of the forgery[10] and substitutions that happen in his prison house, the realm of undeath.) Since Hamlet's "to be, or not to be—that is the question" is a symptom

of obliviousness, you are advised to play it as if you have forgotten it, that is, as if you were waiting for the prompter to remind you of it.

ACTOR PLAYING HAMLET: Should I then play the words, "death, / The undiscovered country, from whose bourn / No traveller returns," in the same manner?

THEATER DIRECTOR: No, because this utterance does not necessarily show that Hamlet has forgotten the specter he encountered, for it could rather indicate that the ghost does not come from that undiscovered country. One cannot return from both *death and the labyrinth*[11]—unless one is resurrected by "the life" (John 11:25). Who then displays to Hamlet some of the characteristics of the dead's prison house?

ACTOR PLAYING POLONIUS (*concerning the diegetic players*): My lord, I will use them according to their desert.

ACTOR PLAYING HAMLET: God's bodykins, man, much better! Use every man after his desert, and who shall 'scape whipping? Use them after your own honor and dignity.

PLAYWRIGHT (*to the interviewer*): Hamlet suspects that the players are not going to follow his instructions, yet he intuits that there may be something redeeming and revelatory about their disregarding them.

ACTOR PLAYING HAMLET (*addressing the three players who are going to perform* The Murder of Gonzago): Anything so o'erdone is from the purpose of playing, whose end, both at the first and now, was and is to hold, as 'twere, the mirror up to nature, to show virtue her own feature, scorn her own image.

ACTOR WHO IS TO PLAY THE KING IN *THE MURDER OF GONZAGO*: I hope we have reformed that indifferently with us, sir.

INTERVIEWER: What are you trying to accomplish with this adaptation of Shakespeare's play?

PLAYWRIGHT: As far as I know, the theoreticians and critics who offered interpretations of *Hamlet* were virtually unanimous about the purport of the play within the play, reducing it to the manifest one that Hamlet explicates in a soliloquy: to catch the king's conscience in a mirror. And yet does Hamlet need a confirmation for himself of what the specter advanced? No: "It is an honest ghost." Through the play, Hamlet wants to catch the king's conscience for others. Any successful play reveals more than the playwright or director intended it to reveal. To read the play within the play—including the dumb show that prefaces it—as manifesting to, and accomplishing for, Hamlet only what he wanted it to manifest and accomplish is to do a great injustice to Shakespeare's art and even to Hamlet. The players "'ll tell all": even that which the ghost could not disclose about "his" prison house.

ACTOR PLAYING HAMLET (*to the actor playing Horatio*): I prithee, when thou seest that act afoot,
Even with the very comment of thy soul
Observe my uncle.

The trumpets sound. Dumb show follows. Enter [players as] a king and a queen very lovingly, the queen embracing him, and he her.

ACTOR PLAYING HAMLET (*aside*): Why are they performing a dumb show? Have I not inveighed in front of them about "inexplicable dumb shows and noise"?

Within the dumb show, the queen kneels, and makes show of protestation unto the king.

ACTOR PLAYING HAMLET: Madam, how like you this play?

ACTRESS PLAYING QUEEN GERTRUDE: The lady doth protest too much, methinks.

ACTOR PLAYING HAMLET: O, but she'll keep her word.

Within the dumb show, the king takes the queen up, and declines his head upon her neck. He lies him down upon a bank of flowers. She, seeing him asleep, leaves him. Anon comes in another man; takes off his crown; kisses it.

ACTRESS PLAYING OPHELIA: What means this, my lord?

ACTOR PLAYING HAMLET: The players cannot keep counsel. They'll tell all.

Within the dumb show, the man pours poison in the sleeper's ears, and leaves him.

ACTOR PLAYING HAMLET: This play is the image of a murder done in Vienna. Gonzago is the duke's name; his wife, Baptista. You shall see anon. 'Tis a knavish piece of work.

Enter the third player, as Lucianus.

ACTOR PLAYING HAMLET: This is one Lucianus, nephew to the king.

ACTRESS PLAYING OPHELIA: You are as good as a chorus, my lord.

ACTOR PLAYING HAMLET: I could interpret between you and your love if I could see the puppets dallying.

The poisoner, along with two men, comes in again. He, along with the others, seems to discover the dead body. The dead body is carried away. The poisoner comes in again with the queen and woos her. She seems harsh awhile, but in the end accepts love. The gestures of the two reflect exactly those of the queen and the late king during the earlier entry. Exeunt (to the side) dumb show.

ACTRESS PLAYING OPHELIA: Belike this show imports the argument of the play.

By now entranced, Hamlet does not answer, but moves somnambulistically—in the manner of a puppet—in the direction of Ophelia.

ACTRESS PLAYING QUEEN GERTRUDE: Forth at your eyes your spirits wildly peep,
And, as the sleeping soldiers in th'alarm,
Your bedded hair, like life in excrements,
Start up and stand on end.
ACTRESS PLAYING OPHELIA: Pale as his shirt, his knees knocking each other,
And with a look so piteous in purport
As if he had been loosed out of hell
To speak of horrors—he comes before me.
PLAYWRIGHT (*to the interviewer*): Having prepared everything to the minutest detail as to both what is to be said by the players and how it is to be performed by them, and readying himself to catch the conscience of the king as the latter apprehends in the play, as in a mirror, his criminal act, Hamlet gets entranced by the doubling he sees in the gestures of the dumb show's two kings, and thus either misses King Claudius's subsequent incriminating reaction to *The Murder of Gonzago*, or—in case the king begins to manifest some subtle reaction already during the dumb show—is unable to

remember what he saw then owing to posthypnotic amnesia.

Hamlet is partly awakened from his trance—but without apprehending what the words signify—by:

ACTOR PLAYING POLONIUS: Lights, lights, lights!

Exeunt (to the side) all but Hamlet and Horatio.

ACTOR PLAYING HAMLET: Didst perceive?
ACTOR PLAYING HORATIO: Very well, my lord.
ACTOR PLAYING HAMLET: Upon the talk of the poisoning?
ACTOR PLAYING HORATIO: I did very well note him.
ACTOR PLAYING HAMLET: Aha! Come, some music!

Enter (from the side) Polonius. Exeunt Horatio.

ACTOR PLAYING POLONIUS: My lord, the queen would speak with you, and presently.
ACTOR PLAYING HAMLET: Do you see yonder cloud that's almost in shape of a camel?
ACTOR PLAYING POLONIUS: By th'mass, and 'tis like a camel indeed.
ACTOR PLAYING HAMLET: Methinks it is like a weasel.
ACTOR PLAYING POLONIUS: It is backed like a weasel.
ACTOR PLAYING HAMLET: Or like a whale.
ACTOR PLAYING POLONIUS: Very like a whale. (*Aside*) Is he still entranced, so that he cannot differentiate between a camel, a weasel, and a whale, or is he being flippant?

The director pushes the playback button.

TAPE: Fittingly the effect of the revelation of generalized substitution is entrancement …
PROMPTER: … a state where one can mistake as identical different things, and as different identical things.

Startled by the interjection of the prompter, the director reflexivily presses on one of the recorder's buttons, but instead of pushing the STOP button, he inadvertently presses the RECORD button, thus replacing what was originally on the tape with the prompter's words. The director pushes again the playback button.

TAPE: … where one can mistake as identical different things, and as different identical things.

Enter Hamlet in his mother's closet.

INTERVIEWER: Why do you need a tape recorder when I already have one?
PLAYWRIGHT: May I remind you that we are on stage—with its asides? (*Aside, into his microphone and recorder*) The dilemma of Prince Hamlet is that he is faced with two monstrous alternatives with regard to his mother's hasty marriage to the brother of her late husband: either a disgraceful lascivious mother or one who has gone far deeper in mourning than him. While in most instances the survivor's substitution of the lost love object signals a resolved mourning, in the remaining cases the survivor's substitution of the lost love reflects the substitutions that the latter undergoes in the undeath realm. It is clear from both the dumb show and the play that follows it, which act as mirrors of the events taking place at the court, that Gertrude begins

a sexual relationship with the brother of her late husband only after the latter's death. Her love for her late husband crosses the threshold of death-as-undeath, following and accepting the substitutions in that realm—where the dead King Hamlet feels *every name in history* [including Claudius] *is I*—so that she no longer perceives any difference between the two brothers, despite their different physiognomies. In the case of *Hamlet*'s Gertrude, love dies, that is, accompanies beyond the threshold of death (Orpheus and *Hamlet*'s Gertrude are, in different manners, counterexamples to the tagline of Coppola's *Bram Stoker's Dracula*, "Love Never Dies")! Hamlet's intuition of this indiscernibility of infidelity and fidelity with regard to the dead[12] dissuades him from killing his mother. While King Claudius's "with mirth in funeral and with dirge in marriage" is merely diplomatic and sly, it accurately and literally applies to the queen's behavior. Although Prince Hamlet's reconciliation with his mother is already virtually established by the time he sees and is entranced by the indistinguishability of the gestures of the two brothers vis-à-vis the queen in the dumb show, he makes yet another effort to recuperate the difference that would allow him to take revenge.

INTERVIEWER: So?

PLAYWRIGHT: Oh, let us set what I said aside.

INTERVIEWER: No, please, I am very interested.

PLAYWRIGHT: Carmelo Bene recalls in an interview Cocteau's proposition that the artist is an exhibitionist among the blind. Don't you agree that it is easier to be that on the stage, with its asides, than in the world at large?

THEATER DIRECTOR (*addressing the actress playing Gertrude*): Up till she learns from Hamlet that her late husband died an unnatural death, Gertrude should be played as an entranced woman. Her entrancement is deepest when she hears Claudius say to Hamlet: "You are the most immediate to our throne, ... our son."

ACTRESS PLAYING QUEEN GERTRUDE: Hamlet, thou hast thy father much offended.

ACTOR PLAYING HAMLET: Mother, you have my father much offended.

PLAYWRIGHT (*to the interviewer*): While Hamlet's conscious innocence is superimposed on unconscious guilt relating to more or less repressed Oedipal incestuous desires for his mother, to whom he confesses, "And, would it were not so, you are my mother" (he also says to Ophelia: "I could accuse me of such things that it were better my mother had not borne me"), and murderous wishes toward the one who declared regarding him, "You are the most immediate to our throne, ... our son"; in relation to her marriage to the brother of her late husband, Gertrude's conscious guilt, revealed by her "our o'er-hasty marriage," is overlaid on unconscious guiltlessness, which is related to the circumstance that the dead assumes all the names of history.

ACTRESS PLAYING QUEEN GERTRUDE: Why, how now, Hamlet?

ACTOR PLAYING HAMLET: What's the matter now?

ACTRESS PLAYING QUEEN GERTRUDE: Have you forgot me?

ACTOR PLAYING HAMLET: No, by the rood, not so!
You are the queen, your husband's brother's wife,
And, would it were not so, you are my mother....
You go not till I set you up a glass
Where you may see the inmost part of you.

PLAYWRIGHT: This is merely the inmost part that can be reached by a glass, thus not the inmost part that, as in the case of the vampire, would not appear in the mirror.

INTERVIEWER: I have been told by some people, including the actor playing Polonius in your adaptation, that you despise much of contemporary theater.

PLAYWRIGHT: "I hate to be bothered when I am thinking about death." (*Aside, into his microphone*) Howard Barker's General Holofernes orders Judith to undress. She finds it prohibitively difficult to do so, most probably because she feels that people who do so would be "so humiliated in their nakedness." She says: "As if I were before the mirror and not before—(*She freezes*)." (The play's directions are often less those, explicit, in italics, than the ones to be gleaned from the characters' lines.) Is she thus also encouraging herself to undress? An average director, not to speak of the legions of mediocre actors and actresses, would play these words as if she is interrupted, implying that the continuation would be: "... his eyes." Who is before the mirror and not before it? Which figure has provided us with this image? It is the vampire, and the undead in general. That is one site where and one sense in which the parting from the body evoked in the title of Barker's play—*Judith: A Parting from the Body*—applies: here it is a parting from her body (the title covers another sense when she later parts from the dead, severed—thus parting from itself—body of Holofernes). Toward dawn, she insists on having sex with the corpse of the murdered Holofernes. May curtains fall before the audience members of a future adaptation by some director other than Barker are tempted to tarry and witness the *jouissance* of the dead (Judith) fucking the (headless) dead (Holofernes).

ACTRESS PLAYING QUEEN GERTRUDE: What wilt thou do? Thou wilt not murder me?
Help, help, ho!

Enter Ghost.

ACTOR PLAYING HAMLET: Save me and hover o'er me with your wings,
You heavenly guards! What would your gracious figure?
ACTRESS PLAYING QUEEN GERTRUDE: Alas, he's mad!
ACTOR PLAYING HAMLET: Do you not come your tardy son to chide,
That, lapsed in time and passion, lets go by
Th'important acting of your dread command?
O, say!
PROMPTER (*aside*): The presentment that by avenging the ghost of his father he would project him indefinitely into generalized substitution inhibits or at least delays Hamlet's revenge, resulting in his being late in avenging the late King Hamlet. Only those who persist in being insensitive to this generalized substitution in the undeath realm are in principle able to take a swift revenge. (*To the ghost*) Do not forget ...
ACTOR PLAYING THE GHOST: Do not forget. This visitation
Is but to whet thy almost blunted purpose.
But look, amazement on thy mother sits.
O, step between her and her fighting soul! ...
Speak to her, Hamlet.
ACTOR PLAYING HAMLET: How is it with you, lady?
ACTRESS PLAYING QUEEN GERTRUDE: Alas, how is't with you,
That you do bend your eye on vacancy,
And with th'incorporal air do hold discourse?

ACTOR PLAYING HAMLET: Do you see nothing there?

ACTRESS PLAYING QUEEN GERTRUDE: Nothing at all; yet all that is I see.

PLAYWRIGHT: It is because Gertrude is already virtually to the other side of death that she, unlike the guards and Horatio, does not see the revenant who is coming back to ask for retribution.

Exit Ghost.

PLAYWRIGHT: Not suspecting that her late king was murdered, she does not sense that he is not in the realm of substitutions and intermingling of identities, in undeath, but rather in the realm between life and death, a revenant, one who thus still asserts his identity, declaring to Hamlet, "I am thy father's spirit," and his difference from others, saying about Claudius, "A wretch whose natural gifts were poor / To those of mine!" so that her replacement of him by Claudius is an infidelity. Once she suspects that he was murdered, she would perceive his specter were it to appear again.

PROMPTER (*to Hamlet*): Nor did you nothing hear?

ACTOR PLAYING HAMLET: Nor did you nothing hear?

ACTRESS PLAYING QUEEN GERTRUDE: No, nothing but ourselves.

ACTOR PLAYING HAMLET (*drawing his sword*): How now, a rat? Dead for a ducat, dead!

He makes a thrust through the arras and kills Polonius.

ACTOR PLAYING POLONIUS: O, I am slain!

ACTRESS PLAYING QUEEN GERTRUDE: O me, what hast thou done?

ACTOR PLAYING HAMLET: Nay, I know not. Is it the king?
ACTRESS PLAYING QUEEN GERTRUDE: O, what a rash and bloody deed is this!
ACTOR PLAYING HAMLET: A bloody deed—almost as bad, good mother,
As kill a king, and marry with his brother.
ACTRESS PLAYING QUEEN GERTRUDE: As kill a king!
ACTOR PLAYING HAMLET: Ay lady, it was my word.
(*He parts the arras and discovers the dead Polonius*) Thou wretched, rash, intruding fool, farewell!
I took thee for thy better.
ACTOR PLAYING KING CLAUDIUS: Polonius may utter in the undeath realm: "I, Claudius."
THEATER DIRECTOR: That's not your line.
ACTOR PLAYING KING CLAUDIUS: Sorry.
THEATER DIRECTOR: That too is not your line.
ACTOR PLAYING HAMLET (*addressing the queen*):
Look here upon this picture, and on this,
The counterfeit presentment of two brothers....
This was your husband. Look you now what follows:
Here is your husband; like a mildewed ear,
Blasting his wholesome brother. Have you eyes?
Could you on this fair mountain leave to feed,
And batten on this moor? Ha! Have you eyes?
You cannot call it love, for at your age
The heyday in the blood is tame, it's humble,
And waits upon the judgment; and what judgment
Would step from this to this? Sense, sure, you have,
Else could you not have motion. But sure that sense
Is apoplexed. For madness would not err,
Nor sense to ecstasy was ne'er so thralled

But it reserved some quantity of choice
To serve in such a difference. What devil was't
That thus hath cozened you at hoodman-blind?
Eyes without feeling (*he sees Polonius's eyes and proceeds to shut them*) ...

ACTRESS PLAYING QUEEN GERTRUDE: O Hamlet, speak no more.
Thou turnest mine eyes into my very soul,
And there I see such black and grained spots
As will not leave their tinct.

PLAYWRIGHT: Hamlet ends up making her faithful to the ghost and to the historical memory of his murdered father, but unfaithful to the late dead-as-undead king and oblivious to the substitutions and forgery underwent by the dead.

THEATER DIRECTOR (*to the actor playing Hamlet*): I repeatedly told you to look awry at the ghost, and (*he turns toward and addresses the actress playing Gertrude*) I repeatedly told you to assume as much as possible, with all your interlocutors, the demeanor of a zombie, since that is how the queen is described by Hamlet: "Sense sure you have, / Else could you not have motion. But sure that sense / Is apoplexed.... / Eyes without feeling ..." Yet just moments ago you were acting vivaciously, and just moments before that (*now addressing the actor playing Hamlet*) you were once again looking straight at the actor rehearsing his role as the ghost. We can't go on like this!

Appendix: A Fourth Wall that Proved to Be a Radical Closure's Gateless Gate

Exeunt the director in frustration, but not toward the wings, rather in the direction of the auditorium, where he sits in a reserved front row seat. The actor who was playing Hamlet follows him with his eyes, then turns abruptly, having heard a sound.

ACTOR WHO WAS PLAYING HAMLET: Nor did you nothing hear?
ACTRESS WHO WAS PLAYING THE QUEEN: No, nothing but ourselves.
ACTOR WHO WAS PLAYING HAMLET (*drawing his sword*): How now, a rat? Dead for a ducat, dead!

Having plunged his mock sword in the prompter's box, he begins moving in the direction of the director.

SOURCELESS VOICE: You go not till I set you up a glass.

He hesitates after a few steps ...

ACTRESS WHO WAS PLAYING THE QUEEN: *What Did He See?* I mean: What did he hear?

He manages to gather enough determination to move ahead, hits against the fourth wall and falls.

ACTRESS WHO WAS PLAYING THE QUEEN: Bravo! That was the best miming gesture I have seen you perform.
THE TWO ACTORS WHO WERE PLAYING HORATIO & MARCELLUS: Why don't you cross to the other side? Why are you acting as if there is a glass wall between us and the audience?[13]
ACTOR WHO WAS PLAYING HORATIO: Was that line yours? I don't feel it was mine, but I also do not feel that I was reading your mind.
ACTOR WHO WAS PLAYING MARCELLUS: That is exactly how I too feel. It is as if that line was inserted in my mind. We both had this

momentary concordance through a thought that belonged to neither!

The actor who was playing the ghost walks in the direction of the director. He recoils before exiting the stage.

ACTOR WHO WAS PLAYING MARCELLUS: How did it feel when you reached that *gateless gate*?

ACTRESS WHO WAS PLAYING OPHELIA: Did you feel you were touching a glass wall, the way certain schizophrenics feel sometimes on touching people or things? Or did you feel that finally you were touching space itself?

ACTOR WHO WAS PLAYING THE GHOST: I underwent a sort of anesthesia at that point. Can one cross a space where one feels absolutely nothing? I got there; I must have felt nothing and recoiled into feeling.

ACTOR WHO WAS PLAYING HAMLET: This stage's a prison.

ACTOR WHO WAS FUNCTIONING AS THE PROMPTER: So, here we are ...

ACTOR WHO WAS PLAYING THE GHOST: Where here?

ACTRESS WHO WAS PLAYING THE QUEEN (*looking around*): How would I know? "Here" is a deictic, a shifter.

The other actors also begin to look around. Foreman's characteristic strings appear all of a sudden and span the theater space in several directions.

ACTRESS WHO WAS PLAYING OPHELIA: Look, strings!

ACTOR WHO WAS FUNCTIONING AS THE PROMPTER: What are they doing here?

Following the appearance of the strings in the radical closure delimited by the fourth wall as a gateless gate, the characters' movements follow only the paths of the strings, whereas before they could trace other trajectories.

THE THREE ACTORS WHO PERFORMED *THE MURDER OF GONZAGO*: It is ironic that we, who contrary to the diegetic director's instructions tried but failed to impersonate the characters psychologically while holding "as 'twere the mirror up to nature," have become imprisoned in this space, exactly as if we were fictional characters who cannot exit the diegetic world to the real world.

ACTOR WHO WAS PLAYING HAMLET: But why did he become so cross with us when in his adaptation of *The Murder of Gonzago* he makes the actors disobey director Hamlet's instructions, going back to their customary ways of acting, and this disobedience discloses a deeper characteristic about melancholia and the realm of undeath?

ACTRESS WHO WAS PLAYING OPHELIA: Look, words!

Two balloons containing visible words have irrupted, one in the space next to the mouth of the actor who was playing Hamlet, and another one between the two actors who were playing Horatio and Marcellus. To whom do the latter words and the thought they articulate belong?

ACTOR WHO WAS PLAYING THE GHOST: Describe them. How do they feel? Are they physical? If so, of what substance?

ACTOR WHO WAS PLAYING THE KING IN THE DUMB SHOW: How would he be able to describe them if the words he would use for the description turn out themselves to be material and external to him?

ACTRESS WHO WAS PLAYING OPHELIA: Vmber ... a heaue, a kissing hill ... so loued Arm'd ... sully and hot, or my complection ... trennowed.

ACTOR WHO WAS PLAYING HAMLET: Words, words, words.

Curtains suddenly appear amidst the performers and between them and the playwright and his interviewer; the latter curtain functions as a demarcation of one of the limits of the radical closure. Some of these curtains seem similar to the ones in Magritte's paintings Evening Falls, *1964, and* Mona Lisa, *1967, and in Lynch's films* Blue Velvet, *1986, and* Twin Peaks: Fire Walk with Me, *1992.*[14]

One cannot predict in relation to any specific performance of a written play instancing a radical closure whether any extra text is going to irrupt during the performance other than through improvisation by the performers (if such an extra text does irrupt, it is experienced as a thought insertion by the performer who utters it). Their interactions having gradually resulted in their becoming invisible behind the curtains on the stage's left side and center, a front curtain closes in two stages at the end of the performance: first hiding the playwright and the interviewer from view—so that all there remains visible on the stage are the curtains[15]*—then the whole stage.*

If You Prick Us, Do We Not Bleed? No

Dedicated to the living memory of Gilles Deleuze, a non-revengeful philosopher

Have we *not* eyes? No: "He [a Japanese man]: 'You saw nothing in Hiroshima. Nothing.' She [a French woman visiting the city]: 'I saw *everything*. *Everything*.... The hospital, for instance, I saw it. I'm sure I did....' 'You did not see the hospital in Hiroshima. You saw nothing in Hiroshima' ... 'Four times at the museum in Hiroshima.... I ... looked thoughtfully at the iron ... made vulnerable as flesh ... [at] anonymous heads of hair that the women of Hiroshima, when they awoke in the morning, discovered had fallen out....' 'You saw nothing in Hiroshima. Nothing.'"[16] (Marguerite Duras, *Hiroshima mon amour*) (Ludwig Wittgenstein: "If a blind man were to ask me 'Have you got two hands?' I should not make sure by looking. If I were to have any doubt of it, then I don't know why I should trust my eyes. For why shouldn't I test my eyes by looking to find out whether I see my two hands? What is to be tested by what? [Who decides what stands fast?]")[17] Have we *not hands*[?] No—the man without hands in Patrick Bokanowski's *L'Ange*. *Organs*[?] No—Daniel Paul Schreber: "I existed frequently without a stomach; I expressly told the attendant M., as he may remember, that I could not eat because I had no stomach. Sometimes immediately before meals a stomach was so to speak produced *ad hoc* by miracles. This was done particularly by von W.'s soul, which in at least some of its forms sometimes showed a friendly spirit towards me. Naturally this never lasted long; the stomach which had been produced by miracles, in any case only an inferior stomach, was usually removed again miraculously by v. W.'s soul during the meal 'because of a change of mind'; great changeability is a marked feature of the soul-character, absolutely divine rays perhaps excluded. Food and drink taken simply poured into the abdominal cavity and into the thighs, a process which, however unbelievable it may sound, was beyond all doubt for me as I distinctly remember the sensation. In the case of any other human being this would have resulted in natural pus formation with an inevitably fatal outcome; but the food pulp could not damage my body because all impure matter in it was soaked up again by the rays. Later, I therefore repeatedly went ahead with eating unperturbed, without having a stomach.... Of other internal organs I will only mention the *gullet* and the *intestines*, which were torn or vanished repeatedly, further the *pharynx*, which I partly ate up several times."[18] *Dimensions*[?] Not if one is subject to "the Alice in Wonderland syndrome, [which is] named for Lewis Carroll's titular character, [and which] is a disorder characterized by transient episodes of visual hallucinations and perceptual distortions, during which objects or body parts are perceived as altered in various ways (metamorphopsia), including enlargement (macropsia) or reduction (micropsia) in the perceived size of a form. Such episodes are of short duration (generally less than an hour), variable frequency (up to several times per day), and unpredictable onset."[19] *Senses*[?] Not if one is a yogi who has achieved *pratyahara* (Sanskrit: "withdrawal of the senses"), "in the Yoga system of Indian philosophy, [the] fifth of the eight stages intended to lead the aspirant to *samadhi*, the state of perfect concentration. The goal of *pratyahara* is to arrest the reaction of the senses to external objects, thus helping to isolate and free the mind from the involuntary intrusions caused by sensory activity. The mind does not cease to experience external phenomena but merely experiences them directly through its own intensified powers of concentration instead of through the mediation of the senses."[20] *Affections*[?] No—the Septimus of Virginia Woolf's *Mrs. Dalloway* "had gone through the whole show, ... European War, death, had won promotion, was still under thirty and was bound to survive. He was right there. The last shells missed him. He watched them explode with indifference. When peace came he was in Milan, billeted in the house of an innkeeper with a courtyard, flowers in tubs, little tables in the open, daughters making hats, and to Lucrezia, the younger daughter, he became engaged one evening when the panic was on him—that he could not feel. For now that it was all over, truce signed, and the dead buried, he had, especially in the evening, these sudden thunder-claps of fear. He could not feel."[21] *Passions*[?] Not if we have achieved Spinoza's third kind of knowledge: "This kind of knowledge proceeds from an adequate idea of the formal essence of certain attributes of God to an adequate knowledge of the essence of things. So ... we readily conceive how effective against the emotions is clear and distinct knowledge, and especially the third kind of knowledge whose basis is the knowledge of God. Insofar as they are passive emotions, if it does not completely destroy them, at least it brings it about that they constitute the least part of the mind" (*Ethics*, Part II, Scholium 2, and Part V, Proposition 20, Scholium).[22] *Fed with the same food*[?] No: "All painted buddhas are actual buddhas.... Because the entire world and all phenomena are a painting, human existence appears from a painting, and buddha ancestors are actualized from a painting. Since this is so, there is no remedy for satisfying hunger other than a painted rice-cake" (Zen master Dōgen, "Painting of a Rice-cake").[23] *Hurt with the same weapons, subject to the same diseases, healed by the same means*[?] No, Daniel Paul Schreber was hurt by the voices ("To be torn from the cell in the middle of the night in order to be drowned was another terrifying possibility which occupied my imagination, indeed was forced on to me by what was said by the voices"[24]; "there had been times when I could not help myself but speak aloud or make some noise, in order to drown the senseless and shameless twaddle of the voices, and so procure temporary rest for my nerves"[25]), and asserted in his memoirs, "Even now I am convinced that I am immune to all natural disease influences; disease germs only arise in me through rays and are removed again in the same way by rays,"[26] and, "One distinguished 'searing' and 'blessing' rays; the former were laden with the poison of corpses or some other putrid matter, and therefore carried some germ of disease into the body or brought about some other destructive effect in it. The blessing (pure) rays in turn healed this damage."[27] *Warmed and cooled by the same winter and summer as a Christian is?* No: "Junkies always beef about *The Cold* as they call it, turning up their black coat collars and clutching their withered necks.... Pure junk con. A junky does not want to be warm, he wants to be Cool-Cooler-COLD. But he wants The Cold like he wants His Junk—NOT OUTSIDE where it does him no good but INSIDE so he can sit around with a spine like a frozen hydraulic jack ... his metabolism approaching Absolute ZERO"[28] (William S. Burroughs). *If you prick us, do we not bleed?* No, or at least not necessarily because of the prick. Was my video *'Āshūrā': This Blood Spilled in My Veins*, 1996, with its documentation of ritualistic bloodletting, a demonstration that Shi'ites too can bleed? If indeed a demonstration, it would be one only for the benefit of the Israelis, so that they would be able to ascertain that we too bleed without having to bombard us in south Lebanon. With my affinity to Shi'ism, I certainly do not need such a demonstration since, irrespective of any wounds suffered in my life (whether as a result of bombardments or otherwise), I already feel even the blood in my veins to be spilled blood, that is, that I am bleeding in my veins. But *'Āshūrā': This Blood Spilled in My Veins* is not really a demonstration that if pricked, Shi'ites bleed: I am not a revengeful person. A disturbance is introduced in the ostensibly rhetorical question, "If you prick us, do we not bleed?" by those who, although they bleed, do so without being pricked or wounded: the stigmata of some saints and of some hysterics of the psychosomatic type; the blood spilled *in* my veins, someone affined to Shi'ism. In Shakespeare's *The Merchant of Venice*, the lawyer informs the Jew Shylock, a revengeful person (Salarino: "Why, I am sure, if he forfeit, thou wilt not take / his flesh: what's that good for?" "... If it will feed nothing else, / it will feed my revenge. He hath disgraced me, and / hindered me half a million; laughed at my losses, / mocked at my gains, scorned my nation, thwarted my / bargains, cooled my friends, heated mine / enemies; and what's his reason? I am a Jew" [Act 3, Scene 1]), that he is indeed permitted by the contract signed by his debtor Antonio to cut one pound of flesh from the latter's body, but that he has to do so without spilling one jot of blood, otherwise he would be persecuted for the attempted murder of a Christian. Did I need to reach the latter part of the discourse of Portia-as-lawyer when she lists all the punishments that Shylock is to suffer to know that she is a revengeful person? Was it not enough her implying to Shylock during her defense of Antonio: "If you prick us [Christians], do we not bleed?"? Shylock's desistance from making an incision in Antonio's flesh to take one pound of it—for fear of spilling blood and of possibly causing the death of a Christian—is still a revengeful gesture. Could not only revenge but also revengefulness have been stopped? Had Shakespeare's play proceeded not with the lawyer's refusal of Shylock's belated proposal to settle for money, and the subsequent revengeful long list of punishments, ranging from religious—conversion—to financial, imposed on him by the lawyer; but, to everyone's surprise, including still untouched Antonio, with the latter's sudden bleeding—whether in a saintly manner (along roughly the same area that was pierced by a lance in crucified Jesus's body) or hysterically—at the precise contours of the area specified in the contract, revengefulness on both sides could possibly have been stopped. Untouched Antonio's bleeding at the precise contours of the specified area for the incision would have provided Shylock with the opportunity to take revenge, since he could then have cut the pound of flesh and nothing would have incontestably proven that the spilled blood is from the wounds inflicted by him (in this play where a woman and her maid assume the role of a male lawyer and his subordinate, where Shylock's daughter disguises herself as a man, etc., the blood from an externally inflicted wound in Antonio's side would have been indiscernible from blood seeping psychosomatically or in a saintly manner [from the same area that was pierced by a lance in crucified Jesus's body]). Untouched Antonio's bleeding at the precise contours of the specified area for the incision would have made apparent to all those present, including Shylock and the lawyer, that when pricked Antonio does not bleed *as a result of that*. Such bleeding would have provided Shylock with the opportunity to take revenge while taking away from him the revengeful logic of similarity. Would psychosomatic bleeding have stopped the Christian Phalangists, and their accomplice, the Israeli army, from massacring the Palestinians in the Sabra and Shatila refugee camps? *If you tickle us, do we not laugh?* I, for one, don't, and not because I am depressed, but because I find this historical period largely so laughable that were I to start laughing I am afraid I would not be able to stop. I remember how when high on marijuana my ex-girlfriend would giggle virtually at everything on and on. I never had this kind of extended laughter on the few instances I smoked pot. Yet I am sure that were I to start laughing in my normal state of consciousness, my laughter would certainly surpass hers. As for her, there was no danger of her starting laughing and not managing to stop, dying of it: she did not find present-day societies that laughable. All I ask of this world to which I have already given several books is that it become less laughable, so that I would be able to laugh again without dying of it—and that it does this soon, before my somberness becomes second nature. This era has made me somber not only through all the barbarisms and genocides it has perpetuated, but also through being so laughable. Even in this period of the utmost sadness for an Arab in general, and an Iraqi in specific, I fear dying of laughter more than of melancholic suicide, and thus I am more prone to let down my guard when it comes to being sad than to laughing at laughable phenomena. The humorous thinker Nietzsche must have been living in a less laughable age than this one for him to still afford the sublimity of: "To see tragic natures sink and *to be able to laugh at them*, despite the profound understanding, the emotion and the sympathy which one feels—that is divine." In a laughable epoch, even the divinities are not immune to this death from laughter: "With the old gods, they have long since met their end—and truly, they had a fine, merry, divine ending! They did not 'fade away in twilight'—that is a lie! On the contrary: they once—laughed themselves to death! That happened when the most godless saying proceeded from a god himself, the saying: 'There is one God! You shall have no other gods before me!'" (Nietzsche, "Of the Apostates," *Thus Spoke Zarathustra*).[29] At this point in history, can one still laugh on reading Nietzsche, Beckett, Thomas Bernhard? Has this age not deprived us of a major facet of these works: their humor? Can present-day humorous people still find Richard Foreman's work, or for that matter my early work humorous—without dying of that? All funny people in laughable periods are not humorous enough; to find the most humorous people in such a period one has to look among the serious, who *need* this seriousness not to expire in laughter. In this respect, I reached a critical point on June 20, 1996. I was standing in a fairly long line at a checkout counter at the Ralphs supermarket on Wilshire and Bundy, Los Angeles. Amidst the many magazines on the adjoining rack, I saw the current issue of *Time*. Its cover story was: "America's 25 Most Influential People." Flipping through the pages to get to the section in question, I was suddenly seized by an apprehension verging on anxiety: that starting to laugh on reading some of the listed names I would not be able to stop, even my aroused seriousness proving this time inadequate to do the job as a defense mechanism. Four months later, I still do not know whether the intense apprehension I felt then was warranted. But from that day on an even more heightened vigilance against starting to laugh has become one of the salient features of my life.[30] *If you poison us, do we not die?* No, we cannot die absolutely from poisoning, whether because we have unfinished business (in a restrained perspective: treacherously murdered King Hamlet; or an extended one: the death and rebirth cycles of Hīnayāna Buddhism); or because we have become fundamentally liberated from any unfinished business, and now when in life are fully in life, when in death are fully in death, life not leading to death, death not leading to life (Zen master Dōgen: "It is a mistake to suppose that birth turns into death. Birth is a phase that is an entire period of itself, with its own past and future.... Death is a phase that is an entire period of itself, with its own past and future.... In birth there is nothing but birth and in death there is nothing but death" ["Birth and Death" (*Shōji*)]). Were we only the living, who at some future date simply biologically die and are no more, there would be only the revengeful morality of identification (don't we too cry, laugh, biologically die, etc.?) to prevent us from murdering others and to prevent others from murdering us. What should persuade us against murder is rather that we are mortals, hence already undead even as we live, and that as undead we undergo *every name in history is I*. The question that directly follows the preceding ones from *The Merchant of Venice* is: *and if you wrong us shall we not revenge?* How insightful of Shakespeare to have detected and intimated that such a manner of thinking that dwells on similarity is a revengeful one. It is revengeful neither simply because one can take revenge only on what has senses, affections, etc., i.e., on one who can be affected by the revenge; nor just because revenge is one more similarity (*if we are like you in the rest, we will resemble you in that* [Act III, Scene I]); but as such. Yes, ultimately, every discourse that invokes a fundamental similarity is a revengeful one, is a discourse of revenge. Nietzsche wrote: "A little revenge is more human than no revenge at all"[31] ("Of the Adder's Bite," *Thus Spoke Zarathustra*). Wouldn't that be also because humanism (don't we too reason,[32] weep[33] ... ?) is revengeful, regardless of any wrong suffered, and even or especially when it invokes a tolerant coexistence based on a fundamental similarity? And aren't many of the aforementioned manners of saying no to such revengeful questions experiments in evading or undoing the generalized revengefulness around[34]—unfortunately, in some instances failing and resulting in yet other, novel kinds of revenge.[35]

Forthcoming

While the God of the Nizārīs and the En-Sof of the cabalists are certainly beyond speech, unspeakable, the Apocalypse or Hell (see the Bible, the Qur'ān, Dante, Hieronymus Bosch, many accounts by schizophrenics, etc.), and therefore the concentration and extermination camps, are not unspeakable (even if one is able to write and speak concerning them only with a voice-over-witness[36]). It is not speaking about the surpassing disasters of the atomic devastation of Hiroshima, the Rwandan genocide, Auschwitz, the Khmer Rouge 1974–1977 rule in Cambodia, the genocidal US-imposed UN sanctions on Iraq, etc., that is indecent; it is any implied attendant disregard of the consequent withdrawal. The tact of Resnais/Duras's *Hiroshima mon amour* is that while showing some of the effects and aftereffects of the nuclear conflagration of Hiroshima and speaking about it, it stresses that there has been a withdrawal: "You have seen nothing in Hiroshima."

What is appropriate past the surpassing disaster is either a "more sober, more factual ... 'grayer' language" (Paul Celan), or the dazzling, colorful language of the messianists.

One way of viewing the difference in Islam between the esoteric (*bāṭin*) and the exoteric (*ẓāhir*) is to consider it a consequence of individual spiritual encounters and events alerting some Muslims to other meanings of what they might otherwise have taken only in a literal sense: this is what one encounters in Sufism. But Sufism did not initiate the differentiation between the *bāṭin* and the *ẓāhir*; such a distinction first appeared among "extremist" Shi'ites (*ghulāt*). The battle of Ṣiffīn between the fourth caliph, 'Alī b. Abī Ṭālib, and the renegade Mu'āwiya was tilting toward a victory by the caliph, when Mu'āwiya ordered his army both to raise all the available *maṣāḥif* (copies of the Qur'ān) on their lances and to say: "Their contents are to be authoritative in our dispute." This order was given in 657, barely twenty-five years after Muḥammad delivered to his community the last revealed words: "This day have I perfected for you your religion and fulfilled My favor unto you ..."; and only a few years after the recension of the canonical version of the Qur'ān in the final years of the third caliph, 'Uthmān b. 'Affān (d. 656)! Lo and behold the five hundred or so copies of the Qur'ān available to the Syrian army were raised on lances. What Mu'āwiya hoped for happened. Led by a band of Qur'ān reciters (*qurrā'*) in 'Alī's camp, a large group of the caliph's followers pressured him to put a stop to the battle. The Qur'ān, extensively cited by many of the combatants during their declamations preceding their individual duels, continued to be cited during the debate concerning whether or not to discontinue the battle. I imagine that becoming weary of resisting the obstinate and insolent pressure of the dissenters, and feeling deserted by many of his followers, 'Alī was on the point of acquiescing when, catching the unsettling sight of the copies of the Qur'ān on the lances, he, known for his vaticinal gifts, had a vision of horsemen shouting with reverence his name while trampling Qur'ān copies and slaughtering pilgrims. I imagine him disconcerted to hear in the vision the *'Alī* of helpless invocation screamed by some of the pilgrims (who, at the approach of the end, were letting go of their *taqiyya* [dissimulation] and disclosing their allegiance to him and his descendants) echoed by the triumphant *'Alī* of the terrific horsemen who struck nonetheless. Instead of persuading him to consent, such a vision would have made him more vehement in his insistence that the battle resume. I envision him saying to the dissenters: "If we do not unintentionally trample the *maṣāḥif* now, in the commotion of the battle, they are certainly going to be intentionally trampled, and justifiably so, around and in the Kaaba itself. I see this happening as I see you." Only after being threatened with murder by Mis'ar b. Fadakī al-Tamīmī and Zayd b. Ḥusayn al-Tā'ī, al-Sinbisī, and a band of *qurrā'*, "'Alī, respond to the Book of God when you are called to it. Otherwise we shall indeed deliver you up entirely to the enemy or do what we did with Ibn 'Affān," did 'Alī, aware, through the quite recent example of the murder of the third caliph, of the catastrophic consequences such an assassination would have on the fledgling Muslim community, acquiesce. "Do not forget that I forbade you to do this, and remember your words to me." One group at the battle of Ṣiffīn remained largely unaware that the Qur'ān was affected fundamentally by being inserted in the conflict: the Umayyads—one more indication of their distance from and basic indifference to the Qur'ān. Another group, the proto-Khārijīs, whose nucleus was the band of reciters of the Qur'ān in 'Alī's camp, intuiting the danger of withdrawal, asserted all the more vehemently the absoluteness of the Qur'ān, refusing the subsequent arbitration between 'Alī and Mu'āwiya, since the Book should and can be the sole arbitrator. Only the (proto-)Shi'ites were really attuned to this gesture, sensing that the Qur'ān had somewhat been withdrawn. The fundamental difference between Shi'ism and Sunni Sufism, giving them their different tones, is not so much the displacement of the spiritual leader from the imām in Shi'ism to the shaykh/pole in Sufism, but that they largely came to esotericism by different routes: the latter mainly through unveiling (*kashf*) and taste (*dhawq*); the former mainly through a withdrawal of the literal.[37] The following words were attributed to the sixth imām, Ja'far al-Ṣādiq: "Coming from Him, this Word [the Qur'ān] returns to Him." His imāmī disciple Hishām b. al-Ḥakam declared: "The Qur'ān is an abrogated concept ... which left the Prophet's Companions and returned to heaven when they apostatized and established Abū Bakr [the first caliph] in place of 'Alī."[38] The dubious gesture of the Umayyads, purported to unite all Muslims around the Qur'ān, instead separated that sacred book from itself by implicating it in the divisiveness and the catastrophic battle. Among the differential symptoms and consequences of the withdrawal of the Qur'ān according to various Shi'ite sects, one can note:

— Viewing it as created, differentiating between it and *Umm al-kitāb* (the Archetype/mother of the book) as the transcendent, uncreated word of God, limiting the withdrawal to the former.

— Differentiating between a *ẓāhir* and a *bāṭin*, a differentiation reportedly introduced by Abū Hāshim 'Abd Allāh, a grandson of 'Alī, and that goes far beyond the basic distinction mentioned in the Qur'ān between sūras that are *muḥkamāt* (clear) and ones that are *mutashābihāt* (ambiguous).

— The primacy given in certain Shi'ite sects to the esoteric sense over the exoteric one, with a consequent downgrading of the messenger Muḥammad:

in Ismāʿīlīsm, Muḥammad is considered just the legislator of the Qur'ān in its exoteric, literal sense, with ʿAlī and the other imāms raised in rank to become those who alone know its esoteric meaning.

— The Ismāʿīlī belief in "cycles of occultation" (*adwār al-satr*), during which the esoteric meaning is concealed behind an exoteric one.

— The discarding of the exoteric sense for the esoteric sense(s), the sole legitimate one even when it is the exact opposite of the literal sense.

— The view of many of the *ghulāt*, but also of such pre-Buwayhid Twelver Shiʿite authors as the Nawbakhtīs and al-Kulaynī that the Qur'ān, in the guise of the canonical version recenced under ʿUthmān, is somewhat forged, parts of it having been altered, and parts not included, suppressed. The faithful recension of the Qur'ān, initially detained by ʿAlī and passed through his descendants, the imāms, is going to be publicly revealed only with the parousia of the presently occulted twelfth imām.

— The Ismāʿīlī notion of the cyclical abrogation of one prophetic legislation by a subsequent one, a descendent of ʿAlī and Ḥusayn being the one who abrogates the revealed legislation of Muḥammad (this in spite of the insistence in Muslim dogma that Muḥammad is the seal of the prophets). This abrogation had its most sublime form in the Great Resurrection of Alamūt and other Nizārī strongholds from 1164 to 1210; it also took place briefly in Yemen under the *dāʿī* ʿAlī b. al-Faḍl.

— The trampling of the *maṣāḥif* around the Kaaba itself in 930 by Abū Ṭāhir Sulaymān al-Jannābī's Qarmaṭīs. The Qarmaṭīs' trampling of the Qur'ān, an action that orthodox Sunni theologians and writers prefer to attribute solely to attempts by Persian, Hellenic, and other non-Arab elements in the land of Islam to subvert the conquering religion, is the reflection, in the distorted mirror of the surpassing disaster, of the placement of the Qur'ān on the lances by the Umayyads in 656. These are two images of a parallel montage across around three centuries.

When the Umayyad army raised the *maṣāḥif* on their lances, they said: "Who will protect the frontier districts of the Syrians if they perish, and who those of the Iraqis if they all perish?" But were the Arab Muslims spared by the raising of the *maṣāḥif* on the lances and the subsequent cessation of the battle? The answer to the sparing of Muslims by the Qur'ān in the battle of Ṣiffīn was the slaughter of the pilgrims by Abū Ṭāhir al-Jannābī's Qarmaṭīs in 930. As customary with the general population, they were offended and scandalized by the Qarmaṭī action but not by the Umayyad one. Can one have enough contempt for the general population? I would answer with a categorical "No" were it not for my knowledge that these people are also mortals, therefore already undead, and thus cannot be limited to their petty measure as living common people.

The same phenomenon of withdrawal of tradition due to the surpassing disaster is encountered in Judaism following the expulsion of all professing Jews from Spain in 1492; the forced mass baptism of the Jews of Portugal in 1497;[39] and the mass reprisals against Jews in Poland during the 1648 Ukrainian revolt, led by Bohdan Chmielnicki (aka Bohdan Khmelnytsky), against the extremely oppressive Arenda system of land use in which many Jews were implicated—these latter events were experienced as particularly depressing and unfortunate since according to many cabalists basing their calculation on *gematria*, 1648 was to be the year of the redemption. This withdrawal is intimated in the messianic movement around Sabbatai Zevi.

"Radical" Sabbatians advocated the systematic violation of the Torah, now viewed, in contradistinction to the Torah of *atzilut*, of the messianic time, as the Torah of *beriah*, of the unredeemed world. From the perspective of the surpassing disaster, the Torah has been withdrawn and this withdrawal has to be made plain through the Torah's transgression or even through apostasy—the latter extreme step required the surpassing disaster of the apostasy of the messiah himself (messianism is a problematic response to the surpassing disaster, not least because it often itself turns into a no less devastating catastrophe). Thus the conversion of some "radical" Sabbatians, the Frankists, to Catholicism; and, following Sabbatai's example, of some others to Islam: the Dönme. It is characteristic of the bigoted journalist Elie Wiesel that he should inveigh against the Sabbatians in his preface to a fiction book on Jacob Frank.[40] He, the ostensible upholder of tradition and memory after the surpassing disaster of the Shoah, the self-proclaimed emissary of the dead, has no appreciation that the Sabbatian response is a just, albeit problematic, reaction to a surpassing disaster—can any genuine response to a surpassing disaster be other than problematic? It is disingenuous and simpleminded to divest oneself from Sabbatians, Nizārīs, and Qarmaṭīs by branding them nihilists. Past the withdrawal of tradition following a surpassing disaster affecting Islam, all Muslims are placed in the position of nihilists, whether they care to assume expressly such nihilism or not; past the withdrawal of tradition following a surpassing disaster affecting Judaism, all Jews are placed in the position of nihilists. Indeed, past the withdrawal of tradition following a surpassing disaster, it is those who do not clearly assume explicitly the nihilism into which they have willy-nilly been placed who are the most treacherous nihilists (Wiesel is more insidious than the reportedly sinister Jacob Frank). Nizārīs and Qarmaṭīs, who abrogated the Muhammadan revealed religion and its law, are Muslims, for it is in reaction to Muslim surpassing disasters that their abrogations were enacted. Similarly, and notwithstanding the bigoted view of their Jewish opponents, "radical" Sabbatians are Jews because their transgressions of the religious law and even their conversions were the consequence of their sensing that Jewish religion and tradition have withdrawn due to the preceding surpassing disasters affecting Judaism, including the apostasy of the Messiah. Excommunicated, the Frankists engaged in several disputations with the rabbis. If I had to side with one of the two antagonistic parties, I would certainly concur with the Sabbatians that they, including those among them who converted to Islam or Christianity, were then legitimately who they called themselves: *the believers* (*ma'aminim*). At that point the rabbis were the unbelievers through their continued belief in a tradition and a religious law that, owing to their withdrawal past the surpassing disaster and in the absence or failure of their resurrection, had become counterfeits of themselves, with the consequence that it had become as sinful to still follow the commandments of the law as it was previously obligatory to act in accordance with them. This reversal, which was also enacted by the Nizārīs under imām Ḥasan *'alā dhikrihi'l-salām*, started with Sabbatai's "strange actions," which included causing ten Israelites to eat "fat of the kidney" in 1658, an act which is strictly prohibited by the Torah and punishable by "excision" (getting cut off from among one's people); reciting the following benediction over the ritually forbidden fat,

"Blessed are Thou, O Lord, who permittest that which is forbidden"; and, in 1665, abolishing the fast of the Seventeenth of Tammuz. It progressed to the abrogation of the Lurianic devotions, "which had now become not only obsolete but almost positively sinful";[41] and culminated in the conversion of the "radical" Sabbatians to Islam or Christianity. The Sabbatians' response to the surpassing disaster revealed that the majority of the official rabbinical authorities, customarily considered the elite, belonged to the common people, those not sensitive to the withdrawal due to the surpassing disaster. I include among the common people those rabbis who excommunicated or banned Sabbatai Zevi solely for abrogating the Law; I do not include among them those rabbis who excommunicated Zevi or endorsed his excommunication not for transgressing the Law and the prohibitions of the Torah, but because he proclaimed himself the Messiah. Nizārīs and Qarmaṭīs are Muslims, and the Sabbatians are Jews, also because their abrogations fundamentally affected respectively Muslim and Jewish religions. The reinstatement of the Sharī'a in 1210 by the grandson of Ḥasan *'alā dhikrihi'l-salām* can be viewed as a diplomatic move to ward off the intensifying threat to his initiates from a Sunnism again on the ascendancy, the Nizārīs again resorting to *taqiyya* while maintaining their esoteric beliefs; or as due to a new cycle of *satr* (occultation); or as a realization that enlightenment and salvation can only be achieved by individuals[42]—in which case the subsequent amalgamation of Ismā'īlī Shi'ism and Sufism would not be solely a result of the Mongols' destruction of the Nizārī strongholds and their persecution of the surviving Nizārīs in the Sunni empire they established. But it is also possible that the abrogation of the Law—a response to the latter's withdrawal—contributed toward its resurrection, and therefore toward its reinstatement forty-six years later. Those Qarmaṭīs who returned to the fold of traditional Islam after the debacle of the episode of the false messiah Zakariyya al-Iṣfahānī with its abrogation of the Muhammadan revelation could validly do that because the preceding Qarmaṭī reaction contributed to resurrecting that religion and its sacred books and places. Those who returned to the fold after the devastating apostasy of Sabbatai did so possibly successfully because of the redeeming measures the Sabbatians took in gauging the measure of the disaster. The rabbinical authorities and the 'ulamā' had the last word because what the Sabbatians, Nizārīs and Qarmaṭīs did probably resurrected what was withdrawn.

The withdrawal of the holiness of Palestine past a surpassing disaster affecting Jews is clear in the Sabbatian outlook, where for the majority of the adherents, including Nathan of Gaza, there was an opposition to the notion of immigration to the Holy Land, which opposition became even more intense in the aftermath of Sabbatai's apostasy, turning toward the middle of the eighteenth century into a distinct anti-Palestinian bias especially among the Frankist wing.[43] Indeed, one of the theses the Frankists submitted in their disputation with the rabbis in Kamenets-Podolsk from June 20 to 28, 1757, was: "We do not believe that Jerusalem will ever be rebuilt." One still finds lapses in the vigilant sensibility to the surpassing disaster even among the Sabbatians: the notion advanced by some of them that one should immigrate to the Holy Land because breaking the Law in Jerusalem is a more effective transgression is still a (negative) stress on, and thus continuing election of, the traditional specialness of the land of Palestine. Similarly, an objection to immigrating to Palestine in terms of eschewing a *forcing of the* [messianic] *end* through the ingathering of the exiles—one of the preconditions for or changes of the messianic era—implies a continuing election of the traditional specialness of the land of Palestine—unless the advanced reason be merely a pretext not to go to a land one senses no longer to be the Holy Land. It is from the standpoint of the withdrawal of the holiness of Mecca that one is to interpret and evaluate the symbolic setting of the pulpit to face west on the day when the Great Resurrection was proclaimed in Alamūt, a direction opposite to the one toward which all Muslims have to turn during their prayer; and, in an even more valid manner (since the Nizārīs' placement of the pulpit precisely in the opposite direction to the Kaaba in Mecca can still be construed to give a negative emphasis to the latter, at least to still refer to it), the sacking and desecration of the Kaaba by the Qarmaṭīs, and their transfer of the Black Stone to their capital, al-Aḥsā'. Can one easily displace the *axis mundi*, which is the closet spot to Heaven on earth, and which cannot be truly viewed outside its complements in the World of the Archetypal Form (*'ālam al-mithāl*), and which is circumambulated not by humans but by angels?[44] I think that the Qarmaṭīs' action was not to consecrate a new *axis mundi*, but to indicate the withdrawal of the traditional one as a consequence of a surpassing disaster.[45] If the Nazi "final solution" to the "Jewish question" was a surpassing disaster, then a withdrawal of the holiness or special traditional significance of Jerusalem has ensued. Therefore the question that intrigues me is not the hypocritically naive one, "How did victims of a racist state (Nazi Germany) become racist oppressors?" but rather: How is it that the surpassing disaster of the Shoah has not produced a widespread attitude among Jewish artists, writers, and thinkers that reveals the withdrawal of the traditional holiness or specialness of a particular land, more specifically of Jerusalem? While a good number of Jewish writers and thinkers have written about the death of God in Auschwitz, rare are those who have written or talked about the demise of the holiness of the land (it seems it is more difficult to relinquish belief in the holiness of a certain land [and in the messiah] than in God!). Notwithstanding the sanctimonious discourse of those Jews who while underscoring the Shoah encourage or at least condone the renaming of occupied Palestinian cities, towns, and villages with Biblical names, and decry the remissness in accomplishing the ingathering of the exiles through the *aliyah*, the ascent to the Holy Land, it is to the Jews' honor that the Diaspora has continued despite the establishment of the state of Israel. I believe that many Jews have not gone to Israel owing to an intuition of this withdrawal rather than because they had become assimilated in the host countries, or because of the dangerous and harsh conditions in the early years of the establishment of the state of Israel, or because of ethical and political qualms concerning the colonial origin of that state as well as its continuing expansionist and racist policies toward its neighboring countries and its brutal illegal occupation of Palestinian land.[46] The continuing Zionist discourse, in its emphasis on tradition and on the ultra-special significance of the land of Palestine; let alone the ultra-orthodox view of Gush Emunim and Rabbi Zvi Yehuda Kook that the establishment of the state of Israel in Palestine is a religious messianic event are thus an obliviousness to the "Final Solution" as a surpassing disaster, through its treatment as a vast, extreme catastrophe with localized effects. The ambivalence that many of the Zionists in Palestine betrayed toward the survivors of the Shoah,[47] especially during the early years following World War II and the establishment of the state of Israel, is to be ascribed not only to a wish to forget the figure of the Jew as a passive victim, but also, possibly, to an intuition that the more the Shoah is underscored and pondered, the more it would reinforce the feeling of the withdrawal of the holiness or simply traditional ultra-special significance of the land of Palestine. Thus while it is fitting that there are memorials to the Shoah at Treblinka, Auschwitz, and in the United States, home to around a third of contemporary Jewry, it is unsettling and dismaying to encounter such memorials in Israel, the "Jewish state" (Jerusalem's Yad Vashem, Nathan Rapoport's *Scroll of Fire* [1971], the Day of Holocaust and Heroism [*Yom Hashoah Vehagvurah*], etc.): only if, consequent of the surpassing disaster of the Shoah, Israel is no longer viewed as the holy land, would the presence of memorials to the Shoah there be valid. One can easily argue that unlike the Qarmaṭīs who were in the tenth century a formidable military power, the Jews, up to the recent establishment of the state of Israel, were in no position to desecrate Jerusalem to reveal the withdrawal of its holiness, for instance by possibly further damaging the remains of the Wailing Wall. But they are in a position to do that now. Yet I do not see any response on their part that comes close to what the Qarmaṭīs did (certainly some of the ultra-orthodox view the secular situation in Jerusalem as already a sort of desecration—but they condemn such a condition).

When it comes to surpassing disasters, the damage is never only the material one; it is also, especially in past eras, the withdrawal of spiritual guides and allies, and of divinities. Reportedly, shortly before his death, the last deputy of the twelfth imām, Abū al-Ḥasan ʻAlī b. Muḥammad al-Samarrī (d. AH 329/940–41), received a note from the imām saying: "In the name of God. O ʻAlī b. Muḥammad al-Samarrī … do not appoint anyone in your place, since the complete occultation has taken place." When Shiʻites came and asked him about his successor, he said: "The matter is in the hands of God, and He will bring it to accomplishment." The Greater Occultation of the twelfth imām was thus ushered in.[48] It is crucial in relation to a certain Shiʻite and Jewish rhetoric of powerlessness and victimization that not only continues unabated even during periods when these communities have achieved political ascendancy, but sometimes intensifies despite that ascendancy, that one take into account that the patterns of response the chronic persecution of these two communities must have inculcated in them cannot fade in a short period. In turn, it is critical that one unmask the hypocritical abuses to which such a rhetoric can lead. In turn, it is vital that one not become oblivious of the withdrawal past a surpassing disaster, which is the reason that would validate the continuation of such a rhetoric. Could the mighty empire and great civilization of the Safavids have genuinely and legitimately, rather than hypocritically, experienced itself as an empire and civilization of disaster? Yes, it could have. Did it experience itself in that manner? Yes, it partly did, since for many Twelver Shiʻites in the great Shiʻite state that was Safavid Iran, the determinant circumstance continued to be the withdrawal of the imām. Once the Greater Occultation began, either it is persisting, in which case the notion, position, and function of the *Nāʼib al-ʻāmm* (the general representative of the Hidden Imām) assumed by the ʻulamāʼ (who argued that what has been canceled by the twelfth imām is not the function of representative as such, but that of an individual representative, of the *Nā'ib khāṣṣ*) is a travesty; or else there is a *Nā'ib al-'āmm* and thenceforth the assumption of a continuing Greater Occultation should be replaced by that of the resumption of the Lesser Occultation. Who among the ayatollahs and 'ulamā' has the audacity to clearly instigate this move, which entails an imminent parousia? At one level, there is a manifest and crucial difference between on the one hand Twelver Shi'ite Safavid Iran, and on the other hand the Nizārī state during the Great Resurrection (1164–1210), the Qarmaṭī state during the Zakariyya al-Iṣfahāni episode in Aḥsā', and the Fatimid state. In the former, past the initial period of the extremist view of the Shah as the imām himself, especially among his Turkmen followers, the Qizilbash, and prior to the time when the notion and function of the *Nā'ib al-'āmm* was introduced—a move alleviating the occultation of the imām—the sensibility to the withdrawal, in the guise of the imām's occultation, continued despite Shi'ite rule; in the latter three, the imām was present in the world in the form of their leader. And yet even in the Nizārī Alamūt of the proclamation of the Great Resurrection, an intimation of withdrawal was maintained, however transiently, amidst the manifestation of the esoteric sense: in his *Khutba* on the 17th of Ramaḍān, during which he proclaimed the Great Resurrection abrogating the Muhammadan religious legislation, Ḥasan *'alā dhikrihi'l-salām* placed himself as the imām's *khalīfa* (deputy). It is only later that his son and successor, Nūr al-Dīn Muḥammad II, explicitly claimed the imāmate for his father and for himself. The process by which the Great Resurrection was proclaimed may be considered sloppy from the strict perspective of the messianic advent as a supernatural event: Ḥaṣan *'alā dhikrihi'l-salām*'s speaking in the name of another could then be fully ascribed to his having been successfully pressured during the reign of his predecessor and ostensible father, Muḥammad b. Buzurg-Ummīd, to publicly divest himself both from the claim that he was the imām and from those of his followers who were making such a claim on his behalf; and/or to a reluctance on his part to assume such a momentous role. But from the perspective of the conflation of a withdrawal past a surpassing disaster with a messianic manifestation, that Ḥasan *'alā dhikrihi'l-salām*'s announcement of the manifestation of the esoteric sense and the abrogation of the exoteric Law is done in the name of another, the still hidden imām, is not sloppy, but rigorous and precise, since it allows, at least until he himself is clearly declared the imām, the maintenance of the tone of withdrawal even amidst the messianic epiphany. The surpassing disaster produces a withdrawal of tradition, which the one proclaimed Messiah/Qā'im "merely" enunciates.[49] In which case, if there is an ominous imprecision to be resisted, it is the danger of mistaking the proclamation of the abrogation to be a performative rather than a description of what has already taken place owing to a surpassing disaster: the messiah/Qā'im does not annul the Law but manifests a condition that has already occurred, namely that the Law has withdrawn. The *Khutba* of Ḥasan *'alā dhikrihi'l-salām*, in Alamūt, with its two-step revelation, minimized this danger.

According to a Talmudic saying, the son of David would appear only in a generation that was "either wholly sinful or wholly righteous"; and in Islamic tradition, the Mahdī is going to fill with justice an earth filled with oppression. If the messiah appears in a generation that is wholly righteous, the manifestation of the esoteric, barred under the law of the cycle of occultation, ushers in the messianic era proper, the cycle of epiphany. The abortive manifestation of the esoteric in a generation that is not wholly righteous can function as an occult sign that the parousia is near, since it indicates that the world has been totally given over to impiety: the highest, secret name of God has so much withdrawn that even its manifestation won't reveal it. *Taqiyya* (dissimulation) and the discipline of the arcane are no longer mandatory in the aftermath of the surpassing disaster, since they are already implemented by the consequent withdrawal. As long as *taqiyya* is still obligatory, the withdrawal has not become maximal and the time of the messianic revelation has not yet come. It is the circumstance that the first manifestation did not reveal anything that announces the necessity of the messianic ushering in of the cycle of epiphany. In such a situation, the messianic manifestation has to be done twice: once, abortive, to intimate the time of total occultation; another, auspicious, the messiah having received, in complement to the holy *nefesh*, *ruah*, and *neshamah*, which he already had, the highest soul-light, the *yehifah*,[50] thus becoming capable of inaugurating the period of redemption.

The surpassing disaster (for the Shi'ites, the slaughter of imām Ḥusayn [imām 'Alī's son and the grandson of the prophet Muḥammad] with most of the prophet's family and many of his companions, etc.; for the Jews, the destruction of the Temple, the *galut* [exile], the expulsion from Spain, etc.) does not, and perhaps cannot, remain an external circumstance. It sooner or later becomes internal: the surpassing disaster for the Ismā'īlīs is the delay in the answer of the Second Emanation in a Gnostic drama in Heaven, which delay produces its retardation to the tenth rank and its subsequent attempt to catch up and ascend again to the third rank;[51] the surpassing disaster for the Lurianic cabalists is the *breaking of the vessels* that were supposed to contain the supernal light, this leading to the dispersal of sparks of that light in the *qelippah*, the demonic realm.

Have the desertion of West Beirut by the Arabs and the rest of the world during the 1982 Israeli invasion of Lebanon, and the continuing sanctions against Iraq, now [1996] in their sixth year, divested these two communities of the rest of the Arab world, undoing any notion of an Arab community? If so, is it accurate on my part to have written in the first edition of my book *Over-Sensitivity* that the conjunction of catastrophes affecting the Arab world in Iraq, Sudan, Lebanon, and earlier Palestine added up to a surpassing disaster? Is the tradition for such communities no longer the one that used to be theirs, but the other communities of the surpassing disaster: Gnostics, Nizārīs, Qarmaṭīs, Sabbatians? Unfortunately, these communities, which have tried to deal with the withdrawal consequent of a surpassing disaster, have been subjected to another kind of withdrawal, a material one enforced by their orthodox enemies: most of the works of the Nizārīs, Qarmaṭīs, and Sabbatians have been burned or destroyed (the Mongols' destruction of the library of Alamūt, etc.).

In his *Heidegger and the "jews,"* setting it against the activism of the resistance fighter Robert Antelme, Lyotard appreciates the attitude of the Jews of Sighet, Romania, on the eve of their deportation to the concentration camps, as described by Elie Wiesel in his book *Night*: obliviousness to the imminent catastrophe—an attitude widespread among Jews then. Unfortunately, the dichotomy Lyotard sets is not only between the Jewish community of Sighet and the community of Jewish resistance fighters, but also between Wiesel and Antelme. To set the latter dichotomy, one has to be colordeaf—and in case one is as attuned to timbre as Lyotard is, one has to colordeafen oneself—to Wiesel's critical tone in *Night* concerning his community's attitude. The discernment of such a tone—an easy enough task for the impartial—would spare one, particularly in a book addressing the shock induced by the depth of Heidegger's involvement with the Nazis, from being taken aback by Wiesel's subsequent lauding of the activism shown by the Israelis, and his total embrace of the actions of the Israeli army in a series of flagrantly prejudiced articles.[52] When the obliviousness to the surpassing disaster continues past it, is it permissible to wax appreciative about such obliviousness? Wiesel's failure to feel the Shoah as a surpassing disaster is shown not only in his extremely negative attitude to the Sabbatians, but also in his very positive attitude to the Zionist enterprise and his unquestioning adherence to the state of Israel.[53] "But Jalal, How can you write about an obliviousness on his part? Are you forgetting Wiesel's express 'This is why I write certain things rather than others: to remain faithful'[54]?" Is it simple to remain faithful to the dead, who, undergoing *every name in history is I*, thought-insertion and doubling, are betraying themselves, betrayed by themselves (Bertolucci's *The Spider's Stratagem*)? Wiesel: "I owe the dead my memory. I am duty-bound to serve as their emissary.... Not to do so would be to betray them."[55] To think and write about the dead as they were when still alive is already a forgetfulness of them—as undead. Wiesel: a bigoted, hypocritical sort of Horatio. How much filtering out and repression of the dead is going on in Wiesel's books for him to think that the dead need an emissary, and to pompously feel the duty to be that emissary. Were Wiesel to harken more, he would discover that while playing his role of the emissary of the dead, they are already interfering with his discourse on them as they were when they still lived. One has to have died before dying to encounter modes of the dead-as-undead, those who do not know and are alien to the laws of the living, the sort of entities Judge Schreber encountered. Were the author of *Twilight*—a novel purportedly revolving around the mad and madness and largely set in an asylum, but that at no point induces in the reader any feeling of anxiety, of the uncanny—to encounter the insertion of ostensibly alien thoughts in his head, and to hear unsolicited voices at inopportune moments that speak in the name of people who died in the concentration camps but sometimes exchange obscene remarks in lascivious, demonic tones (the dead are in one of their modes obscene, as obscene as the Nazi guards at concentration camps), would he listen to them? Would he not so much welcome them—who can welcome the uncanny?—as try not to repress their talk as quickly as possible? Were Antonin Artaud, Maurice Blanchot, Pierre Klossowski, Judge Schreber, the Jean Genet of *L'Atelier d'Alberto Giacometti*, or the author of *(Vampires): An Uneasy Essay on the Undead in Film* to have proclaimed themselves emissaries of the dead, this would be barely bearable; but that Elie Wiesel should do that is the epitome of the derisory. But precisely none of these authors would claim to be the emissary of the dead; they are aware how indecent it is to talk for the dead. Even such a revengeful spirit as Hamlet's dead father has the decency not to do so: "But that I am forbid / To tell the secrets of my prison-house [including of "myself" as dead], / I could a tale unfold whose lightest word / Would harrow up thy soul, freeze thy young blood.... / But this eternal blazon must not be / To ears of flesh and blood." Even the dead (as revenant) does not speak in the name of the dead (as undead); even the ghost, ostensibly a revenant, is not allowed to speak about himself or herself as dead, to fully be his or her own emissary. But then the revengefulness of the ghost of Hamlet's father is as nothing compared to that of Wiesel. Can one blame Wiesel for that revengefulness? No; but neither does one have the right to accept gullibly what he proffers and confer on him the Nobel Peace Prize. The vengefulness of the living is somewhat determined, and limited; even when seemingly indiscriminate, it usually spares someone: one's child, mother, or the stranger. That the vengefulness of the revenant is motivated, a demand for a specific retribution, would thus indicate that the ghost still belongs, however tenuously, to life, that he is not fully a creature of the undeath realm. And when we encounter such sort of restricted vengefulness in the writings of someone, we can be sure that he or she does not speak in the name(s) of the dead (in the undeath realm), for the revengefulness of the latter is not circumscribed. The latter vengefulness is of no use to the revengeful living human, all too human Wiesel. What is also of no use to Wiesel with regards to mortality is that "everything mortal expresses defenselessness. It is just as clearly inscribed above the head of a young bird as above the skull of a human petrified by evil and stupidity. But it requires great spiritual strength to see the likeness and the correlation in it" (Vilhelm Ekelund). The Nazi concentration camp guards, and the torturers in Israeli, Bosnian Serb, and Iraqi prisons are indefensible, that is, both infinitely exposed as mortals (that is, as dead while alive), and, notwithstanding the vile justification the Nobel Peace laureate and journalist Wiesel gives through one of his characters in his book *The Fifth Son* for the torture of Palestinians by the Israeli army ("Now Ilan is convinced: the thought, the prospect of not suffering worries the terrorist. Yet he does not appear stupid. Ilan doesn't understand, but he hides his irritation. Then, he sees a shudder quick as lightning go through the prisoner. It lasts only a fraction of a second but Ilan notices. What is he so afraid of if it is not suffering? And suddenly, the answer is obvious: he wants to suffer. He has prepared himself for suffering, for torture, probably for death. The reason? Perhaps to set an example. To lengthen the list of Palestinian martyrs. To feed anti-Israeli propaganda. And also to force the Jewish adversary to practice torture, therefore to betray himself, therefore, to choose inhumanity"[56]), unjustifiable.

In collaboration with students, Jochen Gerz collected extensive data on the Jewish cemeteries that were in use up to the National Socialist dictatorship. Between April 1990 and May 1993, during the night and with no authorization, the students removed cobblestones from the pathway to the entrance of the Saarbrücken castle, temporarily replacing each with a substitute. After incising on the underside of each removed stone the name of one of the cemeteries, they secretly placed it back in the path, the name facing down. The result was *2146 Stones—Monument against Racism, Saarbrücken*. One can discern in this monument and memorial both withdrawal (the most complete list of Jewish cemeteries in pre-Nazi Germany is provided in an unavailable form)[57] and (through the undetected temporary substitution of the stones) the ever present possibility that what one takes to be what was made available/alive again through resurrection is not what was withdrawn/dead but merely a counterfeit or imposter. Past a surpassing disaster, the memorial and memory are, even when resurrected following their withdrawal, subtly affected with some discredit and disgrace through the ever present possibility that one day one would have the impression that the memorial is a fake and that the memory is a false memory. What would have corroborated that Jesus was "the life" (John 11:25) was not simply that on saying, "Lazarus, come out" (John 11:43), the recognizable body of Lazarus came out from the grave in which Lazarus was buried several days earlier, but also that following the latter's resurrection not once did any of those who met the ostensible brother of Mary and Martha feel, whether fleetingly or for an extended period, that he was not really Lazarus, but a double, a counterfeit—a threat present in any resurrection by anyone other than *the life*.[58]

In countries, such as Bosnia, Lebanon, or Rwanda, that have suffered a brutal civil war, one encounters myriad cases of traumatized survivors. Many of these survivors seek psychiatric treatment to regain a cathexis of the world, including of tradition and culture in general. But that subjective working through cannot on its own succeed in remedying the withdrawal of tradition, for that withdrawal is not a subjective symptom, whether individual or collective, and therefore cannot be fully addressed by psychiatrists or psychoanalysts, but demands the resurrecting efforts of writers, artists, and thinkers. Without the latter's contribution, either the psychiatric treatment fails, or else though the patient may leave ostensibly healthy, he or she soon discovers that tradition, including art, is still withdrawn.

With regard to the surpassing disaster, art acts like the mirror in vampire films: it reveals the withdrawal of what we think is still there. "You have seen nothing in Hiroshima" (Duras's *Hiroshima mon amour*, 1961).[59] Does this entail that one should not record? No. One should record this "nothing," which only after the resurrection can be available. We have to take photographs even though because of their referents' withdrawal, and until their referents are resurrected, they are not going to be available as referential, documentary pieces—with the concomitant risk that facets relating to the subject matter might be mistaken for purely formal ones. A vicious circle: what has to be recorded has been withdrawn, so that, unless it is resurrected, it is going to be overlooked; but in order to accomplish that prerequisite work of resurrection to avert its overlooking, one has initially to have, however minimally, perceived it, that is countered its withdrawal, that is, resurrected it. But how can one speak of a withdrawal of civil war Beirut buildings when refugees still noticed and lived in them? Yet aren't these refugees, who are marginalized because of their lack of political power and their economic destitution, affected with an additional overlooking through their association with these withdrawn buildings? The Lebanese's overall obliviousness and indifference to documenting the carnage through photographs, films, and videos cannot be fully explained by the circumstance that toward the end of the civil war they must have grown habituated to the destruction around them, as well as by the fact that many of these ruined areas were declared military zones, off-limits to cameras. Can photographs of these withdrawn buildings become available without resurrecting their withdrawn referents? It seems such photographs become themselves withdrawn.

There is going then to be "a time of development" of the chemically developed photographs taken during the latter stages of the war. The documentation is for the future not only in the sense that it preserves the present referent for future generations, but also in that it can function as a preservation of the referent only in the future, only when the work of resurrection has countered the withdrawal. He thought that until such photographs become available, one of the appropriate sites for their exposition would be the Stewart Gardner Museum, Boston, next to the spaces left blank following the March 18, 1990, theft of several famous paintings from the museum, thus confronting the viewer with two different kinds of unavailability, a material and an immaterial one. While in the West there has been a proliferation of new museums (Mario Botta's San Francisco Museum of Modern Art; Frank Gehry's Guggenheim Museum, Bilbao, Spain; Steven Holl's Kiasma Museum of Contemporary Art, Helsinki, Finland; Steven Holl's Knut Hamsun Centre, Prestied, Norway; Hans Hollein's Museum of Modern Art, Frankfurt, Germany; Daniel Libeskind's Felix Nussbaum Museum, Osnabrück, Germany; Richard Meier's Getty Center, Los Angeles ...); extensions to existing museums (Daniel Libeskind's Jewish Museum, an extension of the Berlin Museum; the Grand Louvre Project [1981–1999], which involved the doubling in size, to 60,000 m^2, of the exhibition areas of the museum ...); new libraries (Sandy Wilson's British Library, St Pancras, London;[60] Dominique Perrault's Bibliothèque nationale de France; Mete Arat and Hans-Dieter and Gisela Kaiser's German National Library, Frankfurt am Main ...); and cataloguing and inventorying, as exemplified by Macmillan's *The Dictionary of Art* (1996), with its thirty-four volumes, 41,000 articles, 6,802 contributing scholars, and 15,000 black-and-white illustrations, Afghans, Bosnians, and Iraqis have been divested of much of their artistic tradition, not only through material destruction, but also through immaterial withdrawal. Even were substantial parts of the contents of both the National and University Library and the Oriental Institute in Sarajevo to somehow be recovered (in the form of copies that happened to be on loan to other libraries or of microfilm copies of the originals in other libraries ...),[61] this would not be enough to make them once more fully available. Increasingly in the West, absence is affected with a mode of presence through telepresence and telesensing; increasingly in the "developing" countries, presence is affected with an absence through the (negative) matting due to the withdrawal of tradition past surpassing disasters.

After the surpassing disaster, while the documentation of the referent is for the future, the presentation of the withdrawal is an urgent task for the present. If he tried to document specifically Beirut's *Aswāq* (in the central district), it was not that this area was particularly—as a possible consequence of the severe damage it had undergone—withdrawn, but because large sections of it were in imminent danger of being erased without true deliberation, to provide space for the construction of a new city center. He had to explicitly show that some of these severely damaged and/or ruined buildings had withdrawn: as a preventive measure against others, although ostensibly perceiving them, unconsciously acting as if they weren't there. To allow the discussion about the future condition of these severely damaged and/or ruined buildings not to be a foregone oversight, it was crucial not only to criticize the financial interests at stake and the subjective wish to forget whatever had strong associations with so many individual and collective traumas, but also to either resurrect these buildings or make manifest their withdrawal through art and architectural works, so that they would still be available for the argument against their demolition. What contributed to the failure to save these severely damaged and/or ruined buildings in the *Aswāq* area was that artists and filmmakers managed neither to resurrect them nor to manifest their withdrawal, so that the withdrawal not having become explicit, hence not having become a factor that one could consciously and intentionally try to counter when thinking and planning the future of the city, these withdrawn buildings could so easily be overlooked, and thus could so readily be demolished so that a new commercial center could replace them. Did they erase many severely damaged buildings and/or ruins to forget, or was it rather that they were able to erase them so easily because these severely damaged and/or ruined buildings were withdrawn by the surpassing disaster and therefore somewhat already quasi-forgotten, so that the erasure largely implemented the forgetfulness embodied in these severely damaged and/or ruined buildings? Not being part of the community that suffered the surpassing disaster that ravaged Sarajevo, the American architect Lebbeus Woods could notice the severely damaged and/or ruined buildings and recommend in a book their integration into the future reconstructed city. But, as a consequence of the withdrawal, those belonging to that community treated that book with obliviousness, overlooking it and its recommendations. After the surpassing disaster, the duty of at least some artists is to disclose the withdrawal (Duras's *Hiroshima mon amour*, 1961; Godard's *King Lear*, 1987; Boltanski's *Monument: La Fête de Pourim*,

1988) and/or to resurrect what has been withdrawn (Godard's *King Lear*).

Jocelyne Saab's *Once Upon a Time: Beirut* (*Kān ya mā kān Bayrūt*), 1994, is a film about forgetting, unfortunately mainly in the sense that it is an unmindful film: it is grotesque how quickly it forgets even the memorable Duras epigraph with which it starts: "... Like you, I wanted my memory to be inconsolable, a memory of shadow and stone.... Like you, I have forgotten...." Memory is not to be limited, as in Saab's film, to human recollection and archival images. The loss of memory in *Hiroshima mon amour* is implied not only in the French woman's melancholia as to the ineluctability of forgetting her German lover and the nuclear devastation of Hiroshima, but also in the Japanese man's repeated "You have seen nothing in Hiroshima." Forgetfulness is not always the result of subjective factors; it is sometimes an effect of an objective withdrawal of beings (for example, of film images [shadows] and buildings [stone]) due to a surpassing disaster. A memory of that whose withdrawal is in the guise of its abrupt forgetfulness by those belonging to the community of the surpassing disaster is a betrayal of it, a false memory. To accord with the "Like you, I have forgotten ..." of the Duras epigraph with which her film opens would have entailed showing that some of the archival documentary footage Saab presents, for example some of the images of Lebanon in the 1920s, had undergone a withdrawal. Is there a more effective way to hide that certain images that withdrew as a consequence of a surpassing disaster are inaccessible than to have the film's characters enter in them? But past a surpassing disaster, one's appearance in images of an earlier period rather than implying that they are available, and that they thus provide and instance some form of memory, would in a genuine film, on the contrary, suggest that the country that underwent the surpassing disaster was so divested from the others that it turned into a radical closure. The radical closure allows the irruption of unworldly ahistorical versions of the two protagonists in the images,[62] but the images themselves are withdrawn. The film reel that is forgotten in the taxicab and presumably lost gets returned to the two young female protagonists and projected: a missed opportunity to subtly imply the withdrawal of the images. Saab could still have intimated the withdrawal by designing the insertion of the two female actresses in the archival images in such a way as to put in doubt the authenticity of these images; or by having the images of the two characters in the film scenes they shot of each other in early 1990s Beirut manifest the same impression of artificiality and overlaying as the clearly matted shots of them in the 1920s Beirut archival images. Unfortunately this is not the case in Saab's work. It is not fortuitous that Beirut is represented mostly through bad Egyptian movies in a film directed by a journalist, that is, by someone belonging to a profession that has not provided examples of sensing the withdrawal of tradition past a surpassing disaster, let alone of contributing to tradition's resurrection. While, with rare exceptions, commercial culture, which to many is what is most linked to actuality, has not been withdrawn by the series of catastrophes that hit the Arab world and that added up to a surpassing disaster, much of "avant-garde" writing and art, as well as all genuinely traditional art and writing, which is viewed by many as the part of culture least connected to current events, have been withdrawn by the present surpassing disaster. After a public reading from my book *Over-Sensitivity*, I played back *taqāsīm* on *maqām nahawand* performed by Riād al-Sunbāṭī and on *maqām kurd* performed by Munīr Bashīr. Soon after the music started, and except for me, the Middle Easterners present there began swaying their heads to the sounds. After the music stopped, I affirmed: "I am trying to resurrect tradition to be able to really hear this music again, accompanying it then with the quasi-*dhikr* of a musical high (*Allāh! ... Allāh! ...*)." Judging from their reaction to the surpassing disaster, many presumably elitist artists and writers are much more in touch with actuality than commercial culture. Tradition is not merely what materially and ostensibly survived "the test" of time: in normal times a nebulous entity despite the somewhat artificial process of canon formation, tradition becomes delineated and specified by the surpassing disaster. Tradition is what conjointly materially survived the surpassing disaster, was immaterially withdrawn by it, and had the fortune of being subsequently resurrected by artists, writers, and thinkers. Many works one had taken to be part of tradition are revealed by their availability past a surpassing disaster as not really part of tradition; contrariwise, many modernist works of art that vehemently attacked "tradition" are, prior to any reluctant gradual canonization, revealed by their withdrawal to be part of that tradition.

There were two fundamental kinds of out-of-focus and/or sloppy compositions in the photographs, films, and videos of the period around the Lebanese civil war:

— Those from the civil war's period itself were due to one or several of the following factors: the threatening conditions under which the photographer was taking them; the hasty looking away on encountering the gutted, decomposing corpses; the proximity of the dead—come to prevent the world's desertion of those suffering a surpassing disaster from turning into a radical closure—against whose freezing, not as corpses (*rigor mortis* is a form of motion*less*ness, therefore still a variety of motion) but as creatures of the undeath realm, all motions, including the restless motionlessness of the living, appear blurry; and the entranced states in which the encounter with the dead often occurs.

— Those from the aftermath of the civil war were due mainly to the withdrawal of what was being photographed.

Like so many others, he had become used to viewing things at the speed of war. So for a while after the civil war's end, he did not take any photographs nor shoot any videos, waiting until he learned to look again at a leisurely pace. This period of adjustment lasted a full two years. Yet even after he became used to looking at buildings and experiencing events at the rhythm of peace, the photographs of the ruins in Lebanon taken by this Lebanese photographer, who classically composed those of his photographs shot in other countries, still looked like they were taken by a photographer lacking time to aim since in imminent danger, the compositions haphazard and the focus almost always off. He was asked if he was influenced by such works as Vito Acconci's *Fall* (1969): a series of photographs Acconci produced by clicking his handheld camera as he reached the ground while repeatedly falling forward; or Michael Snow's *Venetian Blind* (1970): twenty-four snapshots he took with his eyes closed, each showing a blurred Snow against the accidentally framed background of a section of Venice. He was aware of and attracted by the blurring in Snow's piece and by the random compositions in Acconci's photographs. But he could recognize no basic similarity between these works and his current photographs, since the earth and grass in the Acconci photographs, the sections of Venice in *Venetian Blind*, as well as the road, filmed without looking through the view-finder, in Snow's *Seated Figures* (1988) are available to Acconci and to Snow. The question revealed a misunderstanding, since in his work the out-of-focus and/or the haphazard framings were not a formal strategy but due to the withdrawal and thus unavailability to vision of the material.

They sent him to shoot a photographic portfolio of the destruction in Bosnia. He returned with thousands of largely blurred and haphazardly framed photographs of intact buildings with no shrapnel or shrapnel marks, indeed not even broken glass. He insisted that these photographs should be grouped into an exhibition titled "The Savage War." Some felt offended at what they found to be tasteless humor; others had to admit that they were surprised that so many buildings had weathered the war unscathed. Many thought that he was facetious or that he was apologetic for the aggressors. Someone remarked critically: "One more example of a disciple trying to outdo his master: a Baudrillardian photographer implying that not only the Gulf War but also this one did not take place." He did not care to reply to someone who simplified both his work and that of Baudrillard. Someone unaware that due to the withdrawal past a surpassing disaster something in the referent cannot be localized exactly, whether with regards to framing or focus or both, asked critically whether the blurring and hit-or-miss framings were intentionally created by him to give the sensation they were shot during the war. "No."

Someone had forgotten a high-quality laser reproduction of Boltanski's *Altar to the Chases High School* (1988) in the copy of *The Holocaust Museum in Washington* (Rizzoli, 1995) that he checked out from a library. Is the blurring in Boltanski's reproduction of a graduation photograph he found in a school yearbook an enhancement of the expressivity of the photograph, as curator Lynn Gumpert proposes ("Boltanski transformed them into skeletal vestiges—their eyes reduced to empty black sockets, any hint of a smile metamorphosed into a grimace of death"[63])? Does it render for us the loss of individuation to which those depicted would have been subjected in the camps? Is it to give the sensation that those depicted are already fading from memory? Or is it rather to render the stereotypical association of the dead with haze and furtiveness? None of the above. These blurred photographs disclose to us nothing beyond their referent's withdrawal and possibly their own withdrawal as a result of a surpassing disaster.[64] After looking at that Boltanski photograph for a few minutes, he went back to looking at the illustrations and photographs in the book. He could no longer really focus on them. They had become blurred and distant. He felt that it was with eyes adjusted to the blurriness of that Boltanski photograph that he was looking at the Auschwitz prisoner identification photographs included in the book. Is it conceivable that a curator would place a Boltanski piece such as *Reserves: The Purim Holiday* (1989), based on a photograph of a Purim celebration at a Jewish school in France, 1939, in the United States Holocaust Memorial Museum in Washington DC? It is certainly conceivable, since the vast majority of curators would be oblivious of how this would affect all the items there with blurring. In which case, I would not be surprised were some spectator at the museum's cinema to suddenly yell: "Focus!" Who may have such an experience on seeing Boltanski's blurred photograph?

Is it everybody? Not at all, and this despite what Boltanski himself implies in an interview in the journal *Autrement*, 1996. Only those who belong to the community of that surpassing disaster would have such an experience.

The "You have seen nothing in Hiroshima" said by the Japanese man to the visiting French woman could at one level mean: You, a French woman, removed from both the direct experience of the atomic explosion and its radioactive aftereffects should not have the presumption to consider that you have seen anything in Hiroshima. At yet another level, it includes her in the community, since she is experiencing the withdrawal due to the surpassing disaster. If she reacts negatively to the Japanese man's words, insisting that she has seen certain things, it must be because, being an ethical person, she is not sure she is yet of that community.[65] Those Americans who managed to pressure the Smithsonian to an out-and-out scaling back of the exhibit "The Last Act: The Atomic Bomb and the End of World War II" it planned to hold in 1995 at the National Air and Space Museum are certainly not ones who "have seen nothing in Hiroshima"; they are merely ones who do not want others to see what they presume is perceptible. To very few Westerners would I say: "You have seen nothing in West Beirut" or "You have seen nothing in Iraq." How little has Herzog, the director of *Lessons of Darkness*, 1991, seen in Iraq and the Kuwaiti theater of operations in the aftermath of the Gulf War! With rare people would one progress from "You have seen little in Iraq" (most frequently because they have scant historical knowledge and no direct experience and depend for their political outlook on the biased mainstream media of the West) to "You have seen nothing in Iraq," because they now belong to the community of the surpassing disaster and thus are affected with the withdrawal. The first expression is critical and exclusive; the second is inclusive when in relation to communities that underwent a surpassing disaster. I highly respect Duras for having "seen nothing in Hiroshima"; I feel contempt for her for how little she saw in Palestine and in Iraq. I certainly would not have said to the living Duras: "You have seen nothing in Palestine and Iraq. Nothing"!

In the two film series I curated at the Center for Middle Eastern Studies at the University of California, Berkeley, I did not show any works whose main function is to provide a critique or parody of stereotypes of Middle Easterners, let alone works that do not even furnish such a critique but merely the occasion for subsequent verbose discussions full of resentment. Anyone whose "art" merely revolves around how better to express and convey such a critique reveals that he or she is an academician himself or herself through his or her obliviousness, even at the intuitive level, to the connection of stereotypes to the unconscious. Certainly by now any aspiring academician who intends to once more catalogue the litany of stereotypes the majority of Westerners have of Arabs, Iranians, etc., as his or her contribution to one more anthology negotiating something or other around issues of multiculturalism, orientalism, etc.,[66] has to ask himself or herself how much these stereotypes are linked to the unconscious and its processes—no widespread stereotype is not implicated with the unconscious—and therefore, while arguably effective at the rational, conscious level if not at doing away with these stereotypes then at least at problematizing them, how little effective is the placement of a *no*, a negative sign, a critical attitude before these views whose addresser and addressee is mostly the unconscious, which "knows nothing that is negative, and no negation"[67] (Freud, who elsewhere writes, "'No' seems not to exist so far as dreams are concerned"[68]); indeed how largely counterproductive they are at the level where it really matters with stereotypes, the unconscious level. These critics and academics are playing an important role in the maintenance of these stereotypes at the level of the unconscious; moreover, they are indirectly propagating such stereotypes to sectors previously immune to them, since many people from other cultures and ethnic groups relax their vigilance when dealing with these academics seemingly defending them. I find the encounter with such ostensibly critical academic catalogues of stereotypes of Arabs even more oppressive than the rude transactions with prejudiced airport security officials or embassy employees. All in all, that the representation of Arabs and Iranians in the most simplistic manner (up to denying their existence: the description of Palestine by many of the early Zionists as "a land without a people" ...) can facilitate the Israeli destruction of villages in South Lebanon in the name of a defense against terrorism (even guerrilla operations by the Lebanese against military targets in the part of Lebanon illegally occupied by Israel are termed terroristic!) is no excuse for limiting oneself to criticizing or parodying such widespread misrepresentations. "A woman cannot do much harm to a man. He carries all his tragedy within him. She can bother him, provoke him, she can even kill him—that's all."[69] (That is, even for those who consider that death is the absolute end and a total loss, all is not all.[70] To any totalizing "that is all," we, laconic mortals, have the reaction, and not tautologically: "That's all." That something exceeds all is implied by the difference between *that's all* and *that's all* and confirmed by the difference between *c'est tout* and *c'est tout* [this excess includes but is not reducible to this difference between *that's all* and *that's all* and between *c'est tout* and *c'est tout*].) In other words, they can bother us, for example by their ignorance of our tradition; provoke us, for example with their resultant flagrant stereotypes about us; they can even treat us like potential terrorists and kill us—that's all. But is that all they can do? Kill us—in the hundreds of thousands? Unfortunately, they can do worse: produce a surpassing disaster and thus a withdrawal of tradition.

A Kashaya Pomo chief and scholar recently expressly discontinued the transmission of a tribal dance. Something must have indicated to her that the discontinuation of the transmission of the dance would be less detrimental and problematic than its handing down. Were it the case that their forebears had undergone only a vast catastrophe, the issue for the present-day Native Americans would plainly be to do everything possible to transmit the traditional songs and dances to their youths in spite of the latter's acculturation and indifference. But in case what was suffered was a surpassing disaster, one must be sensitive to the eventuality of the withdrawal, and, in the absence or failure of the resurrection of tradition, of the obligation to suspend transmission, so as not to hand down counterfeit tradition.[71]

You Said, "Stay," So I Stayed

Catastrophes such as the atomic devastation of Hiroshima in 1945, the Rwandan genocide in 1994, the harsh sanctions imposed on Iraq between the two Gulf Wars and that contributed to the additional deaths of tens if not hundreds of thousands of Iraqi children, undermine the "will." Who or how many can will the eternal recurrence of such catastrophes? Nazi Germany, seemingly an episode of *the triumph of the will* (the title of Leni Riefenstahl's 1935 documentary on the Nazi Party Congress in Nuremberg in 1934), was, through the concentration and extermination camps, a cryptic fundamental attack on it. Evil is nostalgic; how much nostalgia, a symptom of the absence or desuetude of the will, have the concentration and extermination camps produced! Nietzsche's "The question posed to each thing you do, 'Do you will this once more and countless times more?'" (*The Gay Science*, no. 341) is to be read as an ethical injunction to do without nostalgia, to do away with it; only that whose eternal recurrence is willed does not produce nostalgia. Nostalgia is basically less a yearning for the repetition of an event than an indication that one did not will the event, that is, did not "will" its eternal recurrence. Nostalgia reveals not only what I feel now about a past event, but also how I "willed" that event when it happened in the past: I did not "will" its eternal recurrence. When it is not merely psychological, nostalgia is basically a facet of the present event; with regard to any event toward which I feel nostalgic, I know that I did not "will" its eternal recurrence when it happened. We are nostalgic beings less—if at all—because we are creatures who remember in an ostensibly transient present than because we do not will events. I really will an event only if I will its eternal recurrence, thus making it recur eternally (Nietzsche's philosophy could be a philosophy of the will only insofar as it was also one of eternal recurrence). Until someone experiences countless recurrence and ends up willing, beneath "willing" some event what we, nostalgic beings, "will" is nostalgia, rather than the event itself. But can't this basic nostalgia itself be genuinely willed? No; only the psychological nostalgia can be "willed." She lamented: "You never talk about or evoke past events. You lack nostalgia. That's why I feel it is so difficult to love you." "Me not nostalgic? I wish it were true!" (From the standpoint of the basic nostalgia, which is related to the inability to will the eternal recurrence of the moment, missing the other while he or she is in one's presence is always the case.) "You wish you were not nostalgic despite what I just told you! It is over between us!" The absence of affective nostalgia, which is linked to memory and desire, does not by itself signal the absence of the basic nostalgia, which is linked directly not to memory but to not having willed the eternal recurrence of the event. With respect to the will, while being our greatest liability, nostalgia is also our chance: we could not will if we did not have the capacity for nostalgia and the possibility of overcoming it.[72] Freedom from nostalgia implies either remaining detached even while the event is happening, considering it "self-arisen and self-liberated"; or, on the contrary, willing its eternal recurrence. One has to totally stop at the event (eternal recurrence) or not stop at all (Takuan Soho's *immovable wisdom*).[73] For example, during a sword duel, the mind has to have no abiding place, not stop and be detained by some matter or aim; or one has to will the eternal recurrence of each of the duel's events. To end nostalgia, one has to go through cycles: the cycles of death-rebirth of Buddhism until one becomes fully detached; or the cycles of recurrence—during which one would die countless times through one's successive virtual versions in similar simulations—until one wills the eternal recurrence of events. Until the conditions for the experience of recurrence become ripe, the feasible way to end nostalgia is through sacrifice, that of the fruit of action (as in karma yoga), thus of linkage: Alexander's sacrifice in Tarkovsky's *The Sacrifice* (1986) includes not only burning his family's house but also not justifying why he did so.

It is only through the experience of recurrence that we may reach the will, that is, will eternal recurrence. Since repetition is a prerequisite of the will, and since according to Heidegger our epoch is that of "the will to will," Kierkegaard was right in his prognosis: "This question [whether a repetition is possible and what importance it has] will play a very important role in modern philosophy."[74] The reason that Nietzsche did not actually carry through the writing of his projected major work, *The Will to Power: Attempt at a Revaluation of All Values*, which was left in the form of notes, was that the conditions for that were not ripe yet. The thought of eternal recurrence is the thought of the untimely in several senses: it makes events untimely through recurrence; it came to the philosopher of the untimely, Nietzsche (the author of, among other books, *Untimely Meditations*, 1873–1876), prematurely, before the conditions for its implementation were ripe; and it came to his character Zarathustra, the teacher of eternal recurrence, when his fruit was ripe but he was not yet ripe for it ("The Stillest Hour," *Thus Spoke Zarathustra*). It is to the credit of Nietzsche that he sensed that pending the right (future) conditions, his eternal recurrence remained somewhat abstract. Are such conditions going to be ripe in the last decades of the twenty-first century (Nietzsche: "What I relate is the history of the next two centuries"[75])? If the will seems to be linked to the future only (up to the use in English of "will" to indicate simple futurity), this is likely because only in a coming historical period in which virtual-reality generators that can produce emulations have been constructed or time travel in the multiverse of the many-worlds interpretation of quantum mechanics has become feasible is it going to be possible not only to think in the manner of a thought experiment, but also to experience countless recurrence (it is a symptom of our inability to will, of our nostalgia, that we place in the past what is going to occur only in the future: the Edenic epoch, in which everything is willed, that is, willed to recur eternally). We would then have reached countless recurrence not only as a relatively abstract and individual selective ethical notion (Nietzsche: "The question posed to each thing you do, 'Do you will this once more and countless times more?'"), but also as a condition for the ontological creation of the will. While in the absence of the possibility of time travel, the many-worlds interpretation of quantum physics makes nonsense of the will, strikes it with irrelevance (it does not make any real difference what I choose, since all the alternatives are actualized in various branches of the multiverse); when connected to the possibility of time travel, such an interpretation of the formalism of quantum physics and of the results of the double-slit experiment is the one that allows for the possibility of the generation of the will, not so much because it proves that I could have done otherwise since different outcomes can issue from the same very long sequence of past events, but because it allows the initiation into countless recurrence and thus the possible production of the will. If the will is linked to computer-simulated worlds, it is not only because some computer simulations are going to be eternally willed, but also, more fundamentally, because simulations make it possible to repeatedly experience, through our or our descendants' virtual versions, countless recurrence until we or our descendants will their eternal recurrence. Thus computer simulation is going to reveal itself as not primarily escapist in relation to this world, but as a major means to fully accept it as it is going to be transfigured by the will. Harold Ramis's *Groundhog Day*, 1993 (script by Ramis and Danny Rubin, based on a story by Rubin) can be viewed as a thought experiment in experiencing countless recurrence (at the level of narrative only, since cinematically no one would bear its countless, let alone eternal recurrence). The experience of countless recurrence spans several phases: past the initial stupefaction at the repetition, one is relieved for a while as one starts the exploration of the variety and complexity of the objects and events of "everyday life," the recurrence functioning then as the form of attention, of meditation, of the otherwise distracted people of our epoch[76] (to explore an event, we, and more so our descendants, have to go through a transversal movement through similar simulations or branches of the multiverse, minor changes making us notice previously unnoticed facets of it)[77]: "To see a world in a grain of sand / And a heaven in a wild flower / Hold infinity in the palm of your hand / and eternity in an hour" (William Blake, *Auguries of Innocence*, 1803). But then this phase that at first seemed to be indefinitely open recedes and one becomes again preoccupied with the repetition itself and resents it. The will is not going to be reached, and thus *amor fati*, without undergoing many times the hour of the great suffocation by and disgust with the recurring events. Sooner or later, one commits suicide through one or more of one's successive virtual versions in similar simulations or some of one's versions in similar branches of the multiverse; the achievement of the will by an overman, a man who experiences the same state of things over and over and ends up willing the eternal recurrence of various events, would include *the death of man*.[78] The one who lives through countless recurrence and ends up willing the eternal recurrence of various events is exceptional in comparison not only to other humans or future cyborgs but also to himself in the guise of those of his virtual versions in computer simulations or those of his physical versions in similar branches of the multiverse who ended up committing suicide. We could give him a term borrowed appropriately from the philosopher of eternal recurrence and the will to power: the overman, or, better, the over-man; we could also give him, once we take the precaution of divesting the term of some of its orthodox religious connotations and of the genealogy various religions and religious sects strictly associate with the one it designates, the title that befits the transfigured, redeemed time ushered in by his achieving the will at the end of so many comings to the same state of things: the Messiah/Mahdī.

Nostalgia is present even in the frustration then anxiety then desperation of *Groundhog Day*'s Phil as the same year's February 2 returns indefinitely. If the same year's February 2 returned even after Phil leapt from a window and smashed against the ground, it was that, despite all his desperation at the day's recurrences, he was still nostalgic in relation to it. It is not manifest in the film why February 3 arrives; I think it is because the protagonist has, after innumerable rehearsals of the recurring day's events, perfected each moment so that he can will its eternal recurrence. A man stuck in the same day tries to get released from it as it repeats itself a stupendous number of times, and he manages to do so only when at last he wills its eternal recurrence! One should not summarily judge a day as imperfect merely because it contains complaints and billiard shots that missed, for these too can be perfect: Phil willed the complaint he addresses to the boy who on once again being caught by him while falling from a tree does not thank him. The criterion for the perfection of a day is whether its eternal recurrence has been willed; the latter is what allows it to pass (so long as the will has not been achieved no day passes [indeed, according to the theory of relativity, events do not pass in the block universe of spacetime], but once the will is realized, one "would no longer be living in the block universe of spacetime of relativity, in which all is preserved, even what is Evil, even what is unforgivable, even what cannot be willed to recur eternally, but would be living in a universe where things are transient but subsist only because they are willed to eternally recur"[79]). Phil is far more Nietzschean and furthest away from the inhabitants of Punxsutawney not when, elitist, he treats them with contempt, but when he wills the eternal recurrence of his stay with them, since, not having attained willing their habitation in their town, they, although bored with the "repetitiveness" of their lives in that small town of 6,782 inhabitants, are separated from it by nostalgia. Compared to him, a TV weatherman, who is first shown superimposed on a blue screen displaying the graphic rendition of the weather, but who attains willing the eternal return of his stay with the town's people, they seem not really integrated in the town but only overlaid on it.

Was Adam's eating of the prohibited tree of the knowledge of good and evil a weighty "act," maybe the weightiest "act," since it apparently caused our entrance into the long historical episode of the lack of the will? Judged from the perspective of any of Adam and Eve's previous acts, each of which was willed, i.e., willed to eternally recur, the transgression of eating from the tree of the knowledge of good and evil was unbearably light. It was, from Adam's perspective, infinitely lighter than the production of Eve from one of his ribs *while he slept deeply* (Genesis 2:21–22); than his displacing his foot one further step while walking; or than his continuing to look at something for one extra "instant," since these were willed to recur eternally. It is one of the gravest *contresens* to connect evil to will. Was Adam's eating from the tree of the knowledge of good and evil evil because it was willful? It was evil rather as his first "act" that was not willed—even his unconscious state while he slept and God fashioned Eve out of his rib, seemingly confronting him with a *fait accompli* on his awakening, was fully willed by him. The one who wills can do no evil, and he or she regrets nothing. The devil did not tempt Adam to will; rather, he tempted him no longer to will. In the Adam and Eve episode with the tree of the knowledge of good and evil, the serpent tries to make them dubious of the existence of the will. In Genesis (3:1), it does so by implying forgetfulness through the question: "Did God really say, 'You must not eat from any tree in the garden'?" How strange is this question in a realm where everything is willed in the mode of eternal recurrence, even God's proscription, and thus cannot be forgotten. How nostalgic is already the insinuation of this possibility of forgetfulness! Since any willed act is willed to occur eternally, it is only with the lack of the will, and consequently with nostalgia, that the past and the future get introduced—nostalgia precedes the past, makes it possible. The nostalgia of Adam is not for Paradise, but for his eating of the tree of the knowledge of good and evil: it is his one "act" "there" that was done without will, it is his one "act" "there" that he cannot will to eternally recur. Having lost the ability to will the eternal recurrence of events, thus no longer able to view them as perfect, he was accordingly already outside of Paradise. Our purported nostalgia for Paradise is not going to lead us to it not only because nostalgia can never be a motive for the will, can never mobilize it; but also and more simply because it is impossible to feel nostalgia for Paradise, that is, for what consists of only what can be willed, that is, willed to recur eternally. Technology and science, avatars of an advanced stage of nihilism—and thus of exacerbated nostalgia—on account of the objective spirit as a symptom of the inability to any longer "will,"[80] and on account of so many catastrophes they have made possible (the atomic bombings of Hiroshima and Nagasaki ...) and whose eternal recurrence ostensibly cannot be willed, are nonetheless going to make it possible to will, thus leading to an epoch where evil is no longer possible: "But where danger is, grows / The saving power also" (Hölderlin, "Patmos"). Evil is that which cannot be willed, that is, cannot be willed to recur eternally, and therefore, for as long as this universe is not willed, is a peculiarity of the world, including of the world of the noble. Hence, Nietzsche's critical exposition of the concept of evil as the outcome of slave morality ("The slave revolt in morality begins when *ressentiment* becomes creative and gives birth to values.... Slave morality from the outset says No to what is 'outside,' what is 'different,' what is 'not itself'; and *this* No is its creative deed.... This, then, is quite the contrary of what the noble man does, who conceives the basic concept 'good' in advance and spontaneously out of himself and only then creates for himself an idea of 'bad'! This 'bad' of noble origin and that 'evil' out of the cauldron of unsatisfied hatred ...

how different these words 'bad' and 'evil' are, although they are both apparently the opposite of the same concept 'good.' But it is *not* the same concept 'good'"[81]) while a fully justified act of resistance is wanting precisely because he is a philosopher of the will. While evil is an exceptional part of the world of the living, the basic obstacle to willing this world, it is a characteristic of the realm of death. In Genesis, through his will-less eating of the tree of the knowledge of good and evil, man became mortal, that is, dead while (physically) alive ("The Lord God commanded the man, saying, ... of the tree of the knowledge of good and evil, thou shalt not eat of it: for in the day that thou eatest thereof thou shalt surely die"[82]). What Adam felt once he performed an "act" that was not willed, i.e., that was not willed to recur eternally, and that, moreover, by turning him into a mortal, i.e., someone dead while alive, changed his body into a potential cadaver, and thus made it include an implicit fall[83] (*cadaver*: "origin late Middle English: from Latin, from *cadere* 'to fall'"[84]), was *the unbearable lightness of being*.[85] The majority of people nowadays unwittingly embody an unbearable lightness of being because, while in no position yet to experience countless recurrence and in the process possibly achieve the will by willing the eternal recurrence of various events, they have long since become oblivious that they carry in them death *as undeath*, a state in which one at least once feels that the fate of the (falling apart) world depends on him, and a realm "in" which, being labyrinthine, one feels one has *always* been. If science and technology are ever to abolish death, this is not going to be simply by ending biological demise through breakthroughs in biology and medicine; it is, additionally and more radically, going to be through making possible the will, since in a willed universe, that is, in a universe where everything is willed to recur eternally, death-as-undeath, a realm to which guilt and evil are intrinsic, is abolished. "Till death do us part" is noncommittal, not so much in comparison to a melancholic response to the death of the beloved, but, more fundamentally, because the process of accomplishing willing the eternal recurrence of any of the joyful days with the beloved is almost certainly bound to include committing at least one suicide (even in the utmost joy that we can bear, we sense that it implies the unbearable joy that will induce us, across one or more suicides, to will its eternal recurrence);[86] and because a world in which one can will the eternal recurrence of being with the beloved is one from which death was abolished. The operation to realize the will is probably going to be aptly called Operation Sisyphus[87],[88] since Sisyphus is said to have experienced countless recurrence, repeatedly pushing a rock uphill to the summit only to then watch it fall back to the bottom. Sisyphus could not have been a possible hero of the will without entertaining a superficial relation to death. During his first encounter with death, he subjugates and chains Hades, sent against him by Zeus. Until the god of war, Ares, releases Hades, no one dies on earth, even those dismembered. Sisyphus is thus linked with the impossibility of death. When Ares hands him to the freed Hades, Sisyphus manages soon to win a temporary reprieve that allows him to go back to the life realm, where he asks his wife to discontinue her offerings to the gods of the underworld, with the result that they end up releasing him so the offerings would resume. Sisyphus's existence in Tartarus, part of the realm of the dead, has and induces none of the uncanniness one encounters in the Orpheus myth. It is symptomatic of how shallow is Sisyphus's encounter with death that in the retelling of the story of his punishment, many narrators forget to inform us that the hill, the rock, and his ordeal are in Tartarus. While choosing Sisyphus as the exemplary figure through which to pose the question of suicide as the "only ... really serious philosophical problem," as Camus does in his *The Myth of Sisyphus*, seems felicitous from the perspective of that hero's punishment by the absurd, it is basically misplaced, since Sisyphus was in Tartarus during his punishment, that is, already dead, hence could not really commit suicide, but only attempt it, futilely. During the first hundreds or thousands of repetitions, Sisyphus felt a short remission during his walk downhill; but then the weight of countless repetition must have resulted in his coming to feel the descent to be as heavy as pushing the rock uphill, thus dreading it equally. The absurd, suicide, and Sisyphus are indeed connected, but in another manner than in Camus's book: since Sisyphus was already in Tartarus, thus ostensibly already dead, he could attempt suicide, and believe that by doing so he was going to succeed in ending it all, only by force of the absurd and not just by dint of desperation. Could Sisyphus have at some point during his ordeal of countless recurrence come to will its eternal recurrence? In that case he, who had temporarily subjugated death at their first encounter, would have led to its abolishment—in which case, yes, one can envision a joyful (rather than merely happy) Sisyphus, having, *across many attempted suicides*, accomplished the will.[89]

One has to be careful when to demand *amor fati*; demanding it before the will has been established is an injunction to nihilism.[90] The initiation into countless recurrence and the consequent accomplishment of the will is a revaluation of all values, at least in the sense that one would then have moved *beyond good and evil* (Nietzsche), since evil would have become impossible. A philosopher of the will has also to be, in addition to a philosopher of eternal recurrence, a philosopher of the eradication of evil, indeed of its erasure even from the past, and thus a philosopher of *amor fati*. The actual world is going to become "the best of all possible worlds" (Leibniz) only by the time the will is accomplished. Those present when the will is accomplished would be in "Eden." The ordeal of the will is not only that one has to go through countless recurrence and, in the guise of some of one's successive virtual versions in similar simulations or of some of one's versions in similar branches of the multiverse, in desperation commit suicide myriad times; but also that once the will is accomplished, one thenceforth is going to have not only to accept everything that happens, but also, since a genuine will is an ontological selector that automatically renders anything that cannot be willed in the mode of eternal recurrence impossible, to affirm its eternal recurrence: *amor fati*. Can genocides be willed? This is possibly an empirical question: if one lives through countless recurrence and ends up willing the eternal recurrence of various events, then if genocides continue to happen, they can be, and indeed *are*, willed (while it may be attained by an individual, the will does not remain an individual faculty, but proves to be epochal). He came to the realization that even the many suicides he—in the guise of some of his virtual versions in similar simulations—committed during his experience of countless recurrence may turn out to be as nothing compared to his having to possibly deal with the implicit not just acceptance, but downright willing, as he had never before willed anything, of what he would have viewed prior to the establishment of the will as unequivocally evil, no longer able to distance himself from it even in the form of being nostalgic about the preceding period. It is our chance, the relative lightness of our condition, that the will is not yet accomplished, that we do not have to affirm, indeed will the eternal recurrence of everything that exists.

Science has tried and has seemingly managed to produce a null balance sheet for the appearance out of nothing and continued existence of the universe: it is "conceivable that the total energy of the universe is zero.... The vast cosmos that we see around us could have originated in a vacuum fluctuation—essentially from nothing at all—because the large positive energy of the masses in the universe can be counterbalanced by a corresponding amount of negative energy in the form of the gravitational field."[91] And yet, it is not enough for the universe to appear that the balance sheet of its energy be zero, and for it to continue to exist that it be a block one of spacetime; it, the outcome of a "dice throw" (presently one of the signs of this is that the values of the dimensionless physical constants, for example, the fine-structure constant [1/137.035999074 (44)], are not deducible from quantum physics and general relativity),[92] has to have the possibility to will itself prior to its hypothesized "death," whether violent in the Big Crunch scenario or cold in the Heat Death scenario. We are not dealing with one universe willed from the outset by the one God of monotheistic religions, but with a multiverse with an infinity of branches that, through the overman, the one who experiences the same period over and over by means of time travel to many of the quite similar branches among the infinity that comprise the multiverse of the many-worlds interpretation of quantum physics, and/or through being recurrently virtually projected in similar computer simulations, generates the will. The excess that time travel is going to produce is neither some extra bodies,[93] nor extra change, nor extra, unearned, unevolutionary knowledge,[94] but, on the long run, that excessive thing, the will, which wills nothing but the eternal recurrence of what is still there once it is established. A sublime hypothesis for a universe that wills itself irrespective of us and our descendants: the generation of the will is going to be accomplished between $10^{-10^{10}}$ seconds and $10^{-10^{123}}$ seconds before the singularity of the Big Crunch (these are the numbers physicist Frank Tipler advances for the upper bound as to when the hypothetical future universal simulation is going to occur).[95] How prodigious then is the expenditure for the universe to will itself irrespective of the overman: an infinity of universes and over 10^{38} years (from the Big Bang to the Big Crunch through expansion then contraction). Were the universe to will itself irrespective of us or our descendants, then it is very probable that it is going to include what cannot be willed even by the overman, what prevents even the overman from having *amor fati*, that is, it is very probable that it is going to be fundamentally nihilistic from the perspective not only of man in general, but even of the overman.

The physicist Frank J. Tipler is finite in a calculated design: "A human being can be in one of $10^{10^{45}}$ [quantum] states at most, and can undergo at most 4×10^{53} changes of state per second;"[96] yet the nostalgia of this scientist who wants everything, including the pettiest, to recur, in the guise of its digital emulation, is boundless. "Naked I once saw them both, the greatest and the smallest human being: all-too-similar to each other—all-too-human, even the greatest! All-too-small the greatest!—That was my loathing for the human! And eternal recurrence even of the smallest!—That was my loathing for all existence! Ah, disgust! disgust! disgust!——Thus spoke Zarathustra and sighed and shuddered"[97] (Nietzsche, "The Convalescent," *Thus Spoke Zarathustra*). Even what Nietzsche found most disgusting, "eternal recurrence even of the smallest!" Tipler, hypothesizing in his book *The Physics of Immortality: Modern Cosmology, God and the Resurrection of the Dead* (1995) "the resurrection to eternal life," in the guise of numerical emulations near and at the Omega Point, "of everyone who has lived, is living, and will live,"[98] considers something to affirm, cherish, and celebrate (Tipler's thought-provoking *The Physics of Immortality* confirms Nietzsche's lament: All-too-human, even the great! All-too-small the great![99]). Qualifying Tipler, I would think that if the will is reached after the point when it becomes feasible to resurrect, in the form of digital emulations, everyone in history, then the vast majority, if not all of those who will have been resurrected are going to vanish again since in a universe where the will has been accomplished anything whose eternal recurrence cannot be willed becomes impossible; and if the will is reached when it is still impossible to resurrect, in the form of emulations, everyone in history, no such universal resurrection would happen—however negligible the cost of doing so in terms of the available computer processing power and memory capacity—but only a selective one.

If events can be changed at all in the same universe, this would not be through time travel to the past; only the frivolous fancy that. Were one to travel to the past before one has achieved the will by going through the ordeal of countless recurrence, possibly no paradoxes, such as the so-called grandfather paradox (the time traveler to the past causes the death of his grandfather before his own father was conceived: how is it then that he was born at all?), could ensue, whether because there is no change in relativity’s block universe of spacetime; or because one traveled to another branch of the multiverse so that one is not changing the past of the same branch of the multiverse but tracing the different past in another branch of the multiverse; or because one cannot yet will and thus makes the same seeming “choices,” ending up doing exactly the same things. What can rend the fabric of reality are not changes that supposedly can be made by some time traveler to the past, but the inaugural appearance of the will. More than to any weird branch of the multiverse, time travel or more probably computer emulation would be an introduction to the weirdest of all for the living: countless recurrence and possibly the will. Mediocre people are going to use time travel or computer emulations to visit different periods. But those preoccupied with the issue of the will are going to use time travel and computer emulation in order to experience countless recurrence. They are going to travel in time less to experience and add to their knowledge of other historical periods than to start their great initiation into willing, in the process of which they, in the guise of either their virtual versions in similar simulations or physical versions in similar branches of the multiverse, are very likely to commit suicide many times. While seeming to be the most cosmopolitan and adventurous, those future travelers who visit conspicuously different branches of the multiverse are really the most restrained. And while, cursorily, the one who experiences again and again the same time and place through traveling to very similar branches of the multiverse would seem the most parochial, actually it is that person who is the most in search of the new: the will.

It is only once one has attained willing the eternal recurrence of an event that volition becomes something that can be felt as such. It is only then that one discovers how devoid one was of any will, how nostalgic one was *all the time* before, suddenly feeling what it is to be truly without nostalgia. How many have truly tasted what it is to will? I haven't, and neither had the philosopher of the will to power: "'Willing' something ... —I know none of this from experience."[100]

Who or what can resist a genuine will (*Groundhog Day*'s Phil is not surprised with his guest's answer to his inquiry as to why she stayed with him for the night of February 2: "You said, 'Stay,' so I stayed")? Shortly before he embarked on his experience of countless recurrence, someone reminded him of Jesus Christ's "If you have faith as small as a mustard seed, you can say to this mountain, 'Move from here to there,' and it will move" (Matthew 17:20). He, rephrasing 1 Corinthians 13:2, responded: "If I have a faith that can move mountains, but do not have will, I have nothing to do with the redeemed world yet." Having gone through this world countless times in the guise of largely similar versions of it in the multiverse or in virtual reality and ended up willing the eternal recurrence of various events, the overman, influenced by Sufi master Junayd, did not consider moving mountains in space, since although seeming steadfast, *they move like clouds* (Qur'ān, 27:90);[101] neither did he, influenced as he was by Zen master Dōgen, consider displacing mountains in space, since although seeming fixed, they *walk* ("Mountains and Waters Sutra," *Treasury of the Eye of the True Dharma* [*Shōbōgenzō*])—he moved a stone on that mountain just a little from where it was in what, with the ushering in of the epochal will, was no longer relativity's block universe but a universe where whatever of the world's past could not be willed, that is, willed to recur eternally, never existed: "A rabbi, a real cabalist, once said that in order to establish the reign of peace it is not necessary to destroy everything nor to begin a completely new world. It is sufficient to displace this cup or this bush or this stone just a little, and thus everything. But this small displacement is so difficult to achieve and its measure is so difficult to find that, with regard to the world, humans are incapable of it and it is necessary that the Messiah come."[102]

Will and goals are not constitutionally linked. We crave goals not because we have will or wish to be induced to muster the will, but, on the contrary, because we would like to avoid the ordeal of reaching the will, since such an ordeal includes experiencing countless recurrence, which divests action from goals—not least because recurrence subverts chronology, what appeared to be later, thus something that could possibly function as a goal, encountered repeatedly as preceding what seemed to be its cause. The will does not lead to a voluntaristic subject but to one who has *amor fati*. It is not those living in the epoch of the actual will who transmute reality, for example so it is no longer a block universe of spacetime: the will does.

The two versions of the woman in David Lynch's *Lost Highway* are not to be reduced to reflections of the desire of the male character: to fantasies. Those who find themselves in a radically-closed space are going to pass through myriad changes in mannerisms, hairstyles, and dress designs; and, in case they happen to be ahistorical unworldly entities that irrupted in the space—appearing then disappearing then appearing again—also through the spectrum of physical characteristics and identities. Moreover the phrases said by the different protagonists are going to be permuted among them and uttered in different intonations and given different interpretations.[103] In Robbe-Grillet's *L'Immortelle*, the discrepancies between the descriptions that the various persons interviewed by the protagonist give of the missing woman are not to be ascribed to mere subjective variations in perception, nor do they disclose a misunderstanding on the part of his interlocutors as to the specific woman to whom he is referring, nor are they the intentional misleading statements of people belonging to some secret organization, for instance one that traffics in slaves and that may have kidnapped the said woman; they rather reveal this passage through all the variations in a radical closure: her first name is Eliane, Liane, Lucile, Lale, etc.; she is French, she isn't French; she is neither as old nor as young as the protagonist says; she is fair-haired, she is very dark ... In a radical closure, one is going to be subject to the permutation in inverse proportion to how intensely one "willed" an event, i.e., to whether one "willed" it to recur twice, ten times, or a thousand times—or be altogether immune to it if one willed the event, i.e., willed it to recur eternally. In a radical closure, only those gestures, responses, and behavior whose eternal recurrence was willed would be repeated again and again amidst the surrounding permutations and attributed to the same person. Place such a character who wills in a space that is merely relatively closed and he is not going to repeat any event, for he wills its eternal recurrence once and for all; but place him in a spatial radical closure and he is going to be the only one who does not go through the permutations affecting even published books and released films.

First Aid, Second Growth, Third Degree, Fourth World, Fifth Amendment, Sixth Sense

During the Israeli army's 1982 siege of West Beirut, the Palestinians faced a double bind: the siege and their desertion by the rest of the world—orchestrated by Israel's main ally, the USA, a UN Security Council permanent, thus veto-wielding, member—may have changed their enclave into a radical closure; yet they were being violently pressured to leave that enclosure. The Palestinian combatants' delay in coming to a decision may not have been caused only by the reluctance to decamp from what had become to many of them a surrogate homeland and to relinquish the elaborate political and administrative apparatus they had established in Lebanon; and by their mistrust of the guarantees they were being offered for the safety of the hundreds of thousands of Palestinian civilians who would be left behind—a mistrust that proved justified by the subsequent massacres in the Sabra and Shatila Palestinian refugee camps. A feeling of radical closure might have contributed to the delay in deciding to leave: "Where should we go after the last frontier? Where should the birds fly after the last sky?" (Mahmoud Darwish, "The Earth Is Closing on Us," *Ward Aqal*, 1986). Ghosts may appear in a quarantined region, not to complete an unfinished business but to intimate to the quarantined living people that the dead are not party to their desertion by the rest of the world. These posthumous entities may appear in time, before the quarantine turns into a radical closure, where apparitions are experienced as impostors not because of the doubling that is a characteristic of the undeath realm from which they apparently issue, but because they are unworldly entities that irrupted fully formed in such a closure.

They may appear there although the quarantined living were, and possibly continue to be, despite the quasi-spontaneous Buddhist-like meditations on their bodies hallucinated as chopped, buried under rubble, or burned to ashes, themselves party to the modern world's desertion and exclusion of the dead. The dead appear there also to maintain the possibility of their continuing remembrance by the living, since were the quarantine to turn into a radical closure, those in it would become disconnected from history. Despite the fact that I had not been in Beirut for the previous four years, the curator Jayce Salloum placed me as residing in Los Angeles and Beirut in his catalogue for the exhibition "East of Here.... (Re)Imagining the 'Orient'" which took place at YYZ Artists Outlet, Toronto, in November–December 1996. His reason for doing this was probably to stress the connection of the included artists to the Middle East. I think such a description of my geographical coordinates was then and continues to be quite accurate only from the perspective of radical closure. Haven't I written: "He left (did he leave?) Beirut—a city where 'nothing [is] left. Not even leaving'—to New York in 1984"? Even if I never go back to Beirut, my coordinates are conjointly the city in which I happen to reside and Beirut.

Radical-Closure Artist with Bandaged Sense Organ

Spaces that are radically disconnected from their environs are open to the diagram (for example, the Red Room in David Lynch's *Twin Peaks: Fire Walk with Me*) or to an unworldly elsewhere or to nothing (the one referred to in the Latin *ex nihilo*, out of nothing). I term such spaces radical closures.[104] An ostensibly finished radical-closure painting may undergo sudden changes, since entities may later irrupt in it, and since what had already irrupted in it may suddenly disappear from it.[105] I would feel no surprise—but apprehension at the confirmation of my wild concepts—were I to read the following headline: "No crows in Van Gogh's ultra-expensive *Wheatfield with Crows*!" Isn't the present owner of that costly painting, the Van Gogh Museum/Vincent van Gogh Foundation, apprehensive about the eventuality of the disappearance of the paint birds from it? I suggest that the owner take out insurance against this eventuality.[106] Moreover, isn't the present owner of the painting apprehensive about the eventuality of the crows irrupting outside the painting? Wouldn't prudence command that the museum and owner of the painting demand from the museum's visitors that they sign a legal release releasing the museum and owner of the painting from any claim or liability for the damage and injury sustained by the undersigned were the crows to suddenly irrupt outside the painting[107] or were he or she to end up cutting off his or her ear in an attempt to stop experiencing the sounds he or she starts to hear on looking at that painting?

In Kurosawa's *Dreams* (1990), standing in a wheat field before his canvas, Van Gogh describes his painter's life as constant slaving and prods his interlocutor into doing the same: work, work. Van Gogh wrote in a September 26, 1888 letter to his brother, Theo: "Today again from seven o'clock in the morning till six in the evening I worked without stirring except to take some food a step or two away.... I have no thought of fatigue, I shall do another picture this very night, and I shall bring it off." It turned out that for *Wheatfield with Crows*, where the two converging lines of grass, which outline the path through the compact field of wheat and trace lines of perspective, meet in the middle of the field not in a point but rather in a green line parallel to the horizon, Van Gogh worked hard to construct a radical closure. In the same *Dreams* scene, Van Gogh says that while painting he gets in a state of trance (from a September 5–6, 1889 letter to his brother: "I am ploughing on like a man possessed" [*je laboure comme un vrai possédé*]) and "the scene paints itself for me." The artist of a radical closure, in which fully formed entities may irrupt sooner or later, is indolent in some measure; Van Gogh, who, in a decade, produced around eight hundred paintings and a thousand drawings as well as a voluminous correspondence, was manifestly a hardworking artist, but he was also, in relation to his painting *Wheatfield with Crows*, in which he constructed a radical closure, to some extent an indolent artist, as indolent as Marcel Duchamp (the artist of, among other things, ready-mades), since part of that radical-closure painting "paint[ed] itself" for him. Obviously, the indolence of artists of radical closures is not necessarily a psychological character trait (although it can be that too); it is basically a consequence of the circumstance that part of the painting, for example the black paint birds of *Wheatfield with Crows*, "paints itself" for the artist, more precisely, irrupts fully formed in the radical closure he produced. Thus Kurosawa's casting of Martin Scorsese in the role of Van Gogh is infelicitous, since while Scorsese gives the impression of someone hardworking, he does not at all give the sense of indolence; David Lynch would have been a far more appropriate choice for that role.

"A third line of thought argues that only the present self-portrait [*Self-Portrait with Bandaged Ear and Pipe*] was ever done by Van Gogh, the other one [*Self-Portrait with Bandaged Ear*] being a pastiche by another hand" (Ronald Pickvance, *Van Gogh in Arles* [The Metropolitan Museum of Art, 1984], 245); if the radical closure Van Gogh constructed in *Wheatfield with Crows* rendered an actual radical closure in the field itself, I would add a fourth line of thought that emends the third one mentioned in the quote: *Self-Portrait with Bandaged Ear* possibly irrupted fully formed. I can quite easily envision this situation: after the death of a radical-closure writer, an incredibly large number of manuscripts are discovered in his house, and years later the editors of his oeuvre preface their introduction to his in-progress collected works with: "We simply note this eerie fact: although all the found manuscripts are in his handwriting, it is *physically impossible* for him to have written them during his life even were he to have stayed awake day and night transcribing in shorthand under continuous dictation."

Van Gogh, who on an outing in Arles from the hospital to his studio in the company of Paul Signac in March 1889 suddenly "tried to gulp down a liter of turpentine that was on his bedroom table"[108] (which made Signac conclude that "it was time to go back to the hospital"); whose brother advised him in a January 3, 1890 letter, "If you know that it is dangerous for you to have colors [oil paint] near you why don't you clear them away for a time and make drawings?"; and who, according to an entry added by Dr. Théophile Peyron when Van Gogh left the St Rémy asylum (May 16, 1890), "had several attacks lasting for between two weeks and a month ... [during which he] is subject to terrifying terrors, and on several occasions he has attempted to poison himself, either by swallowing colors that he used for painting, or by ingesting paraffin, which he had taken from the boy while he was filling his lamps,"[109] ended up producing a radical-closure painting in which *paint birds* irrupted in the represented landscape, did not appear in it from behind the horizon or from amidst the wheat stalks.[110] Duchamp: "Since Courbet, it's been believed that painting is addressed to the retina. That was everyone's error. The retinal shudder! Before, painting had other functions: it could be religious, philosophical, moral.... Our whole century is completely retinal, except for the Surrealists, who tried to go outside it a little";[111] would Duchamp have criticized the black birds that appear over the field in Van Gogh's *Wheatfield with Crows* as retinal? I very much doubt it. The rest of the painting, with its thick brushstrokes of paint, is retinal, but the *paint birds* aren't; they *come across directly onto the nervous system*.[112]

"On Sunday last, at 11:30 p.m., one Vincent Vangogh, a painter, born in Holland, arrived at House of Tolerance [brothel] No. I, asked for one Rachel, and handed her—his ear, saying 'keep this and treasure it.' Then he disappeared. Informed of this action, which could only be that of a poor lunatic, the police went to the man's address the next morning and found him lying in bed and giving almost no sign of life. The unfortunate was admitted to hospital as an emergency case" (*Le Forum républicain* [Arles], December 30, 1888). What kind of treasure was implied when Van Gogh handed a prostitute his severed ear and said: "Keep this and treasure it"? Did his gesture of amputation imply auto-castration, the treasure uncovered to be the phallus? The cutting off of a sense organ by a radical-closure artist has nothing or very little to do with the standard psychoanalytical notion of castration. In Lynch's universe, where characters, as is revealed in his *The Grandmother* (1970), are not sexually conceived, one encounters, rather than castration anxiety, an anxiety induced by the unstoppable irruption of unworldly fully formed ahistorical entities (among them one or more penises?), sounds, and images, sometimes in the sense organs. A person encountering irrupting unworldly sounds in a radical closure or in the falling apart world of psychosis and death may cut off his ear because he still holds the illusory hope that he can stop hearing these sounds by getting rid of the corresponding sense organ: "I the undersigned, Doctor of medicine, Director of the St Rémy mental home, certify that the man named Vincent van Gogh, aged 36, a native of Holland and at present domiciled in Arles (Bouches du Rhône), under treatment at this city's infirmary, suffered an attack of acute mania with visual and auditory hallucinations that led him to mutilate himself by cutting off his ear"[113] (from the transcript of the twenty-four-hour certificate issued by Théophile Peyron, the asylum's doctor, on May 9, 1889). A doctor encouraged his patient, who was a music student, to render through musical compositions the sourceless, obtrusive sounds from which he was suffering. Unfortunately, the student was not a good enough musician to recreate them. In a moment of desperation he severed his ear—to stop the sounds. On coming close to his severed ear to throw it away, he heard diagrammatic or unworldly sounds in it. He realized that he had cut off his ear also to make it easier for others to hear these sounds that were at times a torment to him. Having been told so many times that he was hallucinating them, he now answered the first person who again affirmed that they were only in his head: "Yes, these sounds are nowhere else; they are only in my ear." "So, at long last, you do acknowledge that they are hallucinations." "Not at all. They are *'in'* my severed ear on the floor. Get closer to the ear and listen." "*That's fucking crazy, man!*" Many of those to whom he subsequently told the same thing did not give him the benefit of the doubt; but those few who did go close enough to the ear in spite of the revulsion induced in them by that detached, putrefying organ did, to their horrified amazement, hear in the ear the unworldly sounds he had described to them to the best of his ability. They perceived that in certain circumstances (radical closure), the ear, in addition to allowing one to locate more or less approximately the source of a worldly sound, is sometimes the whereabouts of an unworldly sound. If these sounds were not only in his mind, but were objectively present—as was evident from the fact that others too could hear them—couldn't they be heard in ... ? One day, while in a perverse mood, he told one of his incredulous acquaintances: "Come and listen to the sounds in my remaining ear; put your ear next to mine and listen!" "This provocative manner of talking is bound to lead to a quarrel. I don't think we should have a shouting match over these anomalous sounds you hear sometimes, for basically, except for them, we see eye to eye." "I don't care about seeing eye to eye; what will do our relationship good at this point is to hear ear to ear. Place your ear next to mine!" That there are two Van Gogh self-portraits with bandaged ear could indicate that one of the two was actually painted by Van Gogh while the other, unworldly, irrupted fully formed in relation to some radical closure in the world, or that one, *Self-Portrait with Bandaged Ear and Pipe*, refers to the anecdotal, extrinsic cause of the cutting off of the ear (a fight with the painter Gauguin who had informed him shortly before that he planned to leave him, thus impairing, indeed aborting his wish to establish a painters' cooperative in Arles? Auditory "hallucinations"?) while the other, *Self-Portrait with Bandaged Ear*, implies, through the empty canvas visible in the background to the left of the painter, that what led to his amputation of his ear had to do with a painting. I would think that it is on the referent of the represented empty canvas in *Self-Portrait with Bandaged Ear* that Van Gogh later painted *Wheatfield with Crows*, a painting that evinces a radical closure, the condition of possibility of at least some of the unworldly sounds he was hearing (in Robert Altman's *Vincent & Theo*, having painted the field, the sky, and the two converging, radically-closed paths, Van Gogh hears caws without seeing any crows) but also of the unworldly paint crows that irrupted in the painting. In this case, the relation of music and sound in general to painting is not that of finding equivalents in paint for sounds, but of constructing the condition of possibility—a radical closure—of the irruption of sounds *in* the painting. Whether a critic or not, don't you, the reader, at times hear sounds in Van Gogh's *Wheatfield with Crows*? I do. Van Gogh reached sounds through painting more surely—though in a different manner—in *Wheatfield with Crows* than in *La Berceuse*, which he painted shortly after cutting off his ear and regarding which he wrote in a letter to A. H. Koning, "I call it 'La Berceuse,' or, as we say in ... Van Eeden's Dutch, quite simply 'our lullaby or the woman rocking the cradle.' ... Whether I really sang a lullaby in colors is something I leave to the critics."[114] Who would be the best present-day sound designer for a film concerning Van Gogh in the period in which he severed one of his ears and painted much of *Wheatfield with Crows*? Most probably David Lynch. David Lynch said about one of his early paintings: "I'm looking at this figure in this painting, and I hear like a little wind, and I see a little movement."[115] This movement and sound induced him to change media: from painting to film.[116] In Lynch's *Blue Velvet* (1986), standing with the detective in the coroner's office, Jeffrey, who discovered the severed ear in the field, asks the coroner: "What can you tell about the person from the ear?" "Sex, blood type, whether or not the ear came off a dead person.... It looks like the ear was cut off with scissors." Unlike in Lynch's film, Jeffrey could have responded, to the consternation of the detective: "What about the source of the sounds one can hear in it?"[117] The coroner would have responded: "We are unable to determine it, owing to these areas of total black." In my thought experiment, at first neither Jeffrey nor the detective made out what the corner was referring to: they both persisted in assuming that their eyes would grow adapted to the quite low illumination of these black areas in the ear and begin to discern some outlines. But their eyes did not grow adapted to anything, for there was nothing to get adapted to. Thus it no longer occurred to Jeffrey or to the detective to direct a light at these areas of black. Nonetheless, to shed more light on what he had said, the coroner aimed a spotlight at the ear. While the regions of light and darkness in the other sections of the ear shifted with the variations in the intensity of the illumination directed at them, the totally black regions remained unchanged. How can light not affect the black areas? This can happen if the black is not the circumstantial absence of light, but a zone of inexistence.

In the scene of the crows in Vincente Minnelli's film on Van Gogh, *Lust for Life* (1956), the painting *Wheatfield with Crows* reveals the field in front of the canvas mounted on an easel as radically closed. Although the crows appear from amidst the wheat stalks and are seemingly enduring entities, the shots themselves are then no longer continuous.

Minnelli, who in the ballets of his musicals can connect non-contiguous spaces-times seamlessly, felicitously manages in *Lust for Life* to give, through jump cuts, the impression that the crows suddenly appear and disappear, to be replaced by others, which could imply that the space is a radical closure. Having all of a sudden been assaulted by crows and seeing a peasant-driven cart on the point of going beyond the radically-closed path in the wheat field, Van Gogh exclaims, "It's impossible!" and, minutes later, shoots himself. In this scene, what is impossible? Is it for Van Gogh to continue living despite his anxiety about both the recurrence of hallucinations and his precarious livelihood? Or is it the ostensible progress of the cart and its driver through a radically-closed path? When soon after uttering, "It's impossible," Van Gogh takes out a piece of paper from his pocket and scribbles on it, "No way out," does this portend his suicide? Or does it rather refer to a radical closure? Is death a "way out" of a radical closure? A radical-closure writer, artist, or filmmaker knows or at least intuits that death is not a way out of such a closure (Robbe-Grillet's *L'Immortelle* and *The House of Assignation*). One may intuit that death is not a way out of a radical closure but nonetheless be "suicided by society,"[118] by all those who, like that peasant, would have ostensibly impossibly continued along that radically-closed path and later deplored the supposedly arbitrary distortions of the field and its paths in *Wheatfield with Crows*.[119] Was Van Gogh's suicide a last-ditch attempt to avert the impossibility by providing the imperceptive peasant, who, witless, was not going to supply the comic relief of a makeshift excuse for not crossing the radically-closed *gateless gate*,[120] with a justification to stop and turn back, toward the gravely wounded painter, before he incredibly transgresses the radical closure's border?

Copyright Free *Farm Road*

In the case of a radical closure, the presence in a text of specifications of camera placement and movement does not necessarily indicate that the text is a script; such specifications probably signal the irruption of the cinematic in it or in its diegetic world.

The camera tracks up the windows of consecutive stories and stops on a young woman as she finishes closing the entrance door and moves into the apartment advertised for rent. She removes her hat, revealing beautiful blue short hair. She inspects the bedroom and kitchen, then goes back to the living room and looks ahead into the camera, which pans 180 degrees to show what faces her: a bricked up window. She begins blabbering to herself about Melville's Bartleby. While she likes that the apartment is spacious, she dislikes that it gives onto another building and that the rent is exorbitant. The reason she finally decides to rent it is the bricked up window facing it. One night, suffering from insomnia, she heads to the kitchen for sleeping pills. On her way there, she glances in the direction of the bricked up window and sees a painting. The next morning, she manages to dismiss what she saw as caused by her lack of sleep. When, some time later, she witnesses another irruption of a painting in the bricked up window, she, alarmed, phones her friend Jalal Toufic. They decide to meet the following morning. During their meeting, he asks her whether she could recognize the paintings. "One of the two paintings happened to be one with which I am quite familiar: Andrew Wyeth's *Farm Road*." "You may be dealing with a radical closure." "A what?" It is his turn to exclaim: "Why are *you* the one making coffee?" "I happen to make excellent coffee." Shortly, sitting around the kitchen table, she, bemused, remarks: "Your kitchen looks exactly like mine!"[121]

Middle Eastern Films *Before Thy Gaze Returns to Thee*—in Less than 1/24 of a Second

Did the descent of the standard film-camera lenses from Renaissance Western monocular perspective place early Muslim filmmakers at a disadvantage when it came to a genuine formal contribution in the medium of cinema, since these filmmakers came from a tradition that until only a century or so ago (the age of cinema) was, especially in its Arabic regions, still resistant to, rather than ignorant of, Renaissance perspective? Cinema would appear to disadvantage Muslim filmmakers steeped in their religion's tradition if one pays inordinate attention to the kind of space favored by the standard film-camera lenses and disregards cinema's temporal atomicity facet, which makes cinema very close to the predominant Islamic conception of time but about which comparatively little has been written in works on the basic cinematographic apparatus. The notion of *renewed creation* in the kalām (theology) of the Ash'arites and in the Sufism of Ibn al-'Arabī provides a way of considering the world as subject to processes akin to those of cinema. For Ibn al-'Arabī, the things of the world, unlike God, do not have a necessity of existence, so when God gives actual existence to anything, it reverts instantly to inexistence, disappears.[122] God "then" gives existence to a similar thing the next moment. This process goes on indefinitely, making of the world an ever-renewed creation (Ibn al-'Arabī's gloss on the

Qur'ān's "a new creation" [50:15]). In Paradjanov's *Ashik Kerib*, Ashik Kerib, a poor minstrel who promised his lover to become rich (in order to gain the approval of her wealthy father) and to return, from wherever his instrumental pursuit of riches might lead him, to marry her before a thousand days have passed, has to journey back in that period's remaining two days a distance of one hundred days' travel. He prays for help. It is jarring that the horse rider who appears in response to his prayer flies him to his native town in one day, presumably in a similar manner to the way the *jinn* in the Qur'ān story of Solomon and the Queen of Sheba would have transported her throne to Solomon's palace; I would have expected, in this film of jump cuts, the displacement to occur by a new creation, that is, by means of the disappearance of Ashik Kerib from the point of departure and the appearance of a very similar version of Ashik Kerib at his destination, especially since in Paradjanov's previous two films horses with their riders often suddenly disappear then suddenly appear again (in jump cuts). I would have regretted a missed opportunity here were it not (a) that the one-day miraculous trip that ostensibly covers with no discontinuities (as is implied by the revolving globe in the background) a distance that would have otherwise required a hundred days of travel is introduced by Ashik Kerib's prayer presented in jump cuts and his repeated attempts to mount the supernatural horse also presented in jump cuts; (b) that Ashik Kerib's miraculous trip on the flying horse to his native town is anachronistically preceded by another visit that he makes from that distant land to his mother's ruined house and that does not happen by means of the flying horse; and (c) that Ashik Kerib's proof of his miraculous one-day trip on a flying horse deconstructs itself: through the miracle of healing his mother's blindness with dust from the horse's hoof, Ashik Kerib conjointly proves to his incredulous audience the supernatural power of the flying horse and thus his miraculous trip on it, and disproves that he covered the distance in one day since he was back *before the return of the gaze* of his mother—who became blind years earlier on being told that he died—in other words, in the twinkling of an eye.

If, with very rare exceptions, people are unaware of the universal and perpetual acts of appearance, disappearance, then appearance, it is both that the appearance, disappearance, then appearance occur "before thy gaze returns to thee" (Qur'ān 27:40) and that the form that appears following the disappearance of an earlier one is very similar to it. Is this not reminiscent of cinema, where within the same shot the next frame replaces the largely similar earlier one "before thy gaze returns to thee"? With films as well as the world according to Ibn al-'Arabī and the Ash'arites, very similar frames/things replace each other before the eye can detect this. There are several ways to know of renewed creation. Extremely rare people become aware of it directly, through *kashf*, unveiling. A slightly larger number of people become aware of it indirectly, symptomatically, by sensing that the other person is not identical to himself or herself, but merely a similar person—are some of the cases of the Capgras syndrome to be attributed to sensing such renewed-creation substitutions? A still larger number resort to it to resolve certain paradoxes. By means of it the Ash'arite theologians tried to maintain the absolute omnipotence of God despite the apparent causal linkages in the world. In my case, it has happened that while looking at a half-filled cup of coffee placed on a table, I had the clear impression that it cannot be moved, that no alterations were occurring in or to it, that it does not change. How can I explain then that I myself or someone else did displace the vase a short time later, and that the disjunction between the preceding certain impression of its immovability and its later motion was not strong enough to unsettle me, but induced instead merely a mild surprise? Since while looking at the vase on the table I was certain that I could not gradually displace it, if I nonetheless ended up moving it and was only mildly surprised at my success in doing so, it must be another vase. Both I and the bottle returned back to the nothingness from which we arose (and, it could be argued by others, in relation to which each represents an imbalance, a fluctuation), and then were recreated, appearing again in a changed state, the vase no longer inducing the incontestable impression of immovability and I feeling that it can be moved or already moving it. Is the impression of a progression of time, of change, of movement—that of the cat that has just elegantly glided through the narrow door opening—more incontestable to me than the previous impression of the immovability and, more generally, unchangeability of the vase on the table? No. It is easier for me to reconcile, as a secondary, special effect of it, the ostensible sequential passage of time with this ultrafast recurrent appearance then disappearance then appearance of a largely similar entity than to reconcile the indefinite immovability of the vase with its induced motion a few moments later. From the perspective of ever-renewed creation, gradual change is as illusory in the world as it is in cinema: there is an impossibility (*istiḥāla*) of change of state (*istiḥāla*). Nobody and nothing changes: every thing is recurrently appearing then disappearing then being replaced by a largely similar thing. Peter Kubelka's

Arnulf Rainer remains the best example of the conjunction of stasis and quick recurrent appearance then disappearance then appearance of largely similar entities since it exemplifies both modes: in its projection form as a film of six minutes and twenty-four seconds, it instances the flicker of recurrent appearance-disappearance; in its installation form as 35 mm filmstrips mounted on a wall, it instances immutability. Things, not having a necessity of existence, are directly related to the Being who created them and/or to the nothingness to which they are bound to instantly return, and only indirectly related to the ostensibly previous and subsequent chronological moments. We are constantly, ontologically distracted from the ostensibly chronological, mundane "action": this is our aristocracy—is aristocratic what is detached from other things, other moments.[123] We are constantly returning to nothingness: this is our poverty. With its recurrent appearances-disappearances, Paradjanov's cinema presents a felicitous mixture of aristocracy and absolute dependency. While quick recurrent appearance then disappearance then appearance of a largely similar entity is discernible in pixilation films, as well as in the jump cuts and the discrete replacement of the young by the old in Paradjanov's films from *Sayat Nova* (1968) onward (for example, in *The Legend of Suram Fortress*, 1986, the actress Leila Alibegashvili playing Vardo as a youth steps behind the actress Sofiko Chiaureli playing her as an old woman, this indicating young Vardo's replacement by, not her growth into, the old Vardo), it finds its purest form in two films that are a sort of diagrammatic, abstract tracing of it: Tony Conrad's thirty-minute *The Flicker*, 1966, and Peter Kubelka's *Arnulf Rainer*, 1958–60, with the filmstrip in both an alternation of dark frames and blank ones. Conrad's film is prefaced with a warning and disclaimer, which reads: "WARNING. The producer, distributor, and exhibitors waive all liability for physical or mental injury possibly caused by the motion picture *The Flicker*. Since this film may induce epileptic seizures or produce mild symptoms of shock treatment in certain persons, you are cautioned to remain in the theatre only at your own risk. A physician should be in attendance." Indeed, the exposure to the flicker effect may induce epileptic seizures in the spectator. In the world of Ibn al-'Arabī and the Ash'arites, the material camera projecting this flickering film would itself be flickering in and out of existence. Does the actual witnessing of the ever-renewed creation, of the ultrafast recurrent appearance then disappearance of one entity and its replacement by a largely similar one, induce a more basic kind of seizure, no longer merely "a transient occurrence of signs and/or symptoms due to abnormal excessive or synchronous neuronal activity in the brain,"[124] but an ontological seizure, a *fanā'*, an annihilation in God? The very rare people who actually witness recurrent creation doubly undergo *fanā'*, since, in addition to their recurrent disappearance on account of their not having a necessity of existence, witnessing the flicker of the ultrafast recurrent disappearance of entities itself produces a temporary disappearance of the consciousness of the witness. Were one to manage to accompany consciously this return to nothingness that occurs almost always outside awareness, then the chain of karma would be broken. From this perspective, animals are in the worst situation, since, unlike inorganic matter, which following each of its recurrent creations is limited to returning to God/nothingness, they evince some "attention" to the "durational" "action," albeit in the mode of being "*simply given over*" to it "*without being able to grasp*" it "*as such*,"[125] but, unlike humans, cannot accompany the return to Being/nothingness in an aware manner. Out of the clash of any two images, but even more clearly of any one image, does not arise, unlike in Sergei Eisenstein's films, any concept, but a *dhikr* (invocation, remembrance) of the one necessary Being (and then a heedful absentmindedness regarding the "God" beyond concepts and memory?); or the notion of the absolute dependence of the myriad entities. The jump cut, "the sound of one hand [or image] clapping,"[126] is a silent *dhikr*. Forgetfulness of God is a macro illusion, since creatures, not having a necessity of existence, are always returning to that which alone endures, God. If one is enjoined not to forget God for an instant, it is that that is the maximum that one can possibly forget Him, since one instantly reverts to Him, thus remembering Him. From the standpoint of renewed creation, we are not forgetful of God, but of our return to, of our remembrance of, God. As in Buddhism, where though we are in Samsāra, ignorant and unenlightened, we have Buddha-nature (*busshō*) and Buddha face, in Islam, we—Muslims and non-Muslims—are, through this renewed return to Being/*al-Haqq*, involved in a perpetual *dhikr*. The explicit *dhikr* in the form of the repetitive remembrance and invocation of the one necessary Reality echoes an implicit *dhikr* in the form of the recurrent reversion of the ontologically poor entity to the Reality. The disciple must have meditated enough temporal atomicity and the *dhikr* it implies that however much he reiterates the name of God during a *dhikr* ceremony, "Allāh, Allāh ..." he does become entranced, since trance would be a symptom of obliviousness to the ontological *dhikr*. Our as well as every other entity's (ontological) attention is drawn in the direction of change; if change is the reversion to nothingness/Being rather than continuous alteration then that is where our attention is basically drawn. This detachment from, clinamen in relation to the ostensible chronological change applies not only in the case of humans but also in the case of inanimate matter, including of atoms,[127] which as a result of this askew attentiveness in relation to the ostensible chronological change has a face.[128] "The seven heavens and the earth and all that is therein praise Him, and there is not a thing but hymneth His praise; but ye understand not their praise" (Qur'ān 17:44): the entities' constant going back, from moment to moment, to the Being is this praise. The snapshot, even the one in Harold Edgerton's stroboscopic works, does not capture the instant but is clearly an abstract arrest of the movement,[129] otherwise it would disclose to us a distraction from the apparent chronological "action"; to reach the instant is to reach the element where we see this ontological distraction, where humans are distracted ontologically from psychological distraction, ontologically turning away from any psychological turning away from the mundane "action." What we witness in Paradjanov's films from *Sayat Nova* onward is this askewness of the gaze in relation to the apparent chronological "action." The direction of the gaze in Paradjanov's films from *Sayat Nova* onward is not toward the spectator (whether to trigger or enhance distantiation or in an interactive manner), but, ontologically, toward the nothingness to which the figure instantly reverts. If the characters in Paradjanov's films face the camera, it is because he, intuitively, places it in the non-spatial direction in which the return to nothingness/Being happens. When in *The Legend of Suram Fortress* Osman Aga interpellates Durmishkhan, and the latter looks in the direction of the camera, the film spectator is witnessing the resultant spatial turning of the character toward his interlocutor, but also the facing of the character away from his interlocutor toward the non-spatial direction of his reversion back to nothingness/Being/the camera. Like Muslims in general, during their explicit prayer Osman Aga and his companions turn toward the Kaaba in Mecca, this locus of orientation in exoteric Islam. But this should not mask from the film spectator what *Ashik Kerib* intimates: since Ashik Kerib's prayer is shot in jump cuts, hence in appearances-disappearances, and since the disappearances back to Being are remembrances of the latter, hence a form of prayer, the exoteric prayer is itself full of these other, esoteric prayers. We should thus be aware with regard to the prayer of Osman Aga and his companions that since every entity's disappearance is a turning aside from apparent chronology to the one Being, God, thus a facing toward Him, at that more fundamental level "whithersoever you turn, there is the face of God" (Qur'ān 2:115). Paradjanov's world evinces a different kind of aside than the conventional one in traditional theater. While in the latter the thoughts made manifest in the aside remain related to the progression conflict-climax-resolution, in Paradjanov's films from *Sayat Nova* onward the aside is the turning away from the apparent chronological "action" toward the real action, that is, toward the reversion to nothingness/Being or, in *Ashik Kerib*, to the camera. Moreover, while the conventional theatrical aside manifests various intimate thoughts of the character, the Muslim aside manifests, when in the form of jump cuts, a silent *dhikr* of the only self-subsistent, true ontological reality; or, when in the form of words and thoughts of the character in voice-over, a *ḥadīth qudsī*'s assertion: "I [God] am ... his tongue through which he speaks" (indeed in *Ashik Kerib*, the diegetic songs and music are not fully synchronous with the movement of the lips and of the hands on the musical instrument of the one purportedly singing and playing, Ashik Kerib); or, more frequently, both: Paradjanov's cinema makes clear that there is a correlation of the jump cut, as a symptom of renewed creation, with the voice-over, the "I [God] am ... his tongue through which he speaks." What interpellates the film spectator is not the frontally looking diegetic character but the latter's recurrent disappearance in jump cuts. Unlike the interpellation Althusser conceptualized, this interpellation does not transform each individual into a subject through the always already attempted turn around he or she makes to answer the structural "Hey, you there!" but alerts the film spectator to his or her substitution by another, similar entity, and to his or her subsumption in the one and only Subject, Who is "his hearing, and his sight, and his tongue through which he speaks." Whether such a cinema is popular or not, it has no audience, since it basically recalls the spectator to his or her fundamental nonexistence. Even ghosts and revenants—who ostensibly cannot disappear for good until they settle some outstanding symbolic debt[130]—vanish definitively then are recreated again by God, to haunt.[131] Paradjanov's cinema is an ontological cinema not really because of the stasis of the shots at the chronological level—shots thus ostensibly connected to being rather than to becoming—but because its entities are constantly returning to the only necessary, self-subsistent Being. In temporally atomic artworks and films there is little urge or temptation to return to a chronological source (whether it is assumed to be a golden age, a certain kind of chaos ...), because everything at every moment is reverting back to the more basic and immediate source, Being/nothingness. That is partly why in the case of his films from *Sayat Nova* onward, and despite his pre-twentieth-century characters (in *Sayat Nova*, the Armenian troubadour Sayat Nova [1712–1795] …) and his folkloric references (*The Legend of Suram Fortress* is based on a Georgian folk tale about a fortress whose walls keep crumbling however many times they are restored—until a young man is bricked up alive in them …), Paradjanov cannot be legitimately accused of making retro works.

A view of reality where what seems to be one enduring entity is considered to be actually myriad very similar entities recurring in atomic time is apt to produce at the spatial level if not the arabesque then something akin to it. A sense of recognition occurs to me in front of an arabesque (one that lasts an instant, to be seamlessly replaced by another sense of recognition the next instant), for the person in front of the arabesque is himself or herself a temporal arabesque, myriad very similar versions of himself or herself. The arabesque is a rendition of temporal atomicity at the level of extension. A Muslim who subscribes to atomism knows, if not perceives, that whenever he looks at any entity he is seeing an arabesque—a temporal one. The flower that I see in the courtyard of a mosque whose walls are lined with floral arabesques is itself in reality myriad very similar flowers that momentarily replace each other—the Muslim floral scroll is a bouquet of one flower. The arabesque, especially the one where the figures are juxtaposed rather than interlaced, is doubly my mirror: the multiplication of its basic figure gives me a spatial rendition of my temporal multiplication; the abstraction of its unit figure reminds me of my own abstraction, my being without a nature and proper characteristics. He had seen in museums centuries-old ornamented silver mirrors that belonged to Muslim rulers: in their silver side, which certainly did not reflect as well as modern glass mirrors, he saw that he was one and that he had features, but in their reverse side, ornamented with floral arabesques, he had the inkling that he was myriad entities and that he had no nature and no proper characteristics. Looking in such a mirror, day after day one side showed him that he was aging, while the other intimated to him that he was always one instant old. In a worldview of renewed creation, the flowers of the arabesque of some mirror decorated by a Muslim craftsman can be accurate reflections of the ostensibly much longer-lived human being, since the latter really is as ephemeral, lasts one instant only, and has no nature and proper characteristics. From a temporal atomicity viewpoint, what seems to us even for a moment to be one enduring plant is in actuality myriad ones that replace each other from (atomic) time to (atomic) time; from the related occasionalist viewpoint, what seems to us to be rich in characteristics and possessing a nature is in actuality without them (it is not intrinsic to a flower to have the scent and color we associate with it given its chemistry [and our sense organs and brains]). T. E. Lawrence: "A first knowledge of their sense of the purity of rarefaction was given me in early years, when we had ridden far out over the rolling plains of North Syria to a ruin of the Roman period which the Arabs believed was made by a prince of the border as a desert-palace for his queen. The clay of its building was said to have been kneaded for greater richness, not with water, but with the precious essential oils of flowers. My guides, sniffing the air like dogs, led me from crumbling room to room, saying, 'This is jessamine, this violet, this rose.' But at last Dahoum drew me:

'Come and smell the very sweetest scent of all,' and we went into the main lodging, to the gaping window sockets of its eastern face, and there drank with open mouths of the effortless, empty, eddyless wind of the desert.... 'This,' they told me, 'is the best: it has no taste.'"[132] Many of the Muslim artists who produced floral arabesques would be delighted with tastelessness not only, like the Arabs mentioned by T. E. Lawrence and like Walt Whitman ("The atmosphere is not a perfume, it has no taste of the distillation, it is odorless, / It is for my mouth forever, I am in love with it" [*Leaves of Grass*]), in the case of the air, but also in the case of the most particular smells, those that for others are most likely to evoke and sometimes reactivate the past. Many of these artists could have told Whitman and the Arabs mentioned by T. E. Lawrence that the very sweetest scent of all, the one they are in love with, is that of a flower for the latter, intrinsically, "is odorless," "has no taste." Indeed even the desert air in a non-occasionalist view of reality, where objects have natures and therefore characteristics, is, despite its ostensible tastelessness, still an approximation of the absence of any intrinsic scent of flowers in an occasionalist worldview. From a standpoint alien to occasionalism, one can speak about a procedure of abstraction in Islamic art aiming at eluding the possible accusation of usurping God's prerogative of creation; but judged from the standpoint of the *mutakallimīn*'s occasionalist denial of nature, one cannot legitimately speak about a proper and basic abstraction of Muslim art in relation to everyday reality, for that would imply that the objects outside the artwork have certain qualities and characteristics, when actually they are as devoid of these as the figures in Muslim art. The Muslim floral arabesque does not manifest any abstraction in relation to the flower in the world, since there are, basically, no nature and proper characteristics of the latter. Primarily and fundamentally, in Islam abstraction applies before the Muslim artist plans an artwork and touches his tools; the primary abstractionists of Islam are the atomistic occasionalists. Islamic art abstracts only secondarily, merely accentuates that primary abstraction advanced and argued by occasionalism, through pushing toward a geometrization of the shapes of animals and plants. The incredible colors in Muslim miniatures, for instance the blue, turquoise, green, mauve, or white of rocks and the rose or sky-blue of grass, are not used necessarily to avoid verisimilitude in order to avert the condemnation of the 'ulamā', but are there in many cases because they are allowed by or a result of the occasionalist denial of nature—for a custom of God—and consequent separation of accidents[133]:[134] for the *mutakallimīn*, when a black die touches a white object, the latter is then black not because it was causally changed by its contact with the black die, but because God chose to give it a black color when He recreated it anew—God could possibly have given it a red color. Deploying an amazing practical ingenuity, Muslim artists managed to validly inscribe the same motifs and designs across different media, scales, and materials. This is most probably and cogently a consequence of the absence of nature and proper characteristics of the various media and materials according to the majority of Muslim theologians. Muslim abstraction in the arts is thus double: it is an abstraction not only within a given medium, in the form of arabesques or, in miniatures, human and animal figures with no perspective, shadows, or modulation and with unworldly colors; but also at the level of the media and materials: by creating the same designs across various media and materials, they abstracted such media and materials, intimating that none of the latter has a proper nature,[135] that nothing intrinsically distinguishes textiles, jade, ivory, metalwork, glass, wood, ceramics, bricks, and paper.[136] Undecorated objects are rare in Islamic art, but in Islam one decorates with what has no proper nature, one enriches with what is implied to be poor in characteristics, one clothes with what hints to us its fundamental inexistence—luxurious poverty, in other words, poor luxury. For the perceptive person, the world itself, with its recurrent creation and its absence of nature, of characteristics, is a vast arabesque that ornaments Allāh. The same way that in copies of the Qur'ān arabesques surround many of the words, especially the sūras' titles, the world itself surrounds (while also being surrounded by) God (or, in Ismāʿīlism, one or more of the divine emanations), Who alone has essential attributes.

Even when full with figures and objects, a successful Islamic miniature does not give the impression of overcrowding. Even with figures filling the entire space, leaving no gaps, the Muslim arabesque does not induce the sense of suffocation one experiences in the *regular division of the plane* works of M. C. Escher, an admirer of Muslim arabesques. The void in Muslim miniatures and Muslim art in general, while not seen in the frame, is implied in it: the Muslim miniature breathes not so much through some space left empty in it but by the recurrent return to the void, and thus disappearance, of the figures and objects, and this even if there is no temporal interval between their disappearances and appearances[137].[138] Now you see it—and now you see it. Muslim miniatures and Muslim art in general are virtually as linked to the void as Chinese art, but in a different manner and to a different kind of void. What strikes me as paradoxical about the contorted rocks in many Persian miniatures, which rocks appeared first during the Mongol dynasty of the Ilkhanids, are not their unworldly colors but that they are anomalously connected to two different, virtually antithetical kinds of void, evincing a valid coexistence of the discrete modality of the breath of the all-Merciful (*nafas al-Raḥmān*) that recurrently gives existence to the entities that instantly revert back to God/nothingness, punctuating even the seemingly continuous line; and the continuity of Taoism, where the continuous breath-energy (*chi*) underlies even the seemingly discontinuous brushstroke (Li Jih-Hua: "This means that the movements of the painter's brush must be interrupted [without interruption of the breath that is animating them]"[139]). These rocks most probably belong to *'ālam al-khayāl*, the Imaginal World, which, according to Ibn al-'Arabī, "brings together all opposites (*al-jam' bayn al-aḍḍād*)."[140] How different is the subtle fullness of many a Muslim miniature from the present crowding of the majority-Muslim city of Cairo! The constant meditation on the notion of renewed creation, with its recurrent disappearances, affects the quality of the presence of the people who practice it: their presence is subtle. I recommend placing signs that would indicate the differential capacity of a particular space: "The capacity of this room is ten Ibn al-'Arabī disciples but only six persons who are oblivious to recurrent creation although they too are recurrently created."

The poetic can take the form of:

— the absence of metaphors through the literalization of figurative expressions in altered states of body and consciousness. During his traumatic stay at Count Dracula's castle in Transylvania, how many times did the vampire's victim Harker witness “the mountains … move like clouds”[141] (a time-lapse allowed by the freezing of the vampire in the coffin)? Talking about Harker, who traveled from Bremen to Transylvania ostensibly a few weeks earlier, his yearning fiancée Mina says to her friend Lucy: “I haven’t seen him in ages.” A few weeks after she says these words, Harker appears in Bremen, his hair now totally white.

— the universal extension of the metaphorical. In the Qur’ān, Solomon declared that he wished to have the throne of Bilqīs, the Queen of Sheba, in his court. Someone “who had knowledge from the Scripture” (27:40), Āṣif b. Barkhayā (?),[142] responded: “I will bring it to thee before thy gaze returns to thee” (27:40). According to Ibn al-‘Arabī, he accomplished this by invoking God’s renewed creation. The throne was at the court of the Queen of Sheba, then the cosmos disappeared, and when the cosmos appeared again before the gazes of (very similar versions of) Solomon and his guests had time to return to them (in less than 1/24 of a second), the throne—not the identical throne but an extremely similar one—was at Solomon’s court. “Aṣaf’s only merit in the matter was that he effected the renewal [of Bilqīs’s throne] in the court of Solomon.”[143] Was Solomon aware at that point of renewed creation? No; consequently, he was unaware of the full measure of his fitting response: “This is of the bounty of my Lord …” (27:40). One would have expected that Solomon would have then presented the throne to Bilqīs as a proof of the omnipotence of God, thus inducing her, who “was from a disbelieving people” (27:43), to become a Muslim. Instead—I would imagine to the surprise of those present—Solomon said: “Let the throne be altered, so that we may see whether or not she will recognize it” (27:41). When Bilqīs arrived, she was bidden to enter the palace.

She experienced then an encounter with the figurative in its most manifest guise; mistaking the floor made of transparent glass for a pool, she bared her legs. Solomon was quick to inform her of her error. She was introduced in the palace and presented with what appeared to be her throne. She examined it carefully then she said: "It is as though (*ka'annahu*) it were my throne" (27:42). I imagine that on hearing these words, Solomon underwent a kind of satori ("on a soil very unlike" Japan), a sudden knowledge, becoming aware that the throne that was presently in his court wasn't strictly speaking Bilqīs's throne but as though it (*ka'annahu*), actually its recreation by God. Thus had God favored Solomon over His newest believing slave, Bilqīs, who too received knowledge ("My Lord! Lo! I have wronged myself, and I surrender with Solomon unto Allāh, the Lord of the Worlds" [27:44]), but not of renewed creation—which she might have received had Solomon not altered what looked very much like her throne at his court ("And We had certainly given to David and Solomon knowledge, and they said, 'Praise [is due] to Allāh, who has favored us over many of His believing slaves'" [27:15]). When the hoopoe said to Solomon, who had "been taught the language of birds" (27:16), "I have found out (a thing) that thou apprehendest not, and I come unto thee from Sheba with sure tidings" (27:22), are these tidings to be limited to what he went on to tell him? I would think that they included also the sure knowledge of renewed creation. In Islam, the task of a human is not to be himself or herself (in Islam he or she—who has no necessity of existence—is basically nothing) but to become cognizant that he or she is in the likeness of himself or herself, by becoming aware of God's renewed creation, and in the likeness of God—notwithstanding that "there is nothing whatever like unto Him" (Qur'ān 42:11)—since he or she is at each moment one of the infinite Self-Disclosures of God. Taking into consideration how the poetic function stresses selection over combination (Roman Jakobson),[144] there is a basic poetic modality to an atomistic occasionalist universe, where entities are recurrently replaced by what appears to be them, where we are not ourselves, but rather metaphors of ourselves: *ka'annanā*. It is thus felicitous that this atomistic occasionalistic view was the one prevalent among the Arab Muslim theologians, since Arabs were known to exalt poetry already in the pre-Islamic period. From *Sayat Nova* onward, Paradjanov's cinema, with its atomistic occasionalist world and thus with its jump cuts, is one of the main instantiations of the metaphoric in cinema, since everything is in the image of itself in the jump cuts showing apparently the same entity. Paradjanov's films from *Sayat Nova* onward are cinematic prose poems since the substitution of a term is not by another but by a very similar variant of itself. One can easily remark that the poet Sayat Nova made extensive use of substitution in the production of the poems included in Paradjanov's *Sayat Nova*; but the spectator can also clearly see the substitution of the poet by very similar variants of himself in jump cuts in Paradjanov's poetic film. *Sayat Nova* starts with a voice-over reciting these words from the Bible: "Then God said, 'Let us make mankind in our image, in our likeness ...'" (Genesis 1:26). In the Bible these words are followed almost immediately by: "So God created mankind in his own image, / in the image of God he created them" (Genesis 1:27). Which is more basic, determinant: that mankind is made by God or that they are in the image of God? Is the second half of the quote from Genesis 1:27, where likeness precedes creation and being, a clarification of the first part? In case it is, man would be fundamentally related less to being than to likeness, characterized more as like himself than as being himself. Metaphor is usually based on ontology, derives from it (a poor kind of metaphor); but in Paradjanov's films from *Sayat Nova* onward, metaphor precedes ontology, is more basic. Paradjanov's cinema from *Sayat Nova* onward is doubly a cinema of the image: because of its arresting images, but also and basically because the world it shows is in the image of itself. In comparison with Paradjanov's *Ashik Kerib*, no other film has shown so much love not for the irreplaceable,[145] but for the singularity of the replaceable.[146] In such a universe, that which is extremely similar but not identical to itself does not induce the kind of anxiety encountered in Capgras syndrome, undeath, and, as an unworldly entity, in radical closures. At the outset of Ashik Kerib's journey in Paradjanov's *Ashik Kerib*, his rival tricks him into entrusting him with his clothes while crossing the river, returns to town, announces that Ashik Kerib drowned and exhibits the clothes as proof. The universe of *Ashik Kerib*, a film dedicated to the memory of Tarkovsky (the filmmaker of, among other films, *Solaris* [1972]), not only can be melancholic but actually has an affinity with such a state, because in such a universe the state of death of someone is not a final one, a once and for all occurrence, but is an accident momentarily attached to the person and that has to be recreated by God from instant to instant if it is to appear to last (the Ash'arites' view). While melancholic, this kind of universe does not require the selfsame beloved, but wholly accepts his or her or its replacement by a very similar entity! What would heal Ashik Kerib's lover turned melancholic, and his mother become blind on hearing the convincing report of his death? It is the return not necessarily of Ashik Kerib, but of someone very much like him. Were the temporality of the universe of Paradjanov's *Ashik Kerib* not an atomic one, I would be surprised and somewhat disappointed by the absence of any symptoms that Ashik Kerib was marked by death: even setting aside that, at least in art and literature, episodes of feigned or falsely reported death can be, and frequently are, indicative of dying before dying, the film spectator knows that while Ashik Kerib did not actually drown at the start of his journey, he was nonetheless, prior to his return, and unbeknownst to both his mother and his lover, beheaded at the court of Sultan Aziz. Notwithstanding that he was reported to be dead, Ashik Kerib's mother and his beloved end up wholly accepting him when he appears again after an absence of several years, justifiably at no point feeling any suspicion that he is Ashik Kerib's double or an imposter: once the accident of death is no longer recreated by God, Ashik Kerib is not merely no longer dead, he is not marked by death at all.

We who have no necessity of existence have one passion: to return back to nonexistence. The one act of creatures is facing toward the reversion back to nonexistence rather than toward the seeming chronological change. All other "actions" are actually occasions for the Reality, God, to act. To God and to those who are aware of His renewed creation of the world ("surely He begins the creation in the first instance, then He reproduces it" [Qur'ān 10:4; cf. Qur'ān 50:15]), we, who, lacking any necessity of existence, revert to nonexistence instantly, are portraits; to God, and to those who are aware of renewed creation, there is nothing but portraits. Taking into account the occasionalism of the Ash'arite Muslim theologians, each of these portraits is that of *the man without qualities* (to borrow the title of a Robert Musil novel). Like other things ("The seven heavens and the earth and all that is therein praise Him, and there is not a thing but hymneth His praise; but ye understand not their praise" [Qur'ān 17:44]), the face is praising God—but, if it is not beautiful, it is additionally (irrespective of whether it is laughing, sneering, or that of the dead body of a man or woman) imploring to be saved. That is why we feel that a beautiful face (but not necessarily the man or woman to whom it apparently belongs) is closer to God: it is just praising God (a face that while praising God is not also imploring others to save it is beautiful). While one of the tasks of other portraitists is to manifest the implicit imploration by the face that is not beautiful to be saved, the Muslim portraitist's task is to manifest that the face (but not necessarily the man or woman to whom it apparently belongs) is praising God, Whose face is the only thing that is not perishing ("Each thing is perishing except His face" [Qur'ān 28:88]); and to treat it and show it as a mask, as something that does not change, since, not having an intrinsic necessity of existence, it *instantly* goes back to nonexistence/God.

Paradjanov's ostensibly static *Sayat Nova* (as well as his subsequent feature films) is not an abrupt departure from his hectic preceding film, *Shadows of Our Forgotten Ancestors* (1965), with its pervasive camera motion, but pushes the motion in the latter to a more basic level. To someone who senses the universal and perpetual appearances, disappearances then appearances in Paradjanov's later films, even the exacerbated camera motion in *Shadows of Our Forgotten Ancestors* seems tame. How slow are the most frenetic MTV music videos in comparison to Paradjanov's *Sayat Nova* or *The Legend of Suram Fortress*!

Reaffirming their Islamic faith, during the early 1990s a large number of Egyptian actresses went back to the veil. One is not to expect much from mere actresses, especially ones working in the Egyptian film industry. But one should expect and demand much from Muslim filmmakers, even ones who have not had a tradition of investigating the medium of the art form in which they are working: they could and in a way ought to have indirectly reached this investigation simply by taking into account the kind of temporality most characteristic of orthodox Islam: atomism. Is this atomicity the only temporality to be found in Islam? No: to the highly Hellenized Muslim philosophers, the *falāsifa*, time is continuous; to the Ismāʻīlīs, time is cyclical ... Nonetheless, it certainly is the one most akin to the basic cinematographic apparatus. Cinema is the first medium adequate to represent and reflect the world according to the Ashʻarite view because it functions at the level of the basic cinematographic apparatus in terms of both recurrent appearance and disappearance of entities, and absence of causality between the separate still frames. From *Sayat Nova* onward, rather than being a capitulation of the cinematic to painting, Paradjanov's films manifest, on the contrary, the revolving of the film around a diegetic world akin to cinema, since subject to recurrent appearance and disappearance.[147] Cinema is the first adequate medium to represent and reflect the world according to the Ashʻarite view also because the *mutakallimīn* denied there being a fast or slow movement, the perception of slowness being a result of the recreation of the ostensibly moving object at the same indivisible spatial unit in several "subsequent" moments—a sort of double-framing—so that the more frequent such recreation of the object at the same indivisible spatial unit in "subsequent" moments the slower the object is perceived to be. Here's my Islamic (more specifically, Ash'arite) version of the bet—whether a trotting horse has all four feet off the ground at one time—which reportedly was behind Muybridge's setting up of his cameras, ropes, and diagrams in May 1872 at a racecourse in Sacramento, California: a future rich Muslim patron commissions someone to prove his contention that at certain points the same stage/frame of the horse's trot is repeated. It is unfortunate that Muslim filmmakers have produced very few pixilation films, and that pixilation films are rarely screened in the Islamic world, for pixilation is the kind of filmmaking closest to the kalām's view, where the movement is both atomic and an accident added to the thing that is shown moving, and is slower or quicker according to whether one repeats certain frames or not. With the exception of the films of Paradjanov (who was not a Muslim) from *Sayat Nova* onward, up to now Islamic *cinematography* can be located only in the atomistic temporality of Islam and not in the numerous films and TV programs on Islamic themes, motifs, and figures,[148] which are content with parading Islamic tradition's arabesques, calligraphy, architecture, and music (accompanied by a commentary), and/or, when the film includes among its characters one of the Qur'ānic prophets (Muhammad [Moustapha Akkad's *The Message*], Joseph [Youssef Chahine's *The Emigrant*] ...) or the first four caliphs (Salah Abouseif's *al-Qādisiyya*), trying to tackle the thoughtless prohibition in mainstream Sunni Islam on the representation of not only the prophet Muhammad but also all the aforementioned personages associated with Islam.[149] Youssef Chahine's *Saladin*, Abouseif's *Al-Qādisiyya*, and Moustapha Akkad's *The Message*, three (tasteless and thoughtless) "epics" revolving around major Muslim figures and events, convey far less of Islam than do three consecutive jump cuts in a Paradjanov film.[150]

Notes Toward Cinematic Biographies of Some Qur'ānic Prophets

Dedicated to Wojciech Has for
The Hour-Glass Sanatorium

Whoever is not subject to the dreamwork mechanisms of condensation, displacement, etc., but always appears as himself or herself, and when he or she does not appear thus is not to be interpreted as himself or herself is not to be represented by an actor. This applies to the prophet Muhammad; the great Sufi Ibn al-'Arabī writes in *The Bezels of Wisdom*, "Taqī b. al-Mukhallad, the Imām and author of the *Musnad*, heard that the Apostle had said, 'Whoever sees me in sleep has seen me in waking, for the Devil cannot take my form upon himself.' ... The spirit of the Prophet appears to one in the form of his body when he died, albeit unaffected by decay ..., which form Satan is unable to assume, as a protection from God for the recipient of the vision. Thus, whoever sees him in this way accepts from him all he commands or forbids and all he says, as he would accept his precepts in this world according to whether the sense of the words is explicit or implicit, or in whatever sense they are. If, on the other hand, he gives him something, its [form] is a matter for interpretation."[151] A filmmaker may opt to have the other characters interact with the diegetic prophet Muhammad even while not showing him. In that case, what the writer and filmmaker Duras did regarding her two characters in her film *Le Camion* provides one manner of doing so. In that film, the filmmaker and "screenwriter" Duras sits with the actor or, more precisely, the reader Depardieu around a table on which are placed two stacks of papers. Both take turns reading the text describing the events happening to a female hitchhiker who is picked up by a truck driver. This on-screen reading alternates with shots showing the truck passing through the landscape, the protagonists of the narrative never appearing on screen—even when the inside of the moving truck is shown. The subtlety and complexity of Duras's protocol is that while not showing the protagonists, it is indicated that they are seeable, through the performative that Duras addresses to Depardieu: "You see?" One can thus be made to see the prophet Muhammad through words, performatively, hence without images.

What admits its transfiguration in dreams, appearing under a different form there than it appears in the waking world, permits—disregarding other constraints—its embodiment by an actor. This applies to all the prophets recognized by the Qur'ān except Muḥammad[152] (as well as to the Shi'ite imams—except the Mahdī?).[153] If for some reason a filmmaker still feels some qualms about having actors play these prophets, he or she could problematize and relativize their embodiment by actors through having the same prophet (other than Muhammad)—or for that matter the same Shi'ite imam—at a certain age played by several actors (as Buñuel does with the woman protagonist in *That Obscure Object of Desire*, who is played by two actresses)[154]—some of whom clearly do not fit the verbal description we hear of the prophet; as well as by having one of these actors play also another character in the same film. If I can appear in the figure of someone else in my or another person's dream, with psychoanalytical interpretation, drawing on the material provided by free association, indicating that the one in the dream is me, then it would be legitimate to have an actor embody me in a film. Cinematic fiction films recreating historical episodes are thus essentially related to dreams at least with regards to the embodiment of historical characters by actors. Fictional cinema based on historical characters is a prerogative of creatures that dream; were we not creatures that dream and were it not a facet of dreams that we can appear in them in the guise of other persons, then the filmic representation of a historical personage by an actor would strike us as illegitimate and as so incredible as to be ridiculous. At the premiere of Robert Altman's *Vincent & Theo* (1990), an audience member turned to his companion in the darkness of the movie theater and whispered in her ear, not without licking it: "Do you recall the dream I told you a couple of weeks ago, in which I saw Vincent van Gogh in the guise of the actor Tim Roth?" A few weeks later, his companion also dreamt of Vincent van Gogh: he was in the guise of the American filmmaker Martin Scorsese! Was that inflected by her having seen several days earlier Scorsese's segment around a painter in *New York Stories*, 1989? Taking advantage of the seamless interaction of living actors with bygone film actors made possible by digital technology, the Van Gogh of a future film biography can have several dreams, or a dream with several episodes, in which he is in the guise of the various actors who acted the role: Kirk Douglas (in Vincente Minnelli's *Lust for Life*, 1956), Tim Roth (in Robert Altman's *Vincent & Theo*, 1990), Martin Scorsese (in Akira Kurosawa's *Dreams*, 1990), Jacques Dutronc (in Maurice Pialat's *Van Gogh*, 1991), etc. Such intertextual recapitulation would ground the previous versions' use of various actors to embody the painter.

In his crass *The Emigrant*, which shows a protagonist clearly modeled on the Biblical and Islamic prophet Joseph, the thoughtless Egyptian filmmaker Youssef Chahine failed to take into consideration that Joseph was considered a dreamer ("And they [Joseph's brothers] said one to another, Behold, this dreamer cometh" [Genesis 37:19]). Joseph said to Jacob: "Father, I dreamt of eleven stars and the sun and the moon; I saw them prostrate themselves before me" (Qur'ān 12:4). Fearing that they might get even more jealous of him, his favorite son, and wish to harm him, Jacob told Joseph not to recount his dream to his brothers. Back from an outing on which Joseph accompanied them, his brothers brought back to Jacob his son's shirt drenched in blood, claiming that a beast devoured their brother in their absence. "All his sons and daughters came to comfort him, but he refused to be comforted. 'No,' he said, 'I will continue to mourn until I join my son in the grave'" (Genesis 37:35). Why did Jacob start mourning Joseph when the circumstance that the prophetic dream had not yet been actualized implied that his son must still be alive? Not being a dreamer, the fact that Rachel, Joseph's mother, had already died years before, just after giving birth to Benjamin, Joseph's younger brother, must have made Jacob doubt that the dream was prophetic. Not being a dreamer, when Joseph recounted to him his dream, Jacob did not ask him how he appeared in it.[155] Had he done so, Joseph would have answered: "I was dressed in Egyptian attire!" Years later, a famine devastated the land of Canaan, where Jacob and his sons dwelt. Jacob sent ten of his sons to Egypt to purchase food. They decided that their best bet was to try to have an audience with the overseer of the granaries. Amongst many other imposing, sumptuously attired Egyptian personages in the grand hall, they immediately recognized their man. He asked these Hebrew shepherds: "Who am I?" They answered: "You are clearly the overseer of the pharaoh's granaries." "What is my name?" They could not answer. "He recognized them, but they knew him not" (Qur'ān 12:58).[156] He informed them that each one of them was allowed to purchase at most a camel-load of provisions even if he had the money to buy more. When they reached the land of Canaan, they discovered in their packs the silver they paid for the food. How to interpret that? Could it be the high official's apologetic compensation for allowing some Egyptians to buy portions in excess of the maximum he had insisted on with the brothers? Later, needing more provisions, they went again to Egypt, this time in the company of Benjamin; this way they could have an additional camel's load of food. Once they purchased the provisions, they started heading home, when they were intercepted by a posse of Egyptians and accused of stealing the pharaoh's cup. The cup was indeed found in Benjamin's bag. Benjamin felt greatly confounded for he was certain he did not steal it. How to explain, first of all to himself, the anomaly? Swayed by his earnest protests of his innocence, his brothers too tried hard to interpret why the cup was found among his belongings. They continued their attempt at an interpretation in prison: Was it the high official who had instigated this anomaly—as well as the previous one? But what would be his purport in doing that? Benjamin and his brothers were soon released and brought into the dignitary's presence. He said: "Do you know how I achieved this exalted position? I correctly interpreted the pharaoh's prophetic double dream. Nine years ago, the pharaoh had two disturbing dreams: in the first, he saw seven fatted cows which seven lean ones devoured; in the second, seven green ears of corn and seven dry ones. Being the king of 'The Two Lands,' Upper and Lower Egypt, whose unification ushered in the long period of the reign of Dynasties and whose crowns, thenceforth joined into a double one, he wears, it was natural he should have two dreams portending the same, one for each land. More importantly, he had two dreams with the same signification to indicate that what they portended related not only to the world of the living but also to the realm of the dead. Ostensibly, the interpretation of this dream is: seven years of plenty would be followed by seven years of the severest famine. The pharaoh was horrified when he heard my interpretation. The announced famine threatened mortally not only the living but also the dead, who would die a second, definitive death. During the previous famine, exceptionally large numbers of people boldly attempted to rob the tombs. With worsening famine conditions, some people headed to the tombs they had already robbed, this time for the painted food there, and, on being told by conscientious priests that it was with another kind of mouth that one can magically partake of this food, a mouth that moreover could become functional only by means of the Opening of the Mouth ceremony, in desperation forced the terrified priests to perform that ceremony for them and to invoke the magical formulae that would materialize the food in the tomb's wall paintings." At this point, a priest entered and approached the high official and spoke to him in a language the brothers did not understand. When the priest had taken leave, the high official, himself a priest married to the daughter of Potiphera, priest of On, resumed: "You'll have to excuse me; I have to presently participate, as part of the responsibilities of my office, in a mortuary offering. The task of ensuring there is enough food in Egypt despite the lack of harvest in the last two years is compounded by the duty to regularly provide the dead with a modicum of this world's food, without which counterpart the magical transfiguration of the food painted on the tomb's walls and chiseled into the table of offerings would fail, or the painted food, albeit turning, through the incantation of magical formulae, into meat, beer, etc., would no longer provide any effective sustenance, the mummies' *kas*, although regularly eating, remaining hungry. To give you an idea of what I mean by a counterpart: two fish and five loaves can, in conjunction with the magically materialized painted fish and bread, feed five thousand dead people a meal. By accepting to be in charge of the granaries and the food distribution to the population, I implicitly accepted to be in charge of food also for the dead, in the form of the mortuary offerings." It is then the brothers understood why he had seemed inequitable in his distribution of the food to them as compared to the Egyptians. "With the exception of such offerings at the tomb chapels of a number of women in whose untimely death I was inadvertently implicated years ago, I personally attend only the offerings to the royal mummies at the temples. It is to the tomb chapel of one of these women that I have to head now. You are not allowed within the cultic precincts of the tomb chapel. But you can wait for me outside it." His assistants were intrigued that he would allow the precise whereabouts of a tomb to be known to these Hebrew foreigners, ones who, moreover, had just been in prison on the accusation of theft. What would deter them from robbing the tomb, either on their own or in complicity with others? How to interpret that? Despite their qualms, at the appointed time they brought these Hebrews to the vicinity of the tomb and then left. They must have arrived too early, for the dignitary was nowhere to be seen. Then the brothers heard his voice. Reverberating and distorted along its passage through the tomb's shaft, the high official's voice sounded exactly like Joseph's. They managed to discern the words: "Do you recall what you did to Joseph?" For a moment, they were seized with the uncanny apprehension that they would see the seventeen-year-old Joseph they threw in the pit almost two decades earlier come out of the tomb. Notwithstanding that they were relieved that the one who ascended moments later from the tomb was not the seventeen-year-old Joseph emerging from the past, they exclaimed: "Are you indeed Joseph?" (Qur'ān 12:90). "I know it is hard to believe that I am indeed your brother Joseph. I presume that you must have left me for dead when, back in Canaan, you threw me, a spoiled youth of seventeen, in that pit. I remember the excruciating pain I felt on hitting the bottom. I must shortly have lost consciousness, for when I woke up, I was being pulled up toward a bright light. Potiphar, the pharaoh's captain of the guard who bought me from an Ishmaelite merchant, told me one day: 'What swayed me into buying you despite being troubled by the commotion your beauty was producing in any woman who happened to lay her eyes on you, and what initiated my subsisting regard for you, was one peculiar remark the merchant said: "When we pulled him out of the well in which he had presumably inadvertently fallen, he ecstatically exclaimed: 'Coming forth by day!'"' To this day, I do not know whether I actually uttered these words then, or whether they were added by the merchant to make me, his slave, more desirable to a prospective Egyptian buyer." He took off his shirt and ordered them to return to their father in Canaan and place it on his face, so he would be able to recognize his son from the smell. He asked them to entreat their father to move with his household to Egypt, at least for the duration of the remaining five years of the famine. He provided them with a number of wagons with drivers. They traveled for days on end to reach their destination. Seeing their caravan approaching in the distance, Jacob could not restrain himself from exclaiming: "I can sense it: Joseph is alive!" One of those around, exasperated by what he took to be yet another manifestation of obstinacy—or an initial sign of senility—retorted: "In your dreams!" Wishing to make sure Jacob would have the opportunity to smell what faint scent lingered in the shirt, Jacob's sons wrapped that item of clothing tightly around his face. For a moment, one of the Egyptian charioteers Joseph sent with them had the impression he was looking at a mummy's head. On smelling his son's scent, Jacob fully recovered his sight. Shortly after, in the company of his household, Jacob went to Egypt. When they arrived at On (Heliopolis), they were led to Joseph's headquarters. When he appeared at the entrance, Joseph's brothers recalled that they had once "said one to another, 'Behold, this dreamer cometh.'" Upon seeing his father, Joseph threw his arms around him. He then addressed the old woman standing next to Jacob thus: "I have everything to do with you, mother." "He helped his parents to a dais, and they all fell on their knees and prostrated themselves before him" (Qur'ān 12:100). If we do not view this scene as a dream whose interpretation (in a pre-Freudian manner) by Joseph and his father (the eleven stars stand for his eleven brothers and the sun and the moon for his father and mother) was actualized in life *as a dream*, since a character who in reality was dead, Rachel, was being treated as alive, then we have here, in the omniscient narration *par excellence*, since its author is God, a parapraxis. Most likely, the woman Joseph raised on the dais was Leah, Rachel's older sister.[157] After all, she had already replaced Rachel once before: having accepted to work for Laban for seven years to be given the latter's daughter Rachel as wife, the then still young Jacob discovered the morning following his wedding night that, as a result of a Laban subterfuge, he had lain with Leah, who, as was the custom then, had come to him wearing a veil. If now too Jacob took Leah for Rachel, it was not because she was veiled, but because he was still dreaming even while he believed he was awake. Joseph approached his mother on the dais, wiped her tears, and said: "The eyes, dull, are Leah's, but the signified is Rachel." Jacob was jolted into awareness that he was dreaming. "'This,' said Joseph to his father, 'is the meaning of my old vision: my Lord has fulfilled it'" (Qur'ān 12:100). It should be clear by now that if Joseph was characterized as a dreamer, it was neither because he was unrealistic, seeing that he managed the affairs of Egypt in a rigorously realistic manner during the years of famine; nor simply because at least one of his dreams was later actualized in reality (the interpreted purports of the dreams of the two prisoners and of the pharaoh, people who were not characterized as dreamers, were also actualized in reality, being prophetic dreams); but because he was aware that human life is a dream and that what we usually view as a dream is *a dream within a dream*[158] (how come Joseph was aware that life is a dream? While his brothers did not actually physically kill him when he was a youth, they, unawares, occasioned his dying before dying. The prophet Muhammad indicated, "Men are asleep; they awaken at their death": to die before [physically] dying is not to awaken to a life that is not a dream; it is rather to become aware that one is dreaming while seemingly awake, that is, to become a lucid dreamer); and because the actualization of some, if not all of his dreams in reality was as dreams, which made manifest to at least some of those present that they were dreaming. Indeed, haven't many of the episodes of the sūra of Joseph the atmosphere of dreams? When Potiphar's wife was informed of the rumors circulating about her failed attempts at seducing Joseph, she invited the women implicated in these rumors to a banquet. While the various meals were being prepared at Potiphar's house, the women guests were busy making up: placing cucumbers on their faces; lukewarm olive oil on their hands; lemon, as a conditioner, on their hair; and the solution obtained from boiling lemon with sugar and water, as a depilatory, on their arms and legs. (In a film adaptation of this scene, one would see a parallel montage between these two concurrent activities.) Her role as the hostess momentarily superseding her loathing of her guests, she earnestly inquired of several of them: "How is the food?" One exclaimed, "Luscious," another, "Ambrosial." Noticing one who was not touching her plate, she asked her: "Why are you not eating?" "I am not hungry." She had the impulse to respond, "Then why have you accepted my invitation to a banquet?" but checked herself, for she knew that these women accepted her invitation not for the food, but per chance to espy Joseph. They had began cutting their rarely cooked choice cuts of meat, when Joseph appeared as "a gracious angel" (Qur'ān 12:31) and they, in dreamy enchantment, continued cutting—their fingers. Instead of being revolted by the example of the others, the satiated one was seized with a voracious appetite, and shortly she too was inadvertently cutting her fingers. They seemed unconcerned with the blood flowing from their hands, treating it as if it were not their own or as if it were not blood but red (*pas du sang, du rouge*).[159] Joseph felt certain he was beholding a dream. Years later, listening to the pharaoh's two dreams, he recalled this striking image of people drinking of their own blood, as if it were the only sustenance they could still lay their hands on. He also recalled food that was barely touched. The first confirmed the ominous image of a famine; the other the required solution, that not all the harvest be consumed. As with a dream, the women guests quickly forgot the whole episode: "Yet, for all the evidence they had seen, they thought it right to jail him for a time" (Qur'ān 12:35). Forgetting in Joseph's episode, this tale full of dreams, is not limited to the women at the banquet: for example, having interpreted the dream of the pharaoh's imprisoned cupbearer as indicating his imminent release, Joseph asked him to inform the pharaoh, his lord, of Joseph's mastery of dream interpretation, but the cupbearer forgot to do this for several years. When Joseph died, he was embalmed, and "after they embalmed him, he was placed in a coffin in Egypt" (Genesis 50:26) according to Egyptian custom, with papyri of chapters of *Coming Forth by Day* placed between his feet.[160] Following the ceremony of the Opening of the Mouth, the lector priest recited some further formulae from *Coming Forth by Day*: "Thou shalt come forth in heaven, thou shalt pass over the sky, thou shalt be joined unto the starry deities. Praises shall be offered unto thee in thy boat, thou shalt be hymned in the *atet* boat....[161] May the gods who dwell in heaven ascribe praises unto Osiris Zaphenath-Paneah, when they behold him in triumph, as unto Ra....[162] I am a shining one clothed in power, mightier than any other shining one."[163]

P.S.: Should one dismiss outright the term "dream woman," having become nauseated by its sloppy and facile use in Hollywood, the "dream factory," and by the debased rhetoric of dreams in contemporary American culture ("the American dream," etc. How mundane is any "dream team" when set against a group of surrealists participating in an *exquisite corpse*)? No. Given that, basically, every actor who plays a historical character is a dream creature, the actress Madeleine Stowe is a dream woman as the Mary of Bernard L. Kowalski's *The Nativity*. To be a dream woman in the world or in the diegesis, a rare concatenation of circumstances has to occur. I see a woman during the day. At night, she appears in my dream. Is this significant? Not necessarily: "Dreams show a clear preference for the impressions of the immediately preceding days.... They make their selection upon different principles from our waking memory, since they do not recall what is essential and important but what is subsidiary and unnoticed"[164] (Freud). In the dream, she looks different, having been distorted by the dream-work mechanisms of condensation and displacement. When I see her again in my waking life, she appears, through a chain of circumstances in the world, as she was in the dream. It is this unintended change through the waking world's uncorrelated reasons and means into how the primary processes of the dreamer's unconscious had altered her that turns a woman into a dream woman. Dr. Kathryn Railly of Terry Gilliam's *Twelve Monkeys*, 1995, played by Madeleine Stowe, is such a dream woman. Trying to evade detection by the police, the time traveler to the past James Cole and the psychiatrist turned his accomplice Kathryn Railly hide in a movie theater. It is showing a Hitchcock double feature, beginning with *Vertigo*. Why *Vertigo*? It is in part because of the likelihood that the traumatized protagonist would be tempted to try to make Kathryn look exactly as she appears in his recurrent dream. Did the protagonist see Scottie transforming Judy into his dead beloved Madeleine by making her don the same dress and adopt the same hair color and style? It is undecidable, for when we see him next, he is waking up during the subsequent film. Unexpectedly, unlike *Vertigo*'s Scottie, *Twelve Monkeys*'s protagonist refrains from trying to make Kathryn look as she was in the dream! Is it because, already doubting his own sanity, he is apprehensive that by making her slip into the blonde wig and the dress she had in the dream, he would be making reality indistinguishable from a dream? Is it also because the dream in question was not only desirable but also nightmarish since associated to his ostensible death? It is also because he must intuit that were he to succeed in consciously actualizing the changes that would transform her into the exact look of the woman in his dream, she could no longer be a dream woman, who is for the most part the product of unconscious mechanisms (the Judy who, transfigured by him at long last into Madeleine, appears from the dressing room and approaches Scottie in a greenish penumbra is no dream woman). Notwithstanding her ignorance of how he and she looked in his recurrent dream, by attaching a moustache to her ostensibly awake companion to make him less recognizable to the police, Kathryn, unawares, initiates their transformation into the images of the dream. When he wakes up, she has disappeared—was she only a dream figment? He rushes outside in the blonde wig she placed on his bald head during his sleep—the same kind of wig in which he appears in his recurrent dream. He catches sight of her. She is talking at a public phone. She turns around and starts heading toward him. A snoring sound, faint but unstoppable, like the distant voice of a hypnotist, soon reaches him. The sound has also the tone of an alarm that may wake one from a dream. So then, he first saw her in the blond wig in which she appears in his recurrent dream between two sleeps: his own, having dozed off in the movie theater, and that of the old usher, who is taking a nap on a chair at the cinema entrance. He would have preferred that the old usher be looking at them, gaping at them even, rather than dreaming. There was something voyeuristic about that sleeping usher, as if he were gazing at them in his dreams.

Oedipus in Egypt

Even the sharp contrast between the brutally poor and the extravagantly rich in present-day Egypt did not fully prepare me, when I visited the Egyptian Museum in Cairo, to find in the context of the talkative and noisy culture of present-day Egypt the hieratic culture of silence of the funerary ancient Egyptian statues, these entities to whom talk is not natural, whose mouths had to be artificially opened in a specific ceremony so that they could talk (and eat) again. Physicists inform us of a cosmic background noise (aka cosmic microwave background radiation) of 2.7260 ± 0.0013 K reaching us from the time of the decoupling of matter and radiation, approximately 379,000 years after the Big Bang that started the universe; in the Egyptian Museum, there is a background silence that reaches one, amid the noise of the visitors, from ancient Egypt. Nowhere else do I feel so strongly the exile of the figures of ancient Egyptian statues and bas-reliefs, which otherwise seem (almost) not to be exiled even in death, than in this museum and in present-day Egyptian culture.

The gaze of ancient Egyptian statues and bas-reliefs is directed beyond us (even the frontal eyes in the bas-reliefs' profile faces—a position that seems to be especially directed toward us—do this):[165] sometimes by going through us, thus making us seem to be transparent or overlaid at the spot where we are; sometimes by passing next to us who are standing in front of it (while not determined by physical gravity, this gaze resonates with what general relativity tell us, that even our seemingly straight trajectories are curved); sometimes by going over our heads even when we are standing in front of and level with the statues' and bas-reliefs' eyes, thus implying that we must be comparatively small, and making us aware of its monumentality. The ancient Egyptian figures in sculptures and bas-reliefs are monumental even when having our size physically. The blatant physical monumentality of the colossi of Ramses II at Abu Simbel is largely to impress those who are insensitive to the aforementioned other monumentality: the statues become physically smaller, *but no less monumental*, as one progresses from the exterior of the temple to its sanctuary, off limits to the majority of the ancient Egyptians.[166]

The ancient Egyptian figures in sculptures and bas-reliefs facing in the same direction, and whose gazes, fixed on an area at an indefinite distance beyond, always bypass the present-day human figures who come and stand in front of them (this applies however far back the person originally standing right in front of them may move), are looking at each other and seeing each other at that indefinite area, in a haptic manner. Vision occurs not in the heads of the statues of King Menkaura (Mycerinus) and his queen (2490–2472 B.C., Museum of Fine Arts, Boston) but at the area at which their gazes are fixed and meet. Knowing that in that culture the viscera of the dead person were removed from the body and placed in canopic jars—so that his or her sustenance happened at a distance—I am not surprised by this external, tele-vision. There is at the Egyptian Museum in Cairo a pillar relief of King Senusret I and the god Ptah standing face to face, with the arms of the god around the waist of the king. In this pillar relief, there is an intimacy, since Ptah is hugging the pharaoh, that remains distant, due to the indefinite far-off area at which the gaze of the two happens; and a distance, that of the indefinite area at which the gazes are fixed, that is intimate, since the vision at that indefinite area occurs in a haptic manner. In the case of the Avenue of the Sphinxes, either the Sphinxes in one row do not see the ones facing them, since their gazes are fixed at an indefinite area ahead, or they do see each other but the avenue is incredibly wider than it seems.[167] The only object that was left in the King's Chamber in the Great Pyramid of Khufu was the lidless sarcophagus. Does the fact that thieves managed to get into the pyramid imply that the nearby Sphinx was useless? No: it successfully guarded against the dangers situated at the indeterminate area where its gaze was fixed, as well as against those human robbers who became oblivious of themselves because of its gaze in their direction yet bypassing them.

The following are two of the differences between Egyptian Sphinxes and the Greek Sphinx as it appears on vessels, urns, etc.: the latter's gaze looked down (it was seated on a mound, a column, or a tomb) and in the direction of the Thebans she interpolated. In their encounter with the Greek Sphinx, that so many others failed, but Oedipus managed to solve the riddle ("What creature has only one voice, walks sometimes on two legs, sometimes on three, sometimes on four, and which, contrary to the general law of nature, is at its weakest when it uses the most legs?") was because the answer to it was not *man* but *Oedipus* (in some of the iconic representations, Oedipus answered by pointing to himself). While believing that he was giving a rational generic answer to the riddle (man as someone who walks on four as a baby, on three in old age [since he will use then a staff for support], and on two in between), Oedipus was, unawares, indicating a prophesy specific to him: he will resort to the help of a staff while not yet an infirm old man because he blinds himself. After his excommunication from Thebes, Greece, for marrying and having sexual intercourse with his mother (and killing his father), Oedipus traveled to Egypt. There he encountered again a Sphinx, though this time an Egyptian one; from a distance at which its features were not clear, Oedipus hallucinated or dreamt the riddle (the Egyptian Sphinx, who disregards the human standing in front of it, may address him or her in a dream or hallucination: the future King Thutmose IV is said to have slept at the base of the Sphinx at Giza and dreamt that if he cleared the sand that had engulfed its body, the Sphinx would make him the ruler). Who is naïve enough to consider that the difficulty of the encounter with one of the Egyptian Sphinxes resided solely in the riddle? A good percentage of ancient Egyptians could have solved such a riddle; certainly doing so did not require someone of the resourcefulness of Oedipus, and by no means made the latter outstanding. That so many people failed to solve the enigma of the Egyptian Sphinx they encountered was because it resided not simply in the riddle but also in the disjunction between the riddle and the gaze that by its total disregard of the person in front of it made him forget himself, that is, forget the answer. By what incredible presence of mind and self-centeredness did Oedipus manage to recollect himself in front of the totally disregarding gaze of the Egyptian Sphinx he encountered, a gaze that made people oblivious of themselves? Following his successful encounter with one of the Egyptian Sphinxes, Oedipus knowingly married his half-sister and daughter Antigone in Thebes, in the vicinity of Deir el-Bahri (where many funerary temples and tombs were located and where following her physical death Antigone was buried in the Egyptian manner, then called by name ["Arise ... thou shalt not perish. Thou hast been called by name. Thou hast been resurrected" (*Egyptian Book of the Dead*)], then managed, through uttering the appropriate magical spells, which made actual what was depicted in the bas-reliefs of her tomb, to live physically in the grave and, vindicated, virtually in the Field of the Reeds of the afterlife), but was not exiled for doing so, for incest was affirmed in ancient Egyptian culture (where the paradigmatic marriage was that of the god Osiris to his sister Isis). How utterly beside the point was Napoleon when he said at the start of his conquest of Egypt, "From the summit of these monuments, forty centuries look upon us," and not because the Sphinx, and by implication the statues in the nearby pyramids, do not look (the Sphinx is not an inanimate representation of the king but, as a result of certain rituals, a *seshepankh*, a living statue); but because they look beyond us even when seemingly looking in our direction—had Napoleon said, "From the summit of these monuments, forty centuries look upon *me*," he would have been, unawares, vying with the Oedipus of my thought experiment. In Cecil B. DeMille's *The Ten Commandments*, one scene starts with a long shot of the pharaoh, seated at his court, looking at Moses and addressing him and Aaron. My suggestion for a remake of that scene of Moses's audience with the pharaoh is to begin rather with a medium shot of the seated pharaoh and continue with a sequence of medium shots-reverse shots of the two interlocutors, with Moses saying at one point to the pharaoh, who is still looking at him, "I entreat you to look at me while you are looking straight in my direction," as the camera zooms out to reveal that the pharaoh is seated in the lap of a colossus in the form of a Sphinx with the pharaoh's likeness and whose eyes look at an indefinite area ahead, disregarding Moses. Moses had two encounters with gods and thus with problematic vision: the pharaoh, who, in the guise of a Sphinx, disregarded him even when looking in his direction; and Yahweh/Allāh, Whose glory, face and/or self made him avert his look ("Then Moses said, 'Now show me your glory.' And the LORD said, 'You cannot see my face, for no one may see me and live.' Then the LORD said, 'When my glory passes by, I will put you in a cleft in the rock and cover you with my hand until I have passed by. Then I will remove my hand and you will see my back; but my face must not be seen'" [Exodus 33:18–23]; cf. Qur'ān 7:143, "And when Moses came to Our appointed tryst and his Lord had spoken unto him, he said: My Lord! Show me [Thy Self], that I may gaze upon Thee. He said: Thou wilt not see Me, but gaze upon the mountain! If it stand still in its place, then thou wilt see Me. And when his Lord revealed (His) glory to the mountain He sent it crashing down").

In Cairo, the one searching for graffiti would be well advised to look for it not on the city's walls but on antiquities, for example, the Ibn Tūlūn Mosque; the Mosque of Sultān al-Nāsir and al-Gawhara Palace in al-Qal'a; the King's Chamber in the Great Pyramid of Khufu; as well as on some of the pedestals of the statues in the Egyptian Museum—graffiti becomes a differentiating mark that tells one whether the common Egyptian, and not only the Supreme Council of Antiquities, considers an old building in this old city just another dwelling or an ancient monument. Erstwhile, only Oedipus could have remembered himself in front of an ancient Egyptian figure; but in present-day Egypt, any *insensitive* mediocre living Egyptian can ostensibly do so, inscribing his or her Arabic name on its pedestal.

Like other mortals, ancient Egyptians were already dead even while they lived. That they additionally died physically at one point or another is conspicuous in the Egyptian Museum: the mummies. The mummy is far less uncanny, despite its artificial preservation, than the statues and funerary masks, for notwithstanding the great struggle against history it manifests, it is still fully a historical object. What we witness on the anthropoid coffin encasing the mummy is not only the figure that would hopefully get resurrected following its physical death and then live indefinitely, but also the endless death-as-undeath it would undergo were the resurrection to fail. This endless death-as-undeath is so compellingly implied in ancient Egyptian anthropoid coffins that I almost find it impossible to believe what I presume: the diminutive people walking around in the Egyptian Museum in Cairo—obviously I include myself among them—are themselves always already dead; and that I almost believe that death is the prerogative of only the few (this is what the Egyptians of the Ancient Kingdom believed)[168] and that the people walking around in the museum are wholly within life (while having been rendered spectral by the funerary statues' gaze that totally disregards them who are standing in front of it and sees beyond them), that is, that they tangentially encounter death only as an external event, and that upon physically dying they cease completely. The dwelling of around three-quarter million present-day Egyptians in the "Cities of the Dead" in Cairo[169] remains far more comprehensible than the casual mixing of the living Egyptian museum visitors with the funerary ancient Egyptian sculptures and bas-reliefs.

It is appropriate and symptomatic that in his *The Night of Counting the Years*, 1968, the Egyptian filmmaker Chadi Abdel Salam chose the historical moment when Egyptian mountain dwellers in the region of Luxor in the latter decades of the nineteenth century had become so uncomprehending of the link that relates them to their ancient ancestors that they desecrated the latter's tombs in Deir el-Bahri and sold the enclosed treasures to the highest bidder. Has this chasm largely been bridged in present-day Egypt, where university courses are taught on the language, religion, as well as other facets of that ancient culture? No. It can possibly be bridged only by crossing into death (Chadi Abdel Salam does not appear to have done so), around which that ancient culture revolved. Had Youssef Chahine been still occasionally a fine filmmaker,[170] or a less limited, more spiritual person, then on hearing that he was working on a film on ancient Egypt, I would have expected it to be the occasion for the then sixty-eight-year-old Egyptian filmmaker to deal with death from the other side of that threshold, thus complementing what he had done in *An Egyptian Story*, 1982, his filmic recapitulation of his life occasioned by a dangerous open-heart surgery he underwent. But, characteristically, in the resulting *The Emigrant*, 1994, which revolves around the stay of the foreigner Joseph in ancient Egypt, the exoterically *human, all too human* Chahine treats ancient Egypt as the familiar. With respect to ancient Egypt, the difference between an Egyptian filmmaker and a foreign one cannot reside in some assumed familiarity of the Egyptian filmmaker with that civilization, for there can be no familiarity with that art and culture transfixed by death, since there can be no familiarity with death. I expect to encounter the *unheimlich* whenever a genuine present-day Egyptian filmmaker deals with ancient Egypt, whether the work maintains itself within life: the uncanniness would then relate to the *strange familiarity* of ancient Egypt itself (the religious [for the Muslim Egyptians], racial, national, and geographic other, in the form of the Napoleonic campaign, seems to have also served, through the decipherment of the hieroglyphic language of ancient Egypt by the Frenchman Champollion, to disclose to the Egyptian the otherness he or she hosts as familiar yet most strange: ancient Egypt); or whether it crosses into death: the uncanniness would then be an effect of the undeath realm as such.

Edward Hopper, this painter who did so much to introduce American motifs and architecture in early twentieth-century American painting, and who wrote in 1933, "After all we are not French and never can be," can be easily taken (in his oils rather than in his watercolors) for an (ancient) Egyptian. In both his paintings and ancient Egyptian funerary culture one encounters the contrast between the constriction of the spaces (tombs in ancient Egypt; motel rooms, offices, etc., in Hopper) and the gazes fixed on a beyond (Hopper's *Intermission*), where the otherwise misaligned gazes meet. Light in Hopper is that towards which the figures face (*Pennsylvania Coal Town*, 1947), the one exception to the mismatching, awry gazes of his figures. Because the awry gaze in relation to all other entities becomes accordant in relation to light, the latter is always directional in Hopper, even when the source of light cannot be localized. By looking with an accordant gaze at the light, Hopper's figures, for example, the woman facing the window in *Morning Sun* (1952) and the woman standing at her house's entrance door in *High Noon* (1949), give the impression that they are akin to the departed ancient Egyptians who *manifested in the light*. A voice-over in ancient Egyptian reciting a passage from the *Book of the Dead* reanimates two men and a woman frozen in the exact positions of those in Hopper's *Conference at Night* (1949). The man facing away from the window asks the other man: "Have you heard something?" "No." He then says to the woman facing the window: "I dwell in the building facing you." "I see only light." Doubtful of her assertion, he turns toward the window; to his consternation, there is no building of his, just light.

On Entities Older Than the World

Jalal Toufic, Los Angeles
6/14/1996

Dear Frank Auerbach:
It is not that uncommon in art to encounter figures that are older than the universe in which they are (and not necessarily because they would be unworldly entities that irrupted in a radical closure): the figure in your *Head of E.O.W. V*, 1961, etc. Are at least some of these figures in paintings older than the world because they are coming back from a burial (several days after dying and prior to being resurrected by the Christ, the undead Lazarus lost

in an unworldly labyrinth seemed and "was" older than the world, certainly than the few-thousand-year-old universe of the Bible)? Yes, but not from their own burial; rather from the world's burial. He felt like burying the world that had seemed not to be there when it was needed, that had deserted him and some others. Being a painter, he produced on the canvas a depth that through an impression of limitlessness—achieved in part through a particular thickness of paint—became a fundamental background that buried the world so well it interred even what might return from a traditional burial: revenants. It is from such a background that many of your figures issue. One encounters in *Head of E.O.W. V* a complex impression, conjointly of depth, because of the thickness of the layers of paint, and of shallowness, because, the world and what it interred or repressed having been buried, nothing, not even revenants, can come from behind the figure. The aforementioned figures' concentrated gaze at the person in front of them is perplexing, because while being exclusive of everything else—the world having been buried by the background from which they issued—it is not a fascinated one. Your figures stare totally ahead since nothing can come from the background that buried the world and from which they issued; we cannot reciprocate such a look, with the same totally frontal gaze, since something can appear behind us.

In each of her previous love affairs, she wished that the infatuation would make her and her lover completely oblivious of the world. In each of her previous love affairs, which with their hypersensitivity to the beloved's particularities were states of heightened, if not excessive differentiation, there ensued the temptation not to leave the apartment in which they met, and to gradually drift into a loss of differentiability, disorder spreading, garbage accumulating, electricity and phone line disconnected because of the occupants' disinterest in picking up their mail and the resultant failure to pay the bills—up to the great loss of differentiability of death. They were thus implementing the obliviousness to others and to the outside in general by the paradigmatic consequence of the (relative) closure of a system according to thermodynamics: the rise of entropy. Was it possible for the love affair with her present lover to *cause* both of them to become oblivious of the world? No. She could not demand of him, as she had demanded of her previous lovers, "See me to the exclusion of all others, to the exclusion of the world," since he, who came from a background that had already buried the world, was focused on her because there were no others. What she would see as she looked into his eyes was not her reflection but the darkness of the burial of the world from which he issued. However consuming was her love for him, she knew that she was still aware of others since she could not fully reciprocate his look.

Vampire films have failed to give rise to creatures that are older than the world, but a good number of paintings, whether or not dealing with the undead, have managed to do so. Were I to do a remake of Coppola's *Dracula*, I would have Harker be an artist who brought with him to Count Dracula's castle one of his paintings of his fiancée Mina in which she looks older than the universe. Struck by the look of abjection and extreme old age of his host, and not knowing that the latter was a vampire, who has no (mirror) image, the painter asked his permission to paint him. The vampire accepted, partly humorously because he considered that it is impossible to make an image of him. Soon after finishing his host's portrait, the painter asked him:

"How old are you?" "Had you asked me this question when we first 'met' and before you painted my portrait, I would have answered: 'Around five hundred years.' But since you did my portrait, I no longer know." The painter couldn't believe that the vampire was so old; the vampire couldn't believe that entities as old as the figure in the portrait the painter made of him were possible (several centuries later, the vampire confessed: "I cannot conceive of ever being as old as the figure in the painting he did of 'me'"). The painter wrote in his diary: "A few days ago, as I was going with Dracula over the contract for the house he is to buy, the photograph of Mina that I always carry with me inadvertently fell from my jacket as I was reaching for a pen from my pocket. Count Dracula saw it, held it momentarily in his hand, politely asked who it was, then returned it to me without showing the slightest genuine interest." Several days later, on entering the painter's room, the vampire felt drawn toward "a niche of the room which had hitherto been thrown into deep shade by one of the bedposts." As he got closer, he saw a painting. It was that portrait of Mina in which she appeared older than the universe. The vampire fell in love with this figure rather than with the flesh and blood Mina. He used the flesh and blood Mina merely to provide him with blood to continue his relationship with her figure in the painting, a relationship between an accursed entity who is repeatedly buried but repeatedly comes back for recurrently rejected by the earth[171] and a painted figure that issued from the burial of the world.

The figure in *Head of E.O.W. V*, who is older than the universe *without preceding it historically*, subsists because its excessive oldness makes not only it and the universe but even God, who alone has a necessity of existence, oblivious of its lack of such a necessity, and consequently of its fundamental inability to subsist on its own without being recurrently created (a figure that would subsist for even two moments, rather than disappear after only one, would strike us as older than a figure that appears to be millions of years old but is newly recreated—in the form of similar entities—from moment to moment).

After a number of artists, it is cosmologists' turn to tackle the paradox of entities that are older than the universe from which they ostensibly issue. As reported in the *New York Times* article "Astronomers Debate Conflicting Data on Age of the Universe," dated December 27, 1994, an international team of astronomers led by Dr. Wendy L. Freedman "used the Hubble Space Telescope to get the most precise measurement yet of the distance between Earth and a far-off galaxy. From this they derived a high value for the Hubble constant and thus a relatively young age for the universe of between 8 billion and 12 billion years. Other astronomers praised the complex analysis and could find no obvious errors.... But one aspect gave everyone pause. The new findings made it appear that the universe was younger than the oldest stars, which have been estimated at 14 billion to 16 billion years old.[172]"[173] Before scientists rush to solve this paradox,[174] they would probably benefit from looking at your paintings. Were this particular avatar of the paradox of entities older than the universe of which they are part to be solved by science, the paradox will be encountered again and, in the case of at least one phenomenon or class of phenomena, will prove unsolvable.

Monstrous Units over the Plateau

For Larry Ochs

Most music pieces take sounds ready-made. A few generate them through an encounter with chaos, whether before they start, as their prehistory, or along their endangered progress, presenting, in the latter case, the origination of some or all of their already heard sounds. In music, chaos is fundamentally less some noisiness than the possibility of the generation of the sounds. In rare musical pieces, for example *Triceratops*, composed by Larry Ochs for Rova Saxophone Quartet's offshoot saxophone octet, Figure 8, one notices not only such an encounter with chaos within the piece, but also the construction of a sound plateau that is recognizable aurally by the effacement of the differentiability of the respective sounds produced by the various musicians, and functionally by the burial of the world it accomplishes. The distinguishable sounds that emerge above the plateau that buried the world never function as an accompaniment. The following are, at the two ends of the spectrum, two sound relations to the background: that of John Cage, accepting so-called background sounds as music (*4'33"*); and that of a music that establishes plateaus that bury the world and hence instances a total absence of ambient worldly sounds—in some cases only to construct its own (unworldly or otherworldly) aural background. Cage's proposal that there is no silence, that there are always sounds, usually downplayed as background, non musical ones, is an illegitimate generalization, since it holds neither in dance and death, with their frequent silence-over, nor in the works of musicians who construct plateaus that bury the world, including its sounds. Any sound, however complex, that appears above this aural plateau that buried the world is, and effectively gives the impression of being, an unanalyzable unit, an element. In not so rare limit cases, the whole music piece up to the construction of the plateau the musicians produced and that buried the world may appear again, this time having issued from the plateau as an unanalyzable sound. In some instances, the same sounds that were ungenerated and analyzable at the music piece's beginning are generated through the encounter with chaos and issue as unanalyzable units over the plateau the musicians produced and that buried the world. Ochs's music is historical not only through inspirations and influences (in *Pipe Dreams* [Black Saint, 1994], he provides a partial listing of these through the dedications of the pieces: Albert Ayler, Pete Townshend, Ray Charles, Steve Lacy, Anthony Braxton, Morton Feldman, Iannis Xenakis, and Roscoe Mitchell); but also because it generates its sounds through an encounter with chaos—it is historical up to the establishment of the plateau that buries the world.

In the paintings of Frank Auerbach there is an equivalent production of a burial of the world, partly through a particular thick layering of the paint. The painter must have required his models to stay motionless during the painting sessions in part because such motionlessness, reminiscent of that of corpses, made the burial easier. The circumstance that the painting's figure of the model comes from the burial of the world as it were gets replayed, deepened at another level: Auerbach never seems to be satisfied with the first painted figure, scratching it and painting over it, i.e., burying it. How many times have Juliet Yardley Mills (J.Y.M.) and Stella West (E.O.W.) been buried while posing for Auerbach! For any discerning model, the hardest aspect of posing for Auerbach would not be the "deformations," which might make it difficult for him or her to recognize himself or herself in the painted figure, or may make him or her feel that his or her image has been subjected to violence, violated; but the burial, and, even more, perhaps, the dispossession, through the figure that issues from the model's burial, of the possibility of "having" a ghost. I can envision Stella West lamenting to Auerbach in 1973: "You divested me even of my ghost and now you discard me!" Overall, Artaud's assertion that "there are no ghosts in the paintings of van Gogh"[175] applies even better to the work of Frank Auerbach—were one to, exceptionally, encounter a ghost in an Auerbach painting, this would be due to human, all-too-human artistic misjudgments, where a figure was judged to be a botched one and consequently buried, when actually it had issued from the burial of the world. The fact of this kind of painting is not the model before the painter, but the unanalyzable figure that issues from the burial of the world. The figure in each of the forty-one sessions ending in Auerbach's *Portrait of Sandra*, 1973–1974, does not result from the modification of the previous ones, since, when not valid, the resultant figure of the previous day's work is scrubbed. Along the painting sessions, Auerbach becomes more adept at painting not the figure, but the burial of the world from which the figure issues. Robert Hughes's discussion of *Portrait of Sandra* in his book *Frank Auerbach* (Thames and Hudson, 1990) is inadequate since it concentrates on the alterations the figure underwent, ignoring the changes the painter made to the thick background from which the figure issued. Auerbach is one of the great portraitists by being a great painter of the background from which the figure issues. In some artworks, what is a matter of judgment in terms of success or failure is not the figure in front of the background or the sound over the plateau, but whether the background or plateau buried the world. The figure or sound that issues from a successful background or plateau that buried the world should not be subject to revision, erasure, or destruction by the musician or painter since (the music work or painting implies that) he or she was buried along with the rest of the world. Once the musician or painter has produced the musical plateau or painted background that buried the world, *including the musician or painter himself or herself*, he or she is as effaced as, if not more effaced than John Cage once the latter had established the chance procedures by which a given music piece was to be generated. The unplanned in Ochs's music is not limited to the improvisations in certain specified sections of his pieces; it includes the sounds that issue from the plateau that the Rova Saxophone Quartet and Figure 8 musicians produced and that buried the world. That the same few figures issue from the burial of the world in Auerbach's paintings is symptomatic of an obsession of the image rather than of the painter. I picture Auerbach protesting: "It is not I who am obsessive; it is the figure who is obsessive!"

Few music works are as little interactive as a Larry Ochs music piece once the Rova Saxophone Quartet has produced the musical plateau that buries the world. And few artworks are as little interactive as a Frank Auerbach painting once he has buried the world through painting; the stare of Auerbach's figures cannot be arrested by anything or anybody in front of it, everyone, indeed the whole world, having been buried by the background from which the figure issued. How insensitive must the spectators or listeners of such works of art or music be to continue to be distracted!

The Anamorphic Skull's Aside

If one has not died physically prematurely, one day one may, like Rilke's Malte Laurids Brigge,[176] learn to see. If one has not ceased to live prior to the initiation of dying before dying, one day some artworks may learn to gaze at one. He was standing before a vanity in the National Gallery in London. A man and a woman in their late twenties or early thirties approached the painting. Most probably in associative reaction to the skull in the artwork, the man started reciting some of the words Hamlet utters while holding the skull of Yorick, the late king's jester: "Here hung those lips that I have kissed I know not how oft. Where be your gibes now, your gambols, your songs, your flashes of merriment ... ? Quite chop-fallen?" He wondered why this man standing in a museum, this array of visibility, did not extemporize a supplement such as: "Here were those eyes ..." He moved away from the couple into the next room. He could still see them in the distance, but their conversation was no longer audible to him. What drew his attention while standing in front of Hans Holbein the Younger's *The Ambassadors* was both the amorphous shape between the two standing men, and that the cylindrical sundial showed the date of the painting, April 11, 1533, as well as the following times: 9:30 and 10:30. This last observation reminded him that he was scheduled to meet a friend at the museum's entrance at 4 p.m. He looked at his watch: it was 3:50. He would have to head immediately to the exit if he wished to spare his friend the inconvenience of waiting. Having reached the end of the room, he turned. Why? He sensed that he was being gazed at from behind. The spot at which he turned was the exact point from which the blurred, amorphous shape appears in focus and it becomes clear what it actually is. Anamorphosis is an art of the aside. The anamorphic skull, presently in focus, had gazed at him not with its eyes, since it had none, just empty sockets; but in its entirety.[177] The anamorphic skull gazes at us as vanities. He twice did not see it while seeing it: the first time because, looking at it from the wrong standpoint, he only saw a shapeless smudge; the second time because while he saw it, now in focus, for what it actually was, he turned into what it disclosed to him, a skull, something that lacks eyes with which to see—this blindness is implied by the disappearance, through blurring, of the rest of the world as the skull becomes in focus (unlike the skull held by Hamlet, the anamorphic one does not belong to the world). He quickly averted his eyes. They rested temporarily on the couple: the man and the woman were now frozen. Anxious, he averted his look again, toward others who were still animated and talking. But soon silence-over began spreading in the rest of the museum, more and more of its visitors and employees becoming frozen. While this dreadful silence-over was spreading elsewhere in the museum, he suddenly heard, in a sort of whisper, but one quite clear, so that he could locate it a short distance behind his back, a voice reciting part of that same Hamlet speech: "No one now to mock your own grinning?" Startled, he turned around. There was nobody there! Suddenly, with an ineluctable certainty, he knew that the voice was the skull's in the anamorphosis. Who is a more exemplary locus of the aside: Hamlet saying, "to be, or not to be," or the anamorphic skull in *The Ambassadors* inducing voices in one's head that although they seem to one to belong to the outside world are, like the theatrical aside, though no longer conventionally, not heard by others? He was seized by anxiety and started running, afraid of being frozen any moment into some kind of statue (as in the case of one of the dancers in Maya Deren's *Ritual in Transfigured Time*). He ran for what seemed a very long time. At some point, he realized that he was moving in a labyrinthine space, and that he must have been undergoing over-turns. He slowed, then stopped, doubtful of the efficacy of moving. Having despaired of ever exiting the museum, he unexpectedly "found" "himself" actually at the door, opening it and leaving. "Why the hell are you so late?!" The loud voice of his friend snapped him out of his somnambulism. While his friend drove in tense "silence," he realized that thenceforth he could still exist outside the labyrinth only through the latter's twisted space and time, where the inside is outside (and vice versa).

On Names

Jalal Toufic

Lyn Hejinian:
I don't know at this point whether the following episode, which I remember as having occurred in the aftermath of the publication of *(Vampires)*, happened in actuality or in a dream. During that period I would still experience, although at increasingly longer intervals, attacks of anxiety. It was during one of these, with their slow reaction time, that while closing the cabinet's glass door after getting a Band-Aid, I glimpsed in it, while it was coming to a stop, the image of my face not still as mine was, but in the last phase of a turn to face me; indeed I

could for a very brief moment espy a small stretch of the back of my neck (with a barber's, "Is the haircut of the back of the head fine?" passing through my mind). For a short period, whenever I thought back on that episode, I tried, without much success, to convince myself that that furtive movement was an effect of the mirror's own motion compounded by my anxiety-induced slow reaction time.

The nymph Echo was one of the many suitors shunned by Narcissus. One day, she followed him. She could not address him, since her punishment for distracting Hera, Zeus's wife, with stories while the god's concubines managed to escape was that she could only repeat what had just been said, not initiate an utterance. At one point during his walk, feeling unsure of where he was, Narcissus inquired: "Is anyone here?" Echo replied: "Here." Looking around, but not seeing anyone, he asked again: "Why do you avoid me?" Echo replied: "Why do you avoid me?" She rushed toward him, but he extricated himself from her embrace, saying: "I will die before you ever lie with me!" Echo replied: "Lie with me!"[178] During another of his solitary walks, he sensed her presence. He resolved not to utter any words so as not to give her the opportunity to have a conversation with him. He soon came upon a spring. As he looked into its limpid water, he saw his image, facing him. Somehow, he felt that such a thing did not go without saying. And indeed he heard right then a voice say: "Narcissus!" Deeply entranced by the image in the spring's water, Narcissus did not even instinctively turn away from it to look in the direction from which Echo's odd utterance came. But when the word "Narcissus" was repeated, he became aware that these two calls were Echo's. But if Echo could only repeat, not initiate, then that first call he heard must have been a repetition of some initial utterance of his name. Who could have been the addresser of that initial interpellation? He came to the realization that he himself must have voicelessly called himself (this voiceless interpellation of oneself is virtually the beginning of the interior monologue),[179] and that the circumstance that his image in the water was facing him was the result of a successful interpellation. It is only when he voicelessly interpellated himself that Echo learned his name and called him by it. Prior to this scene, his suitors, Echo included, did not call him by his name, did not know how to call him; this is partly why he gave them his back, seemingly shunned them.

At a stage when the child still lacks coordination of motor functions, he or she anticipates this coordination in the mirror image. The anticipated motor control includes—it is disappointing it doesn't in Lacan[180]—the ability to turn around to answer a call. To see one's mirror image facing one presupposes not only the standard Lacanian imaginary identification with the unitary mirror image, but also the Althusserian symbolic turn to answer an interpellation.[181] Two possibilities:

— Whenever the infant looked in the mirror, he saw his image facing him. If that is so, then the mirror image not only anticipates for the child his future unity, but also, and in this it is one of his earliest and most accomplished teachers, rehearses for him the 180° turn of response to the voiceless interpellation he will one day, using the name he would have been given by his parents, address to the image he sees in the mirror, in the process preparing him to respond in the future to others' interpellation (as with any rehearsal, glitches may occur, the child perceiving then, as in a dream, his figure with its back to him in the mirror). In which case, one would have to admit that unlike with the other objects to which he ascribes animation,[182] the child would be justified in ascribing animation to the mirror image. If there is misrecognition in this context, it would not be limited to the child's identification with his mirror image, but would also include the mirror image's turning to answer the interpellation.

— What the child facing the mirror sees prior to what Lacan termed *the mirror stage* is what the figure facing the mirror in Magritte's *Reproduction Prohibited*, 1937, witnesses: a similar figure but with its back to him. It may be objected that this could not be the case not only because it contradicts the laws of optics, but also because the child does not recall such a scene. Is that scene then mythical? A *Gedankenexperiment*? A structural presupposition? If it is none of these, but something actually witnessed, why doesn't the child remember it? Is it on account of its traumatic uncanniness? It is also because it is witnessed by someone who has no name yet, thus by an indeterminate one, one who cannot be called and consequently recalled. To the objection that such a configuration cannot be the case since it contradicts the laws of optics, one can retort: "Because, as he says, the geometric laws of the propagation of light map space only, and not vision, Lacan does not theorize the visual field in terms of these laws." Why then does he, but also Joan Copjec, the author of the preceding quote,[183] as well as others who elaborate on his mirror stage, assume an image facing the one looking at the mirror? While in Magritte's painting, the mirror image of the human figure is turned 180° in relation to what we, adults, normally experience, the mirror image of the book placed on the mantelpiece is not, because objects aren't subject to over-turns. Since the mirror image's facing a human is not natural, but something that has been mastered, it may fail to take place: a condition actually encountered in psychosis or undeath.

While he was waiting for his blind date at a party, a child asked him: "What's the name of this dog?" He answered: "I have no idea—anyway, a dog has no name." A passing servant who happened to overhear this conversation volunteered: "The dog's name is Max." The dog pricked up its ears and glanced in their direction. The child looked at the thinker, partly feeling vindicated and partly awaiting a rejoinder to what the servant had just said. The thinker thought with dismay: Why isn't a servant who proffers such misinformation to an impressionable child fired promptly? He resumed, not addressing anyone in particular: "Moreover, animals never turn. For the poet Rilke, they are in the Open: 'With all its eyes the natural world looks out into the Open.... We ... take the very young child and force it around, so that it sees objects—not the Open, which is so deep in animals' faces.'[184]"[185] He then yelled to the dog: "Max!" Before the child had time to interject that the dog turned, the thinker said to him while attentively following the dog's movement: "You see? Exactly as I told you." Disconcerted by the child's confusion, the thinker looked aside. He saw a woman standing a few feet away staring at him. "Nadja?" "Yes. Jalal?" "Yes." Annoyed with him for confusing the child, she said: "Why are you telling the poor child confusing untruths?" "Untruths? In Genesis, God tells the man (from Hebrew *'āḏām*) to give names to animals. He does. A while later, he performs two acts of naming his wife. Initially, he calls her "Woman" (a common name even though there was then only one specimen of the one it designated). This is the same sort of naming he had performed in relation to the animals; it confirms that the names that he gave them were generic names, rather than proper ones. Subsequently, the man and the woman eat of the prohibited tree of the knowledge of good and evil, becoming fully mortal, dead even while still physically alive: "And the Lord God commanded the man, saying, ... of the tree of the knowledge of good and evil, thou shalt not eat of it: for in the day that thou eatest thereof thou shalt surely die" (Genesis 2:16–17, King James Version). Thenceforth the Hebrew *'āḏām* is to be rendered as Adam, a proper name.[186] Past the surreptitious introduction of mortality, Adam again gives his wife a name; this time, it is a proper name: Eve. The animals are not offered by God the opportunity to eat of the tree of the knowledge of good and evil and therefore do not, *while continuing to be physically alive*, die as a result of eating of such a tree. Thus their death is not of the same kind as that of the humans; it is only biological demise. Whatever its owner may believe, strictly speaking the individual animal has no proper name, only a generic one. With the possible exception of those animals, such as chimpanzees and orangutans, who can recognize themselves in a mirror,[187] and of whom it may be the case that they see themselves facing themselves in the mirror because they called themselves, the mirror image of an animal faces it because animals' relation to the mirror is from the outset fully within the established laws of optics. Thus the animal essentially never has the occasion to call itself, and therefore it does not properly have a name. It could be that animals also see themselves in the mirror not only frontally but also with their backs to themselves, but, taking into consideration that they would be doing both *simultaneously*, this would be because they exist, according to Rilke, in the Open, thus do not see only half of existence." She drew close and kissed him: "You brought me round!"

The animal does not undergo over-turns; consequently, despite the blandness of the human back, certainly in comparison to the rear side of many animals, especially during their courtship, the great paintings of the back are of the human figure. The face has certainly been investigated in twentieth century thought (Levinas; Deleuze and Guattari's "Year Zero: Faciality";[188] Deleuze's "The Affection-Image: Face and Close-Up";[189] Pascal Bonitzer's "Bobines ou le labyrinthe et la question du visage,"[190] etc.) and cinema (Ingmar Bergman [*Persona* ...], Dreyer's *The Passion of Joan of Arc* ...). But a subterranean investigation of the back has also been taking place in thought (Jalal Toufic's concept *over-turn* ...), cinema (Beckett's *Film* ...), and art (Magritte ...). Magritte is one of the great painters of the human back, of the mortal's back: *Pandora's Box*, 1951; *The Ready-Made Bouquet*, 1956; *L'ami intime*, 1958; *The Spirit of Adventure*, 1962; and *Decalcomania*, 1966. To render the back in the way it appears in these paintings, or at least to provide the right conditions for it to be painted in this manner, it is not enough to walk to the other side of a person facing one and paint what one sees then, nor to simply ask him or her to turn around. The aforementioned Magritte paintings cannot be fully appreciated irrespective of his *Reproduction Prohibited*, 1937, the pivotal and greatest painting of the mortal's back, which shows a man with his back to us both inside and outside the mirror in front of which he is standing, and which functions as their key. To reach the non-accidental back we witness in *Reproduction Prohibited*, one has to have had trouble naming, for example, calling Edward James, the ostensible model of *Reproduction Prohibited*, by some other name, or one must have reached the condition of possibility of such a back, the over-turn, which the dead man or woman undergoes and which undoes his or her turn to answer the call by his or her proper name. It is thus fitting to find in the oeuvre of the painter of *Reproduction Prohibited* at least one painting that can be viewed as instancing trouble naming: in Magritte's *Dream Key*, 1930, an egg is "called" "Acacia," a woman's shoe, "The moon," a hat, "Snow," a glass, "Storm" (and in his *The Treachery of Images* [*La trahison des images*], 1928–29, one can read under what clearly looks like a pipe, "Ceci n'est pas une pipe" [This is not a pipe][191]). Is it at all surprising that a film with the epigraphic intertitle "A Picture Shot in the Back" should raise the question of naming: "Suppose we made a mistake at the very beginning and we called red 'green,' how would we know today?"/"What if I have called the flower by another name?"/"Suppose we call it 'image' but the real word is 'reality'" (Godard's *King Lear*, 1987)? Already at the time of *Prénom Carmen*, 1983, Godard was proposing that "cinema should show things before they receive a name, so that they can be given a name, or that we can give in to the business of naming them," and advancing that "the real title of the film [*Prénom Carmen*] could be *Before the Name*. Before Language, in other words, *Before Language (Children Playing Carmen)*."[192] It is much more difficult to reach this condition for humans than for flowers. Reaching the condition prior to any name requires that one get to a time that precedes one's interpellation of oneself (in the mirror) or that instances its undoing: to an infant up to around a year old, or to someone undergoing the psychotic experience of the over-turn of the mirror image—the transitory madness of King Lear would have provided an occasion for the latter scene. The parenthesis of the alternate title for *Prénom Carmen*, "(Children Playing Carmen)," prepares one for the first eventuality; *King Lear*'s intertitle "A Picture Shot in the Back" for the second. Both would have provided a complementary exploration to that of the face in such Godard 1980s works as *Passion*, 1982 (mainly the video shots of the face of Hanna Schygulla), and *Grandeur et décadence d'un petit commerce de cinéma*, 1986. Unfortunately, *Prénom Carmen* and *King Lear* present a mundane investigation of the back, Godard failing in the latter film to develop the "picture shot in the back" beyond the thematic of betrayal—that of King Lear by two of his daughters, that of himself by the producers of the film, etc.—and a critique of the customary seating arrangement in cinema theaters, in which the spectators have their backs to each other. Therefore *First Name: Carmen*, the English title of Godard's *Prénom Carmen*, is more appropriate than the original, French title.

A doctor who used hypnosis in his work was treating a patient with an intractable case of amnesia. Even after several weeks of lack of progress, he still felt that the patient, who could not remember his own name, may be healed. After one more fruitless session in his office, the doctor accompanied the patient to his room. On the way there, the patient slowed down. Sensing this, the doctor turned around and saw that the patient had stopped in front of the mirror hung in the hallway. On the spur of the moment, the doctor called him. He quickly remembered that his amnesiac patient did not recall his name and so felt no consternation that his patient did not turn toward him but continued to look in the mirror. He gingerly approached his patient. To his amazement, the mirror image of his patient was giving the latter its back. Witnessing this anomaly proved traumatic for the doctor. He himself became amnesiac—although not fully so:

only apparently could he no longer remember his name, since when he faced a mirror, the figure in the mirror faced him.

The prognosis of the prison's doctor was that the prisoner would die within three months of an incurable disease—the doctor was "a great deal more reliable ... than most" not only because his diagnoses of sicknesses were medically accurate, but also because those of his prognoses that indicated imminent death were accurate even when the sick man or woman ostensibly survived the deadline he proffered since they were performatives that turned the person into a dead one come the deadline. A few days before the aforementioned deadline, the prisoner made a desperate attempt to flee the prison. He was caught, and it was decided that his punishment would be death by firing squad. A few days later, as he stood with his back to the firing squad, he heard the commander yell, "Hey, you there!" As far as he knew, he turned, yet he continued facing the wall (his turn was overturned by an over-turn—had he already died by then in conformity with the doctor's prognosis?). The commander then yelled the prisoner's name, yet the latter did not turn, for he did not recognize that name as his and so disregarded what he took to be a call to another man. At this point he heard the commander order his soldiers: "Turn him forcibly!" As the soldiers approached him, he heard the commander yell in panic and dread: "Stop! Were you to turn that mortal, who did not turn when called, around would space itself rotate with him, or would we discover then that the condemned still has his back to us?"

The back turned to us not accidentally, but as a result of an over-turn, is even more the site of the ethical than the face (Levinas: "Access to the face is straightaway ethical";[193] "the ethical relation, the face to face, ..."[194]). Ethics regarding mortals, who are dead while alive and hence, insofar as they are dead, undergo over-turns, is basically related to the back.

Someone has his back to me. I call what I take to be his name, for example: "Friedrich." The person does not turn. One possibility is that he is not Friedrich, that he merely happens to look like Friedrich from the back; another possibility is that he "is" Friedrich but, having died before dying, he assumes other names—for example Prado or Chambige—if not every name in history, and therefore does not turn as he considers that the call is addressed to another man; yet another possibility is that he "is" Friedrich and that notwithstanding his having died before dying and his resultant assumption of every name in history he turned —since "every name in history" includes "Friedrich" (his name while he lived)—but his turn was overturned by an over-turn and so he continues to look away from me. What I am describing as a two-stage process in which the dead man turns to answer the call but his turn is overturned by an over-turn that undoes the initial turn is experienced otherwise by the dead man: he turned to answer the call but, to his bewilderment, he continued nonetheless to face in the same direction;[195] and it is experienced differently by the caller: the one called did not respond to the call, did not turn at all. Unless he has died before dying, the one calling again and again someone whose back is to him without the latter appearing to respond to the call by turning toward him is most likely to sooner or later consider that he is calling the wrong person, cease calling and leave. Hence it is unsettling to undergo over-turns not only because one continues then to look in the same direction notwithstanding one's turn (again and again) in the opposite direction, thus becoming disoriented in a labyrinthine space, but also because, as a consequence of one's repeated failure to answer their calls, one ends up being abandoned even by those who love one in such a manner that they are unable to mourn one successfully, to let go of one, in the process losing the possibility of leaving the labyrinth, since one way to get out of the labyrinth (as well as not to enter it "in the first place") is to manage not to be separated from at least one (other) living human. Why is it that, unless they died before dying physically, even those who love melancholically the one who died end up in all probability abandoning him or her? It is because they don't heed what they should intuit as mortals, that is, as dead while alive, that the dead cannot, due to the over-turns they undergo, successfully turn to answer a call, and so they end up deducing that they are calling the wrong person.

When one is deserted or betrayed by everybody, one looks in the mirror to confirm to oneself that one can still count on oneself. It may be that one will then discover to one's dismay and horror that one has been deserted even by oneself: he saw his back to himself in the mirror. Frightened, he screamed, but no sound issued from his mouth. He soon became even more scared that the figure in the mirror would manage somehow to sense his fearful voiceless call than of seeing the mirror image with its back to him. But his mirror image did not seem to hear his *sous-entendu* call. Maybe what one fears most is no longer to successfully interpellate oneself (in the mirror). At its intensest, fear not only stifles my voice, rendering me speechless, but it also extends my speechlessness to the *sous-entendu* call of myself in the mirror, the one to which, as long as I have not died before (physically) dying, the figure in the mirror responds. After a while, the figure in the mirror not having turned toward him, he felt disconcerted no longer because he took it as natural that the mirror image faces the one looking in the mirror, but because the figure, which, because it had its back to him, he no longer viewed as a mirror image, did not appear to sense his gaze and thus turn. He felt that if the figure did not do so, it was that he did not exist. He was apprehensive that were someone to pass by, that person would not notice he was there. While he was preoccupied with these thoughts, someone bumped into him! Later that day, the dread that had taken hold of him then having subsided, he tried to account for that incident by hypothesizing that the person who bumped into him was absentminded. Why was his anxiety tinged with shame and guilt? When he became less anxious, he realized that the guilt or shame he was feeling was the result not of some specific act he had done but of the connection he, unawares, was allowing to take place between the anomaly he was seeing in the mirror, the figure with its back to him, and the expression *lost face*.

To view interpellation as basically and mainly related to guilt is to be guilty of a double misrecognition. This is because the paradigmatic interpellation is not that of being hailed in private or public, for example, by a policeman in the street, but that of hailing one's image in the mirror—in the primary interpellation, it is the weakest, most fragile who hails: a child who has no motor control or unity yet. It is also because such a view implies that one is paying attention exclusively or at least inordinately to the one who answers the interpellation; in the case of the paradigmatic interpellation, to the figure in the mirror but not to the one in front of the mirror. While many scholars have argued that the main state of the one who turns to respond to interpellation is guilt (while the example of the policeman as hailer in his text on interpellation is neither accidental nor innocent, Althusser is more circumspect than the aforementioned interpreters of his text: "And yet it [the 180° physical turn to respond to the unspecific hailing by a figure of authority] is a strange phenomenon, and one which cannot be explained solely by 'guilt feelings,' despite the large numbers who 'have something on their consciences'"[196]), I think that the main state of the one initiating the primary interpellation in front of the mirror and witnessing the responsive turn is trusting gratitude, for, except in psychotic states, every time there is interpellation in front of the mirror, there is, in response, the 180°-turn of the figure in the mirror. The narcissism of mortals always contains an element of gratitude: mortals, who can undergo over-turns, are grateful to the figure in the mirror for turning toward them when interpellated—even the mother does not always, "automatically," do that for her child.

The Dancer's Two Bodies[197]

His fascination with her started during a multimedia dance in which she performed. At some point, she looked toward the section of the auditorium where he was seated. He was sure that it was as a general audience member that her look happened to rest briefly on him. Soon, she lost her mirror image; not surprisingly her movements were then shortly mirrored by another, physically dissimilar dancer. Later, the stage became dark and he could see her close-up on a large screen. Something uncanny took place then, something he should have expected, having written about it, but that nonetheless made him feel anxious when it happened so unmistakably.[198] He had the unsettling feeling that she was gazing at and addressing him specifically. It was a quasi-psychotic moment, of the sort schizophrenics sometimes feel on watching a TV program or hearing a radio broadcast: that the broadcaster is addressing them specifically. He attended all her subsequent performances of that dance in its brief run. Soon he was dating her. One day she invited him to come see her rehearse a new dance. They arrived early at the studio. She wanted him to hug her. She did not ask him to do that but started to dance. Feeling she was partly disappearing, by being projected as a subtle dancer into dance's realm of altered movement, space, and time, he hugged her. Soon, her dance partner arrived, and the two dancers started a *pas de deux*. Shortly, he could feel that she was no longer fully in the room. (She was also not fully in the realm of altered movement, body, space, and time into which her dance projected a subtle version of her.)[199] On various occasions he mentioned to her this impression he had on looking at her dance. "You keep telling me that I am not fully present where we happen to be when I dance! You'll quickly forget me were I to prematurely die." It perplexed him to hear her say this. In the second half of Hitchcock's *Vertigo* and Robbe-Grillet's *L'Immortelle*, rather expectedly the bereaved protagonist revisits the places that ostensibly convey the beloved's earlier presence and current absence, except that, and this is partly what makes these films two of the major cinematic works of melancholia, this earlier presence itself was already not a full one, but affected with absence! In *Vertigo*, this absence assumes the guise of Madeleine's trance states and her possession by a dead woman; the accompanying episodes of posthypnotic amnesia; and her mysterious disappearance from a hotel (having followed her into the building, Scottie is told by the desk attendant that she did not see the woman in question come in, and he ascertains for himself that she is not in the room whose shutters he saw her open). Precisely because as dancers they are not fully where they ostensibly are, since they are conjointly projected as subtle dancers into dance's realm of altered movement, body, space, and time, dancers are most apt to induce melancholia when they die (*Giselle*). But doesn't the circumstance that the immobilizations in dance allow a backward-in-time motion in dance's realm of altered movement, space, and time, so that in principle death can be reversed, reduce the eventuality of melancholia following the premature death of an intensely loved dancer? On the contrary, it heightens such an eventuality since it makes it very difficult for the dancer in love with another dancer to accept that the latter's death is final, a refusal that undoes the normal process of mourning, ushering in melancholia. The limit towards which dance (that produces a projection of a subtle dancer into its realm of altered movement, space, and time) tends and therefore the temptation and predilection specific to it is not death but definitive disappearance: not of the subtle body, since the latter exists in a realm in which immobilization (which, as the genetic element of movement, makes all kinds of extraordinary movements possible) can take place, therefore where backward-in-time movement is possible, hence where disappearance is not final; but of the material body, the dancer having been *completely* refined to a subtle body in dance's realm of altered movement, space, and time. She advanced so far in her projection as a subtle dancer, she began to feel that she could linger longer and longer in dance's realm of altered movement, body, space, and time. She asked him: "What if one day I don't come back from dance's realm of altered silence, body, space, and time, having become so refined as to be reduced to the subtle dancer?" He replied that such a feat is much more difficult to accomplish than she anticipates; that it took all the discipline and enlightenment of a Dzogchen master to manage a feat that was not identical but nonetheless somewhat analogous: *the great transference into the body of light*.

In Carlos Saura's *Love, the Magician* (aka *A Love Bewitched*, 1986), Carmelo is told that the only way to release Candela from being haunted by Jose, her slain husband, is to manage a substitution between her and the dead man's mistress, Lucia. The latter accompanies Candela and her present lover Carmelo to the ruined location haunted by Jose. They advance in space toward their destination. Jose's ghost appears. In dance movements, Candela and Carmelo start moving backward in time—to before they headed to the encounter. Lucia advances toward Jose, thus toward the past, which has come to meet her in the figure of a revenant with unfinished business.[200]

It is unfortunate that Francis Ford Coppola's foray into the musical and the vampire film took the form of two independent films, *One from the Heart*, 1982, and *Bram Stoker's Dracula*, 1992. Had Coppola joined the two realms of death and dance in one film, the following situation would have become possible. As she, a dancer, stood "with" Count Dracula in the great hall of his castle, she, horrified by them, closed his eyes that gaze at the undeath realm. Then, in order to regain her composure and to partly be elsewhere, in dance's realm of altered space and time, she began to dance. While she was dancing, he, an undead, who did not appear in the mirror in the hall where they ostensibly were, asked her: "Where are you now?" "Also in a forest" (on the two other occasions on which they were again in the same hall and he asked, while she was dancing, about her whereabouts, she answered the first time, "Also in this hall," and the second time, "Also in this hall as it was fifty years ago"). As he began to respond, "I do ..." she placed her finger on his lips momentarily. He resumed, "see the ..."—at this point he, while his eyes were still closed, outlined with his hands her figure—"hidden in the forest."

Did he, as a writer, accompany her into dance's realm of altered body, movement, silence, music, space, and time? In a way, through his writing, he did, but only in a general, abstract manner. He had to admit to himself that he could not do it specifically, as her dance partner could. The seamless tele-interaction of his beloved with her dance partner across the two separate branches of the realm of altered space and time into which their dance projected subtle versions of them made him feel that his relationship with her in the same world was, however intense, a commonplace one. And so, he told her that he would no longer attend her dance performances. It was for ethical reasons that he did not ask her to put a stop to her dancing career: he was aware how futile such a demand would prove to be since he still remembered the twisted last scene in Michael Powell and Emeric Pressburger's *The Red Shoes* (1948). In this film, arriving at the principal ballerina's room backstage just before the ballet performance was to begin, her selfish husband crudely insisted that she cease her dancing career, giving her an ultimatum to either immediately leave with him or bear the responsibility for the premature cessation of their relationship. Soon after, while waiting for the train, he saw her in the distance running toward him. Spotting him from the edge of the balcony overlooking the station, she tried to quickly join him—with one leap. Psychologically, at the level of a character torn between her passion for dance and her love for her husband, the leap was a suicidal gesture. And yet, this gesture by which she indicated her failure to resolve the conflict between these two exclusive options simultaneously intimated that she chose dance: the leap was a throwback to dance, which allows the seamless direct connection of spaces that are not contiguous. While dying, she beseeched him to take off the slippers. He then recognized that even while imploring him to help her get rid of the ballet shoes,[201] and thus seemingly synecdochically of dance, she was still implicated in the latter, for he remembered that she made the same entreaty—to the diegetic priest—in *The Red Shoes* ballet in which she starred.

Although she did a striptease during her next dance, she started the performance with a duet with another female dancer who made the same gestures, quickly becoming her double, she losing through the doubling the mirror image. Consequently it became extremely difficult not only to distinguish the two different-looking women, but also, and despite the ostensible enactment through the striptease of a reduction to the bodily image, to properly see the image. "Will you some day have sex with the dancer who doubled me during a performance in which I lost my mirror image, feeling no guilt at the personal level, brushing it off as not being at a 'basic level' an act of infidelity?" "The doubling lasts only for the duration of the dance."

The body image of the dancer is not limited to the mirror image, since it also involves the subtle dancer induced by dance and projected by it into its realm of altered body, movement, silence, music, space, and time, who could be taller, thinner, etc. Thus the dancer is surprised when someone is interested solely in his or her flesh and blood body, feeling: What about the subtle body? It is those who have a problematic relation to the body, those who cannot stand the suffocation of a reduction to the (flesh and blood) body, who are most attracted to dancers, who while being the closest to the (flesh and blood) body are also the most distant from it. With the dancer, it is less a matter of having a body and a soul than of having two bodies: the flesh and blood one and a subtle one.

So many dancers are training in front of the large mirror covering one of the studio's walls, all doing the same gesture, mirror images of each other. What is exasperating at the level of training, this multiplication, this absence of uniqueness, becomes of no importance, the lightest to bear, once one accomplishes dance and is thereby projected into dance's realm of altered body and movement where one is already in another time and place than the others, something often indicated by the change to solos. With others as the flesh and blood dancer in one of those formations dear to Busby Berkeley;[202] alone as the subtle dancer in one of the separate branches of dance's realm of altered movement, silence, music, space, and time.

The revelation that the *pas de deux* is performed across the two separate branches of the realm of altered body, silence, music, space, and time into which dance projects subtle versions of the two dancers can, as in *The Belle of New York*, take the form of an odd awkwardness and mismatching of the couple's dance movements in what was until then and what will subsequently resume being perfectly matched dance movements by the couple. Or it can take, as in *The Red Shoes*, the form of the absence of one of the dancers: the final performance of the ballet despite the death of the principal ballerina, while functioning at the story level as a tribute of the ballet company's director to his star ("Ladies and gentlemen, I am sorry to tell you that Miss Page is unable to dance tonight—nor indeed any other night. Nevertheless, we've decided to present *The Red Shoes*; it is the ballet that made her name and whose name she made"), also implies that even the first time the ballet was performed, when she was physically present, she and her partner tele-interacted seamlessly across the separate branches of the realm of altered body, silence, music, space, and time into which dance projected a subtle version of each of them.[203]

Gilles Deleuze: "For antiquity, movement refers to intelligible elements, Forms or Ideas which are themselves eternal and immobile.... Movement, conceived in this way, will thus be the regulated transition from one form to another, that is, an order of poses or privileged instants, as in a dance.... The modern scientific revolution has consisted in relating movement not to privileged instants, but to any-instant-whatever."[204] Classical ballet (*Giselle ...*) was a mixed regime of transcendent poses and immanent immobilizations. It tried to make the immanent immobilizations that are a characteristic of the realm into which dance projects a subtle body of the dancer and that the subtle dancer may undergo at any-instant-whatever artificially coincide with the transcendent poses (other than through the immobilization in dance and death, an unnatural dead stop brought about by silence-over, one cannot exactly superimpose over the Idea, over the ideal posture, eternal and immobile, since every other kind of stopping leaves a rest as it comes to rest—this remainder, which is one of the differences between the resultant motionlessness and immobilization, allows everything else to remain in its place rather than acquire auto-mobility). The following words of

Deleuze, "The privileged instants of Eisenstein, or of any other director, are still any-instant-whatevers; to put it simply, the any-instant-whatever can be regular *or* singular, ordinary *or* remarkable,"[205] apply even better to Maya Deren's *Ritual in Transfigured Time*, where one of the sculptures in the park is, unlike the others, which are embodiments of Forms, reached through the freeze-framing of a dancer who shortly before was mingling with others at a party. The subtle dancer of classical ballet was affined to the Idea and the ideal pose and posture since the latter, entailing no residue, have no past and since the immobilizations in dance's altered realm of body, movement, silence, music, and time make possible backward-in-time motion, a kind of bodily anamnesis divested of psychological remembrance.

Dance, which, in the altered realm of body, silence, and movement into which it projects a subtle version of the dancer, makes possible immobilization, the genetic element of motion, allows all sorts of extraordinary movements, including an auto-mobility of the inanimate. The first couple of times when its winding mechanism came to a stop, the doll became again motionless, while in its vicinity a number of dancers were frozen. The third time the winding mechanism came to a stop, its faint sound no longer audible, the doll continued to move, having acceded to the auto-mobility allowed by dance in its realm of altered body, silence, and movement in which it projects a subtle version of the dancer (in the "Olympia" section in Powell and Pressburger's *The Tales of Hoffmann*, after the puppet's dismemberment, its leg continues to dance on its own, manifesting the auto-mobility of the inanimate allowed by dance).[206] When the mechanical doll attains the state of dance, a cessation of its movement would be due to its becoming frozen in dance's realm of altered body, movement, silence, and music. The notion of rewinding the doll's mechanism occurred to its erstwhile master, but, being himself a dancer, he dismissed it—he must have sensed that he would not be able to do so since the doll was then frozen still, thus withheld from time, with the consequence that the action of rewinding it, one that takes place in time or is a form of time, could not be effectuated until the doll was no longer frozen but subject to time again. The doll resumed its movement on its own once the silence-over had receded.

Heinrich von Kleist: "'And the advantage ... a puppet would have over a living dancer?' 'The advantage? First a negative gain ... : that such a figure would never be affected. For affectation appears, as you know, when the soul (*vis motrix*) locates itself at any point other than the center of gravity of the movement. Because the puppeteer absolutely controls the wire or string, he controls and has power over no other point than this one: therefore all the other limbs are what they should be—dead, pure pendulums following the simple law of gravity, an outstanding quality that we look for in vain in most dancers.... It would be almost impossible for a man to attain even an approximation of a mechanical being. In such a realm only a God could measure up to this matter.... Grace ... appears to best advantage in that human bodily structure that has no consciousness at all—or has infinite consciousness—that is, in the mechanical puppet, or in the God" ("On the Marionette Theatre," translated by Thomas G. Neumiller). While the flesh and blood dancer cannot be as perfect as the puppet, the subtle dancer projected by him or her into dance's realm of altered body, movement, space, and time certainly can; it seems that in his "On the Marionette Theatre" Kleist sticks to the dancing flesh and blood person, not perceiving superimposed on him or her the subtle dancer he or she projects. The training of the dancer is not to change his or her flesh and blood body into a perfect one adequate to that most spiritual, incorporeal earthly thing, music (a crazy temptation and goal), and to the spatial and temporal possibilities produced by dance, such as entering and moving in what were up to then two-dimensional objects, etc.; but rather to enable him or her to project the subtle body that alone can be adequate to music (-over) and the space and time of dance's realm of altered movement and body. What the protagonist of Twyla Tharp's dance *The Catherine Wheel* (1981) does not grasp is that it is not she, but her subtle dancer who has to emulate the electronic dancer. Once more the writer tolerantly listened to the litany of the dancers' complaints about not reaching the perfect state of body and movement while dancing. It amused him that dancers did not seem to know about the subtle dancer they project. Although not expressly knowing about this subtle dancer they project, they must intuit his or her presence, since this litany of dissatisfaction is the result of a comparison with the subtle dancer. It is not in relation to any other flesh and blood dancer, not even an Ulanova or an Astaire, that the dancer compares himself or herself and feels dissatisfaction, but, unawares, to the subtle dancer he or she projects into dance's realm of altered body and movement.

They were out with a friend at a nightclub. She walked to the platform and started to move to the music. His friend asked him: "Why this admiration for dancers?" "I admire dancers because they are graceful in the realm of altered movement, music, silence, space, and time into which dance projects a subtle version of them, a realm with many dangers, for example, silence-over, immobilization, the loss of the mirror image ... How comparatively sheltered and limited is the elegance of many fashion models, and even the poise of cats, which are playful, but risk nothing. Right now, she is not projected into dance's realm of altered movement, music, silence, space, and time, and therefore her grace has no occasion to manifest itself—her movements are merely elegant." On returning to her seat, she remarked: "I need to come here a few times a week, to sway to the music-in, in order to mitigate the awe that as a dancer I feel for music-over, whose appearance and disappearance is out of my control and which, angelically, can save me from being immobilized by silence-over."

On Portraits

Jalal Toufic, Los Angeles
1/24/1998

Christy Turlington, New York:[207]
Toward the end of a recent session of my class "Dance in/and Film" at California Institute of the Arts, I put forth: "What fashion supermodel will ever have the grace of a dancer? None. What fashion supermodel would have given Heinrich von Kleist, the author of 'On the Marionette Theater,' the taste to write on the grace of models? None." I was asked: "Jalal, do you deny that models walk more elegantly than dancers?" "No, I don't deny it. Dancers find it more difficult than others to walk because they are used, as dancers, to connect directly non-contiguous spaces-times.[208] Yet it sometimes happens that while seeming to be simply walking, they have already, as is revealed by how time and the space around them have become altered, began dancing, and then who can compete with the graceful 'walk'

of the dancer? Anyway, while elegant, is supermodels' walk graceful? No supermodel will ever achieve the grace of walking of Henry David Thoreau, the author of 'Walking.'" A student came to me afterward and asked if I had seen Robert Leacock's *Catwalk* (1996). I said no. She requested that I watch it—in its entirety. I promised to do so. In the last scene of the film, while handing you the portrait he had just painted of you, Francesco Clemente said to you: "This is what you're going to look like in heaven." How conceited is Clemente here and how false is his assertion![209] A real portrait of a beautiful woman would, among other things, make those who witness it, *including herself*, feel that "beauty is nothing / but the beginning of terror, which we still are just able to endure, / and we are so awed because it serenely disdains / to annihilate us" (Rilke, *Duino Elegies*). I can easily endure the Clemente "portrait" of you, and I am sure that you too can easily endure it. During the portrait session with Clemente, I did not hear you exclaim: "Like others, I have passed through the mirror stage in my infancy, but, unlike most of them, I have also, looking at my portrait, passed through the portrait stage." You show enough deference while Clemente works, and enough disappointment with the result to give me a taste to do a portrait of you. How to go about the extremely difficult task of accomplishing a portrait?

When a producer proposed to him to direct a remake of *Dracula*, why did he accept to do it, in this period glutted with remakes of that work? Was it because his last film had plunged him in debt? They had already shot a substantial part of the remake and were now beginning to film the scene in which Doctor Van Helsing, Doctor John Seward, Arthur Holmwood (the fiancée of the late Lucy), and Quincey Morris, having heard various reports that a woman with Lucy's features was stalking children by night and leaving two punctures in their necks, wait outside her empty grave until she shows up and then intercept her. The director had instructed the actress playing Lucy to act slightly mechanical and yet more seductive than when her character was alive; she managed to pull this off after five takes. In the next shot, as Arthur, seduced and still yearning for his prematurely dead Lucy, began to move toward her, Van Helsing yelled, "Stop!" The shout failed to jolt Arthur out of his entrancement. He continued to advance. Van Helsing screamed: "Arthur, this is not Lucy!"[210] What happened next, while the shot was still in progress, took the crew by surprise: the director suddenly screamed, "But that's not Arthur!" He had felt dissatisfaction not only with his portrayal of Lucy prior to her turning into the undead double of herself who no longer appears in mirrors, but also with his portrayal of all the other characters, including those who did not turn into the undead doubles of themselves. It is then that he realized why he had accepted to do a remake of *Dracula*; obscurely, he was drawn to make such a film to render more explicit a nagging suspicion that his portraiture in his previous films was inadequate.

With their problematizing of identity, horror and comedy are the two genres of mainstream cinema that have had the most exacting attitude toward portraiture, the ones that have been most skeptical in relation to, and least easily satisfied with the illustrative, traditional portrait. Instead of, or alongside reading Jack Finney's *Invasion of the Body Snatchers* as a fictional version of Capgras syndrome ("He looks, sounds, acts, and remembers exactly like Ira.... That is not my uncle Ira") or as a novel about the sort of entities that may sooner or later irrupt in a radical closure, one can view it as a coming to terms with the extreme difficulty of portraiture. In Finney's novel, the events are narrated and the portraits of the other characters are drawn by the protagonist, a doctor, rather than by the diegetic writer. Were one to provisionally treat Finney as a writer, then his recourse to a fictional narrator who is not a writer—nor an artist—would be a defense mechanism against having to face head-on the extreme difficulty, if not the impossibility of portraiture. There is something strange about the nonchalance with which Finney and his narrator continue to describe people, make their portraits, when their subject matter, impostors, should have given both of them pause as to the adequacy of traditional portraiture. Were I to write a remake of that novel, I would first allow the diegetic writer to survive, and I would make him the narrator. I would also eschew making emotion what distinguishes humans from their alien impersonators. The book would begin with the diegetic writer indicating that he is going to start his account of the anomalous events simply by reproducing the sort of "portrait" entries he penned in his journal before he ceased writing such "portraits" as he began to hear alarmed complaints from one friend that her ostensible mother is not her mother, from one acquaintance that his ostensible sister is not his sister, etc. He remarks at the end of these entries how surprised he is at the ease with which he was managing to churn out "portraits." Having survived the encounter with the alien impostors, would he while recounting the events be able to simply write when introducing a character: "He's big, well over six feet, a little shambling in his gait now, but still a vigorous, shrewd-eyed, nice-old man. And this was him ..."? No. If carried through, such a remake would result in a book that, past the irruption of the imposters, is either experimental in its portraits or avoids portraiture altogether. Even while problematizing the portrait (doubles), exhibiting its apparent impossibility (for example through the nonappearance of the vampire's image in the mirror) and/or evincing a dread of it (Oscar Wilde's *The Picture of Dorian Gray*, etc.), the horror genre has nonetheless frequently been one of the main means to accomplish it.

Had I been given the opportunity to do a filmic remake of Finney's novel *Invasion of the Body Snatchers* when Francis Bacon was still alive and he agreed to be part of it, I would have had the events be narrated by a young painter.[211] "It all started around the time a friend asked me to do her portrait. I apologetically declined her request, because I was experiencing extreme difficulty doing portraits." He arranges for her to have her portrait done by a painter he admires, Francis Bacon. A few weeks later, she returns to the young painter and insists that he do a portrait of her. "You owe me this for the 'favor' of sending me to your eccentric friend. Notwithstanding his assertion to the contrary, the painting he did of me is definitely not my portrait. I don't want it to circulate. Towards that, I intend to buy it. I want you to make the necessary arrangements for this transaction; I cannot myself do that, having insulted him while in the state of shock in which I was plunged on seeing the portrait for the first time. The recognizable image I see in the mirror has proven powerless to make me forget, however minimally, the portrait he did of me. I want you to restore my image by painting me. You know that I am not an uncultivated person: I do not expect your portrait of me to resemble my mirror image. All I ask is that it not induce in me so strongly the urge to repeatedly protest, 'That is not me,' and that it take my mind off his haunting usurping portrait. To ascertain that I am not being unjust to your friend, I suggest you visit him and see for yourself the painting." "No. If I agree to do your portrait, I cannot go see the one he did of you. First of all, it might strike me as definitive ..." "Were you at all listening to me? I told you it is not me. Anyway, and this seems to me to be elementary, indeed obvious, I am constantly changing, so how could it be a definitive portrait?" "It may nonetheless strike me as definitive, and then I would be unable to do something different. Second, it was his portraits that plunged my painting into a crisis—one which I don't think I've overcome yet. For months, this refrain reverberated in my head: 'How can one make portraits after Bacon?'" He started working on her portrait. Soon after, and unbeknownst to him, the city began to be invaded by extraterrestrial impostors. The portrait sessions dragged on for several weeks. Repeatedly he would tell her that they should desist, that he felt unsatisfied. Each time her desperate insistence would persuade him to persevere. The night they were to visit Bacon to buy the portrait was no different. Following yet another frustrating session, they drove as scheduled to Bacon's house. They were ushered by a servant to the library, where Bacon was in the company of a writer. The host and his guest were discussing two paintings Bacon did of another writer, Michel Leiris; Bacon, "I think that, of those two paintings of Michel Leiris, the one I did which is less literally like him is in fact more poignantly like him. What is curious about that particular one of Michel is that it does look more like him and yet, if you think about Michel's head, it's rather globular, in fact, and this is long and narrow.... Being rather long and thin, that head in fact has nothing to do with what Michel's head is really like, and yet it looks more like him."[212] Shortly after greeting his two new guests, the host went to his studio and came back with the wrapped portrait of the woman. The writer, although usually reserved, insisted that they be allowed to have a look at it. After receiving the reluctant permission of the model, Bacon exhibited it to his guests. The young painter was disconcerted. He fully trusted Bacon as a painter and was certain that the latter would have destroyed the painting had he not felt that it was a fine work. And yet, the young painter felt that the painting was inadequate as a portrait, did not render her. While looking at the portrait, Bacon realized that the woman standing in front of him was not the female model he had painted weeks earlier, because *now* the discrepancy between the long and narrow face of the figure in the painting and the globular one of the woman in front of him made the painting as a portrait look inadequate. The extraterrestrial impostor could fool everyone except ... the portrait. This could be for the age of feasible genetic cloning and/or digital emulation a criterion for a valid portrait: that it prove to be the most sensitive detector of the impostor—even of one who fooled mother, sibling, husband, and the painter when he or she was not working or looking at the portrait. In the era of cloning and digital emulations, the portraitist is going to be someone who *discovers through creation* the crucial detail that differentiates the person from himself/herself, and thus derivatively from his clones and computer emulations; we could thus be on the threshold of a golden age of portraiture.

Chronological time fashions our "portrait" as people who are moving toward death at a future date. But—so long as we have no will—the thoughtful, artistic, or literary portrait has to draw our portrait as mortals, that is, as already dead even while we live. The successful portrait of a mortal is one in front of which he or she acknowledges: "It's me!—as someone who can feel, at least at times, *every name in history is I* [Nietzsche, who had attended his funeral twice on the day he wrote these words]."

Have you seen Jacques Rivette's film *La belle noiseuse*, 1991? If you haven't, I recommend that you do. After doing a number of sketches of Marianne, the painter Frenhofer, feeling the imminence of a valid portrait, tells her to defend herself. But shortly after, he declares that he is giving up. She insists that they continue. The next morning she is already in his studio by the time he arrives there. In his presence, she takes the liberty of rearranging the studio's sparse furniture, decides where to place the mattress and the sheets on which she is to lie and assumes a particular pose on them. You would think that she has taken charge. But what does she do then? She begins to tell him about her past: that his studio reminds her of the boarding school she attended, where she was frequently ill; that the fever she was afflicted with in those days has returned since the portrait sessions started. One might "think": she is acquainting him with herself so he would come to know her better and thus, supposedly, be able to draw a more faithful portrait of her. Notwithstanding that he doesn't really listen to her, he feels encouraged by her defensive reaffirmation of her past and identity: as a symptom of unease at the approach of a valid portrait. (In Bergman's *Persona*, Elizabeth draws the portrait of Alma: in a preliminary manner in a letter she addresses to her husband, describing the nurse, and incorporating some of the private information the latter confessed to her while inebriated; and then fully through the close-up where the compound face is composed of half of the face of Elisabeth [played by Liv Ullmann] and of the complementary half of the face of Alma [played by Bibi Andersson]—this shot is a great portrait of Alma, even while it is no longer possible to distinguish the two women's heads. Why would it be a portrait of Alma rather than Elisabeth if we can no longer distinguish the two? Alma's prior defensive measures of restating who she is and what her plans are and of recounting her past [sexual encounters ...] imply this.) Indeed, such a portrait is soon after presumably accomplished. That Marianne, whose lover asserted prior to the beginning of the portrait sessions that she is a writer, and who wrote a children's book, does not mobilize writing in her defense of herself against the portrait, that all she falls back on are her memories, indicates clearly that she is not yet a writer. This does not preclude her becoming one later on. This could be the subject of a later film that would complement *La belle noiseuse*. It would chronicle her progress toward becoming a writer, her production of a textual portrait of herself, and her subsequent visit to the Frenhofer home in search of the portrait that painter did of her and then walled up. If the painter Bernard Dufour, whose hands we see as Frenhofer is shown painting, has in the meantime managed to actually paint such a portrait, then the film's spectators will at long last see it (they didn't in *La belle noiseuse*) when she retrieves it. And they will probably hear over it, as a voice-over, the portrait of herself she wrote (the painted portrait entombed again behind a wall of words?).

When I next saw my student, I told her that I had watched Robert Leacock's *Catwalk* and that it had provided me with an occasion to think about portraits. She mentioned that you are presently enrolled at New York University. It would be felicitous if you are studying literature or art, so that were you to find yourself in a situation where a valid portrait is being made of you, you would be better equipped to produce a different valid portrait in the process of defending yourself.[213] Were a correspondence to issue from this letter, such an epistolary exchange could become a training that would make you better equipped for the confrontation with a portraitist, for example, me.

A Hitherto Unrecognized Apocalyptic Photographer: The Universe

"[Paul Gsell:] 'Well, then, when in the interpretation of movement he [the artist] completely contradicts photography, which is an unimpeachable mechanical testimony, he evidently alters truth.' 'No,' replied Rodin, 'it is the artist who is truthful and it is photography which lies, for in reality time does not stop, and if the artist succeeds in producing the impression of a movement which takes several moments for accomplishment, his work is certainly much less conventional than the scientific image, where time is abruptly suspended.'"[214] While I tend to concur with this Rodin view generally, I do not agree with his assertion that "in reality time does not stop." To disagree with this assertion, I do not have to invoke the freezing in dance and undeath, under silence-over; I can invoke relativity. The Schwarzschild membrane of a black hole is an event horizon not only because once an entity crosses it that entity can no longer communicate back with us this side of it, but also because from our reference frame the entities at the horizon do not undergo any events, being frozen due to the infinite dilation of time produced by the overwhelming gravity in the vicinity of the black hole. Was photography invented not so much to assuage some urge to arrest the moment, but partly owing to an intuition that it already existed in the universe, in the form of the immobilization and flattening at the event horizon? "Windbag, watching Goulash from a spaceship safely outside the horizon, sees Goulash acting in a bizarre way. Windbag has lowered to the horizon a cable equipped with a camcorder and other probes, to better keep an eye on Goulash. As Goulash falls toward the black hole, his speed increases until it approaches that of light. Einstein found that if two persons are moving fast relative to each other, each sees the other's clock slow down; in addition, a clock that is near a massive object will run slowly compared with one in empty space. Windbag sees a strangely lethargic Goulash. As he falls, the latter shakes his fist at Windbag. But he appears to be moving ever more slowly; at the horizon, Windbag sees Goulash's motions slow to a halt.... In fact, not only does Goulash seem to slow down, but his body looks as if it is being squashed into a thin layer. Einstein also showed that if two persons move fast with respect to each other, each will see the other as being flattened in the direction of motion. More strangely, Windbag should also see all the material that ever fell into the black hole, including the original matter that made it up—and Goulash's computer—similarly flattened and frozen at the horizon."[215] By superimposing the reference frame of the outside observer and that of the astronaut approaching the black hole, one has at the event horizon a flattening and a suspension of motion—a photograph—of the still moving three-dimensional person who crossed into the black hole. The universe automatically takes the astronaut's photograph as he crosses its border, the event horizon, in a sort of paradigmatic farewell. Do photographs induce nostalgia because they show a moment that has vanished? Both relativity, with its spacetime,[216] and Zen master Dōgen, with his time-being (*uji*),[217] tell us that that moment has not vanished. I rather think that this gloomy nostalgia is linked to an intuition of the resonance of the man-made photographs with the aforementioned naturally occurring photographs, which signal the irretrievable loss to the universe of the one who has been thus photographed. From a local reference frame, an artistic rendering in the Rodin manner of the astronaut at the event horizon might very well be less conventional, more truthful, than a photograph of him; but from the reference frame of an outside observer, a photograph of the astronaut at the event horizon is less conventional than an artistic rendering of him in the Rodin manner, for at the event horizon not only is the person flattened, but also time is so slowed it comes to a standstill.

If the radical-closure work presents only one, exclusive frame of reference, then the crossing into such a closure happens in a lapse of consciousness, in other words, is missed, one finding "oneself" to the other side without having been introduced there; but if two reference frames are provided, then the crossing both does not happen and is continuous! From the reference frame of an outside observer, those at the black hole's event horizon are flattened and frozen, turning into quasi photographs; but from their local reference frame they have gradually crossed that boundary as three-dimensional persons. In Robbe-Grillet's universe, from one perspective, exterior to the radical closure, the protagonists and the objects are frozen and flat; but from another perspective, interior to the radical closure, they are three-dimensional and undergo events ("I am closing the door behind me, a heavy wooden door with a tiny narrow oblong window near the top, its pane protected by a cast-iron grille.... The wood around the window is coated with a brownish varnish in which ... I have discerned human figures for a long time: a young woman lying on her left side and facing me, apparently naked.... From the left part of the frame spreads a cone of harsh light ... : the shaft of light has been carefully directed, as though for an interrogation.... Yet it cannot be an interrogation; the mouth, which has been wide open too long, must be distended by some kind of gag.... Besides, a scream, if the girl were screaming, would be audible through the thick pane of the oblong window with its cast-iron grille. But now a silver-haired man in a white doctor's coat appears in the foreground from the right.... He walks toward the bound girl"[218]). If, in the narrative, there is a subsequent freezing that is again accompanied by a flattening, the reader would be once again looking from outside the radical closure. This would indicate that the fiction writer has not relinquished the ubiquity and omniscience of the traditional novelist, but truly accomplished it: what could be a clearer sign of an omniscience of the narrator than to be able to report on what is happening to either side of the event horizon?

There is a sort of photograph that is specific to a radical closure: the photograph that irrupts in it without being shot by anyone within it[219].[220] Were one to want to list David Lynch's photographs, one should include not only those that were shown in exhibitions and/or published,[221] but also *Lost Highway*'s photograph of the two look-alike women, and *Twin Peaks: Fire Walk with Me*'s photograph handed by the old woman and the child, who suddenly appear on the sidewalk, to Laura Palmer, and in which she later appears. Similarly, in order to complement one's view of Robbe-Grillet the writer and filmmaker by Robbe-Grillet the painter and photographer, one has to include as part of his oeuvre the paintings, ostensibly by others (Magritte ...), that irrupted in his novels (*La Belle Captive* ...),[222] and the photographs that resulted from the freezing and flattening of various characters at the gateless gates of radical closures in his novels as well as those that irrupted in his films, for example, the photograph that the woman's suitor hands her to convince her they met the previous year at Marienbad and that was taken by no one, not even "the third who walks always beside you" (T. S. Eliot)—her husband?[223] While made possible by the radical closure presented by the film, these photographs do not fit fully in the film in which they irrupted, making the latter a mixed media work. The absence of any mention of, let alone a separate section on the photographs in Robbe-Grillet's *Last Year at Marienbad*, *L'Immortelle*, and *The Man Who Lies*; the photographs in Lynch's *Twin Peaks: Fire Walk with Me* and *Lost Highway*; and the photograph of Jack Torrance among the other guests at the July 4th ball that took place in 1921 at the Overlook Hotel, where he apparently first arrived as a middle-aged man sometime in the 1970s, in Kubrick's *The Shining* is a significant omission in historical surveys of photography. Francis Bacon frequently painted not directly from models but from photographs of them taken by other, camera-wielding humans ("I've had photographs taken for portraits because I very much prefer working from the photographs than from models"), in the process allowing, from a reference frame external to the radical closure, the fashioning of the figure into a photograph at that radical closure's border, as in *Study for Self Portrait 1982*, 1984, *Study from the Human Body after Muybridge*, 1988, and *Triptych*, 1991, where the figure is three-dimensional in the left panel, but two-dimensional in the right one (what is presented consecutively in Robbe-Grillet's novelistic radical closures is presented simultaneously in Bacon's artistic radical closures);[224] or the irruption in the radical closure of a photograph not taken by anyone,[225] often in the form of a portrait hung on the wall (*Three Portraits: Posthumous Portrait of George Dyer, Self-Portrait, Portrait of Lucian Freud*, 1973, and *Three Studies of Isabel Rawsthorne*, 1967).

The scientists at the space program had asked the astronaut to take a fitting pose once he was almost at the event horizon, as he would appear, from an outside reference frame, as a photograph (that would look increasingly dimmer and redder as he got ever closer to the event horizon from their reference frame), and had programmed the main computer on the spaceship to provide him when he had gone beyond the Schwarzschild radius with a convincing simulation of a photograph showing him at the event horizon. Some perverse engineer had even arranged for the click of a camera to be suddenly audible as the spaceship crossed the event horizon. Supposedly, by looking at this photograph, he would still feel himself to be virtually outside the event horizon. A few psychiatrists and a thinker cautioned him that it would be unsettling to look at a photograph that uncannily reproduced one that could exist only in a frame of reference from which he was excluded, warning him that he would have the impression of being at two places or even three places at the same time: in the spaceship inside the black hole, where he would actually be; back at the event horizon; and in the reference frame, at a distance from the event horizon, from which his freezing and flattening would be observable.[226] They cautioned him that by seeing this photograph in his spaceship beyond the event horizon, indeed by merely knowing of its existence in his spaceship, he would feel dissociated. But was such a warning really necessary in this peculiar case? If, as Bergson avers, memory is not localized and preserved in the brain, but presupposes the subsistence of the past, and if "whenever we are trying to recover a recollection, to call up some period of our history, we ... replace ourselves, first, in the past in general, then, in a certain region of the past" where "little by little it comes into view like a condensing cloud ... [and] from the virtual state passes into the actual,"[227] how can the person who crosses the event horizon continue to have his memory if by crossing it he becomes disconnected from the spacetime to the other side? According to Kip S. Thorne, Paul Davies, and other physicists, setting aside the intensifying gravitational tidal forces, hypothetically the astronaut would not feel anything special at the Schwarzschild membrane or just after he crosses it. But, since the spacetime outside the event horizon is no longer available to the astronaut who crossed that boundary, my contention is that starting at the event horizon the astronaut suffers an automatic, instantaneous loss of memory. There is thus a weighty difference between the traditional photograph taken by a human using a camera, and this other photograph into which he or she would turn at the edge of the universe, the event horizon: while we still have our memories when photographed by humans, the person whose photograph is taken at the event horizon, as it were by the universe, loses memory (as a result of being separated from the spacetime to the other side of the event horizon he has just crossed). To the other side of the event horizon of a black hole, a photograph showing the astronaut would not elicit any nostalgia from him or her because he or she would have become amnesiac—and because such a photograph might be an unworldly, ahistorical entity that irrupted in the black hole as a radical closure. (Similarly, to the other side of the gateless gate of the radical closure in Resnais and Robbe-Grillet's *Last Year at Marienbad*, the photograph her suitor presents to the woman and that shows her in the hotel in Marienbad does not elicit any nostalgia from her not only because she has become amnesiac but also because it is an unworldly, ahistorical entity that irrupted in the radical closure.) Many physicists resort to robots in their description of what may happen to the entity that crosses the event horizon (Kip S. Thorne: "The spin of the [black] hole intrigues you. Never before could you observe a spinning hole up close. So with pangs of conscience you ask for and get a volunteer robot, to explore the neighborhood of the horizon and transmit back his experiences"[228]); is this merely to allay the empathetic reader's concern by sparing the human astronaut, his *semblable*, death by gravitational shredding? Or is it possibly because they intuit that only one of the two forms of memory that Bergson differentiates ("The past appears indeed to be stored up ... under two extreme forms: on the one hand, motor mechanisms which make use of it; on the other, personal memory-images which picture all past events with their outline, their colour and their place in time"[229]), "the bodily memory, made up of the sum of the sensori-motor systems organized by habit,[230] [and which] is ... a quasi-instantaneous memory"[231]—the only one available to the robot, indeed the one that the robot embodies[232]—continues to be available to the entity that crosses the event horizon? Convinced by Bergson's views, the astronaut was less apprehensive of being shredded by the gravitational tidal effects or the singularity to the other side of the event horizon of a gargantuan black hole than of suddenly becoming amnesiac just as he crossed the event horizon. To appease him, some scientists "explained" to him that since the brain is the locus where the traces of the past are preserved through a series of modifications to the circuits of that complex biological organ, the entity that passes to the other side of the event horizon maintains its memory up to its death by enormous tidal forces; and a philosopher told him that there was a conflict between the largely spatialized time of relativity, especially in its Minkowski rendition, and the unextended time of Bergson, and that he had to choose between the two: "If time is unextended, then you cannot be separated from it by a border in space." He was not convinced, exclaiming: "Can one cross beyond the end of the universe and conserve one's memory intact?" Deleuze on Bergson: "The present changes or passes. We can always say that it becomes past when it no longer is, when a new present replaces it. But this is meaningless. It is clearly necessary for it to pass on for the new present to arrive, and it is clearly necessary for it to pass at the same time as it is present, at the moment that it is the present. Thus the image has to be present and past, still present and already past, at once and at the same time. If it was not already past at the same time as present, the present would never pass on."[233] The two different frames of reference with regard to a black hole manifest the two consequences of a present divested from the past, which "is preserved by itself, automatically,"[234] and which allows the present to pass: at the event horizon of the black hole, and from the reference frame of an outside observer, the present that does not pass, in the form of the freezing of the astronaut as well as any object whatever; inside the black hole, from the reference frame of the astronaut who crossed the horizon, the present that is not preserved, thus an astronaut that not only is amnesiac but also irrupted fully formed ahistorically, so that if he or she does not at some point suddenly perceptibly disappear, this would be only because he or she is being recurrently created. While of the view that modern physics is not Leibnizian, since it contains many absolute borders, for example, relativity's light cone,[235] which makes "the connexion of all matter in the plenum" (*Monadology* #62) impossible; and since, as is made clear by quantum physics's Bose-Einstein condensate, it contradicts Leibniz's principle of the identity of indiscernibles, the astronaut nonetheless wondered what would happen to him at the border of the black hole in case he were a monad. One could consider the world delimited by the event horizons of all the black holes as the expression of monads. What is outside the incorporeal monads is not the world, which is enfolded in the monads, but what is external to the world, what borders it: invisible black holes. This side of the event horizon, there is no world out there, but only its expression by the incorporeal monads; beyond the event horizon, there is an external world, but, given that black holes do not allow what renders visible, light, to escape, one that can be detected this side of the event horizon only indirectly, through the effects, enfolded in the monads, of the mass, electric charge, and angular momentum of what ostensibly imploded or fell into the black holes. At the event horizon, there is an abrupt switch from one extreme closure to another: from the monad, which has "no windows, by which anything could come in or go out" (*Monadology* #7), to the black hole, a spacetime region that is radically closed.[236] What we have around the event horizon is the ever-increasing unfoldings of the monad, which contains all the information in the universe past, present, and future ("each created monad represents the whole universe" [*Monadology* #62], in other words, "every substance ... expresses, although confusedly, all that happens in the universe, past, present and future" [*Discourse on Metaphysics*, IX]). A monadic entity's camera-less photographic portrait in the vicinity of the event horizon is also that of the photographer, the universe:[237] in the vicinity of the event horizon, we have, from an external reference frame, a photograph of the astronaut, or, to be more accurate, the astronaut turned, through flattening and freezing, into a photograph; but also, through the infinite unfolding of what he, as a monad, enfolds, the baroque photograph of the universe. While in the last moments before one's death, one's whole life reportedly flashes before one, at the universe's end, at the event horizon, all the universe's events unfold. From this perspective, any monadic entity that ostensibly crosses the event horizon, but certainly a human being, is an apocalyptic event. Jorge Luis Borges wrote in the "Afterword" to *The Maker* (1960), "A man sets out to draw the world. As the years go by, he peoples a space with images of provinces, kingdoms, mountains, bays, ships, islands, fishes, rooms, instruments, stars, horses, and individuals. A short time before he dies, he discovers that that patient labyrinth of lines traces the lineaments of his own face"[238]; one can paraphrase his words thus regarding a monadic astronaut in the vicinity of the event horizon. "A man sets out to draw the world. Years go by as he travels to the nearest black hole. Then some extremely long-lived patient futuristic outside observer discovers, as the years go by from his or her reference frame, that the labyrinth of lines into which the face of the monadic astronaut a short time before the latter crossed into the black hole and died in his local reference frame indefinitely unfolds traces the lineaments of provinces, kingdoms, mountains, bays, ships, islands, fishes, rooms, instruments, stars, horses, and individuals; that 'there is a world of created things, of living beings, of animals, of entelechies, of souls, in the minutest particle of matter'; that 'every portion of matter may be conceived as like a garden full of plants and like a pond full of fish'; that 'every branch of a plant, every member of an animal, and every drop of the fluids within it, is also such a garden or such a pond'; and that 'although the ground and air which lies between the plants of the garden, and the water which is between the fish in the pond, are not themselves plants or fish, yet they nevertheless contain these.'[239]" To be precise, the portrait of the universe that unfolds, from an outside reference frame, as the monadic astronaut approaches ever closer the event horizon would take an infinite time to do so fully since the wavelengths of the electromagnetic signal, which undergo gravitational redshift, keep rapidly increasing, with the consequence that some of them "take forever long to climb out of the hole's gravitational grip"[240]—by which time the world, according to numerous scientists, would have imploded in a Big Crunch or endured a Heat Death.

He had first seen her in a cafe at the space program. She turned when someone called: "Shanna!" A couple of days later, he wrote the following letter: "In Duras's *India Song*, is the French vice-consul of Lahore Leibnizian or enunciating a Leibnizian truth during his conversation, in voice-over, with Anne-Marie Stretter: 'I didn't need to dance with you to know you. You know that.' 'Yes.' 'There's no need for us to go any further, you and I. We haven't anything to say to each other. We are the same.' 'I believe you'? Sitting at nearby tables at the cafe, he felt they were two monads, windowless, and that not only all that had happened or would ever happen to her is plicated in him, albeit as quite confused perceptions, but also that all that would ever happen to him was folded in her who might refuse his advances. Which did he prefer: to meet her in a world where one learns about others through observation, writing that receives through creation the *aparté*, French kisses, slips of the tongue, in short, intercourse? Or, rather, to express a Leibnizian world in which he never meets her, a world where each monad, himself included, expresses the universe, Shanna included, past, present, and future? Which did he prefer: to meet her in the former kind of world and know that whole zones of her life will remain totally unknown to him? Or never to meet her but for both to be monads, with the consequence that he expressed her past, present, and future, though in a confused, unconscious manner?" He did not end up mailing or giving in person the letter to her. They were soon after chosen for the first mission to a black hole. Along the training process, they became lovers. They quickly came to view that coming trip into the black hole as a double suicide. She began avidly reading any biographies and letters she could find of Heinrich von Kleist, who shot himself in 1811 in a suicide pact with Henriette Vogel. He surrounded himself with reproductions of Francis Bacon paintings, since for him that painter's work made gravity visible. He was particularly attracted to Bacon's triptych *Three Studies for a Crucifixion* (1962). Like Bacon, he was not interested in crucifixion from a religious point of view. It rather captured his interest as the fate awaiting him as a consequence of the quick increase in the excruciating difference of the gravitational pull on various parts of his body that he would suffer as his spaceship approached the black hole. He told her: "We will be together until the end of the world." And indeed at the event horizon, they were, from the reference frame of an outside observer, together until the end of the world; notwithstanding his aversion to being photographed, he could not refuse her a photograph with him at the event horizon since they both became, from the reference frame of some outside observer, a photograph. But immediately beyond the event horizon they were, in their own reference frame, separated from each other as no two sane living humans were ever separated. The only kind of separation that might be equivalent would be that between oneself and one's double, who is oneself divested from all the others with whom one is, insofar as one is alive, intermingled.[241] He was preparing himself to possibly encounter alien beings and exotic kinds of matter to the other side of the event horizon, but the first things that he encountered as alien were the other astronauts in his spaceship. The one who crosses the event horizon is divested of the world, not only because he can no longer cross to the other side, but also because he or she is then no longer a monad, no longer enfolds the world. By crossing the event horizon one exits this universe, but also the universe exits one, in the sense that it is no longer enfolded in one, that one is no longer a monad. In which case, no information is lost to the black hole, because the astronaut *as a monad* never crosses the event horizon, and because anyway all the information is enfolded in each of the other monads "outside" the black hole. The separation he had to accept inside the supermassive black hole was not only with the universe to the other side of the event horizon, but also with the other travelers on the spaceship, no longer feeling any affinity with them: they presently gave the impression of being, indeed were possibly, ahistorical, unworldly entities that irrupted fully formed. Moreover, to the other side of the event horizon, the astronaut, now no longer a monad, could notice all the unworldly entities that were irrupting in the black hole.[242] That we do not perceive the irruption of unworldly entities in a world that physics tells us has absolute ends (in the form of the singularities of the Big Bang and black holes) could be either because such entities are localized in black holes or because we are what Leibniz considered us, monads, and the entities that irrupt do not belong to the world all monads express. As monads, enfolding the same world, at the most basic level *we are always only in our own company*.[243] As they, monads, ever so closely approached the event horizon, unfolding ever more, they appeared from outside reference frames to be less and less distinguishable, since they both expressed the universe; but to the other side of the event horizon, and from their local frame of reference, they, no longer monads, immediately became alien to each other. Looking at his beloved as they crossed to the other side of the event horizon, he felt that she is as alien as a sphinx. I envision the sphinx of Bacon's *Oedipus and the Sphinx after Ingres*, 1983, asking a twenty-first-century Oedipus, now an astronaut, a different riddle at a black hole's event horizon: "What is it that conjointly crosses a gateless gate and doesn't, is two dimensional and three dimensional, and although ostensibly the same totally alien?" Some time after they had crossed into the massive black hole, he was again gradually getting acquainted with her, but the intimacy was gone since it was no longer the case that whatever happened to her was folded in him (albeit in such a manner that for the most part he could perceive it only in a confused way). He realized now which of the two alternatives he had listed in his Leibnizian letter to her he preferred—by far.

Natural Apprehension at Human Burial

While in some cases, it is felicitous to disregard a doctor's prognosis giving one "only weeks, or at best months, to live," the prognosis proving to be mistaken (Thomas Bernhard's *Wittgenstein's Nephew*); in others, it is ill-advised to do so, since that prognosis was a performative that, past the deadline, turns one into a posthumous creature, a revenant who never departed (Maurice Blanchot's *Death Sentence*). One is also ill-advised to disregard the prognosis of a butterfly that does not fly away even when one moves the hand on which it is resting, for that butterfly already senses that the body on which it is resting is that of the late (Sokurov's *Mother and Son*).

Burial is dealt with in two complementary Sokurov films: *The Second Circle*, 1990, and *Mother and Son*, 1997. The first deals with the arrangements on the part of humans to symbolically "lay the deceased to rest," this requiring many legal and administrative procedures, the execution of which is complicated by the poverty of the film's protagonist, a son trying to bury his dead father. The second film shows nature's accommodation to take in the recently dead body. Even the trace of spirit that lingers in such a body (the son addresses thus the body of his dead mother: "You can hear me. I know. Listen, I want to tell you something") is a challenge for nature to accommodate. Nature disregards us as spiritual beings as long as we are alive. This is not because spirit interacts weakly with nature, but rather because as long as we are alive, we seem to be able to fully contain the spiritual in us, shielding nature from it. While alive, we remain, as spiritual beings, like neutrinos, weakly interacting entities passing undetected through nature. It is only while dying or when we have just died that nature becomes disturbed by us as spiritual beings, for we no longer contain the spiritual in us (in *Mother and Son*, the dying mother's dreams become permeable to her son: "Last night I had a dream.... For a long time, I was walking along a path and someone was following me.... Finally I turned around and asked him why he was following me. Guess what he said." "He asked you to remind him of several lines." "What lines?" "'I am seized by a suffocating nightmare. I awake terror-stricken, covered in sweat. God, dwelling in my soul, affects only my consciousness. He never extends to the outer world ... [*he utters the continuation of the sentence concurrently with her*] to the course of things ...' I saw and heard all of this." "In your dream?" "Yes, in my dream")—how momentarily relieved must nature have been when Lazarus was resurrected and could contain the spiritual in him. Human death is simultaneously humans' separation from nature—leading to their projection in the form of a mental/Imaginal/subtle body into the realm of undeath; and, in the guise of their recently dead physical body, their intensest point of contact with it. The modicum of spirituality that nature envelops is implied by its apprehension of the trace of spirituality in the human body being interred in it—a nature devoid of the spiritual would not feel any such apprehension at the burial of what was earlier the living body of someone endowed with spirit. The recently dead human body, which as matter slightly curves spacetime, twists, through its inability to contain the trace of spirit that tarries in it, nature into extreme distortions. Insignificant in relation to the vastness of nature as long as, alive, it can contain its spiritual life, once recently dead or dying, thus no longer able to fully contain the spiritual in it, the human body triggers extreme convolutions on the part of nature in the latter's attempt to deal with it and accommodate it. This dying human body that elicits from the son the remark, "But how small you are, my little one!" that once placed in a given position tends to remain in it so sick and frail it is, that cannot stand still without falling, so that it has to lean against a tree, none-theless forces that tree, but also the mountains, to contort and elongate, as if nature, shown in its vastness, in long and aerial shots of mountain cliffs, and its power, during a storm, is not large enough and strong enough for that remnant of spirituality that clings to the recently dead body. Given that in many societies, forty days is conjointly the assumed time it takes for the soul to fully separate from the body, and the *customary* period of mourning, it is likely that these effects of elongation and twist-ing to which nature is subjected last no longer than this period. Thenceforth, the corpse having become divested of spirit, nature resumes its indifference.

Especially during and in the aftermath of vast catastrophes and surpassing disasters, we are disappointed, if not horrified that *life goes on* in the case of nature, by the latter's indifference, which is less obvious in harsh winter, when many animals hibernate and many plants are dormant ("You may confidently / regale me with snow" say the opening lines of Paul Celan's *Breathturn*), but glaring in sum-mer ("Like the fear of dying in summer / when you decompose more quickly" [Peter Handke]). Could the "modern" sensibility to the event, where the phrases are connected with the barest, most tenu-ous link, apposition,[244] be viewed as already a coun-ter to, a shielding from the traumatizing encounter with the continuance of life after an immense disaster that one considered to be the end of the world, this persistence of life itself experienced as a disaster? Does one end up preferring the anxiety that there might be no next event to the trauma that *life goes on* despite the catastrophe or surpassing disaster? It takes an intensely spiritual person to reveal to us this nature that goes on (in the form of grass appearing on mass graves ...) as twisted and elongated to accommodate the remainder of the spiritual in *each* of the hundreds of thousands of bodies buried collectively or left unburied to rot in the fields of Rwanda. Nature is even more disturbed by one dying or freshly dead human body than by the ecocide human societies are apparently wreaking on it. If in Sokurov's *Mother and Son* the son is characterized as a head person by his dying mother, it is not that he is not tender (returning with a book to read to her, and finding her already asleep on the garden bench, he gently places his hand for her as a pillow), but that he is aware only of her fragility, remaining unconscious of the incredible spiritual power she contains—one that twists the rock behind the bench on which she is sleeping—because such power is, unbeknownst to him, countered by a similar one in him.

The moribund old mother confesses: "I am afraid of dying." Nature too is apprehensive of dying—the old woman's; nature is agitated by a recently dead human body and apprehends it as strange. This agitation is much more intense when the recently dead human body is that of a saint, and reached a cataclysmic, incredible level with the death and burial of Jesus Christ. The stigmata, paralyses, and/or other kinds of alterations and deformations that the bodies of saints undergo, and that are considered in the religious literature as miraculous happenings and in the clinical literature as psychosomatic symptoms, can be viewed also from this perspective: what the spiritual in the recently dead human body is to nature, the saintly or divine is to the human body; both require an inordinate effort of accommodation from their receptacles. That the body of Jesus could accommodate the divine nature of Christ without explicitly looking distorted was already a miracle. A Christian, for example, the resurrected brother and Mary and Martha, would have sensed that were the crucified Christ's dead body not to remain uncorrupted (Hans Holbein the Younger's *The Body of the Dead Christ in the Tomb*, 1521–22, shows the dead Christ's body putrefying) or were his spirit not to be raised to Heaven before his dead body began to decay (Jesus Christ said to one of the two men crucified alongside him, "Truly I tell you, today you will be with me in paradise," then he "called out with a loud voice, 'Father, into your hands I commit my spirit.' When he had said this, he breathed his last" [Luke 23:43–46]), his words about the imminent end of the world (from the infinite convulsion it would have undergone in its effort to accommodate even a trace of the divine Life passing into it from Jesus Christ's corpse—a convulsion even more intense than that at a gravitational singularity) would be actualized right then.[245] For the minimal delay before Christ's spirit totally left the dead body, "the earth shook, the rocks split" (Matthew 27:51). Were it not the case that Christ's spirit had already totally left the decaying body shown in Holbein's painting, then the tomb (the only part of the world visible in that painting) would not have remained unaffected, but would have undergone either the sort of distortion the skull undergoes in Holbein's anamorphic painting *The Ambassadors*, 1533, or the reverse deformation that affects everything else as the skull becomes in focus and manifest as such in the anamorphosis. The dead body of the saint is not raised to Heaven like that of Christ, but through not decomposing it spares nature the cataclysmic deformation it would otherwise undergo in its attempt to incorporate the saintly: of the forty-two saints who lived between 1400 and 1900, at least twenty-two are said not to have decomposed after their deaths. The halo surrounding the divine and the saintly is an additional shield for nature; if in the Imaginal World (*'ālam al-khayāl*), gardens and other environments are not twisted and elongated although the bodies of imāms and Sufi masters there, who reached them by dying (before dying), are not surrounded by halos, it is that that world is in its entirety one where "bodies are spiritualized."

Rilke's *The Notebooks of Malte Laurids Brigge* (1910) and Sokurov's *Mother and Son* (1997) complement each other across almost a century. Rilke demanded that, contrary to the spreading tendency of the age of the masses ("Already in the time of King Clovis people were dying here [the Hôtel-Dieu], in a few beds. Now there are 559 beds to die in. Like a factory, of course.... The desire to have a death of one's own is becoming more and more rare. In a short time it will be as rare as a life of one's own"[246]) and of science of assuming a death "that belongs to the sickness you have (for since all sicknesses are well known, it is also known that the various fatal endings belong to the sicknesses and not to the people; and the sick person has, so to speak, nothing more to do),"[247] you undergo the death you have "*inside* you as a fruit has its core"[248]: the awesome dying of Chamberlain Christoph Detlev Brigge, which introduced a voice that "didn't belong to Christoph Detlev, but to Christoph Detlev's death," and which "when night had come ... began screaming, it screamed and groaned, it howled so long and continuously that the dogs, which at first had howled along with it, fell silent and ... were afraid," and which "refused to let itself be hurried. It had come for ten weeks, and for ten weeks it stayed. And during that time it was master, more than Christoph Detlev Brigge had ever been."[249] What is glorified in Sokurov's film is not death as much as spiritual life, the incredible power in even the trace of spiritual life that lingers in the freshly dead body. Have you heard the scream of nature, in Sokurov's film, not in empathy with a dying woman, but in panic of having to take in that mostly (although not radically) alien element, the spiritual?

P.S.: Did the one other spectator in the cinema theater during my second viewing of Sokurov's *Mother and Son* see me become contorted and elongated in all dimensions (not only the "well-known" three dimensions of space and one dimension of time but also six or seven extra dimensions?) to be able to accommodate the film?

Notes

1

Bram Stoker, *Dracula*, revised edition (London: Penguin Books, 2007), 21.

2

Jalal Toufic, *(Vampires): An Uneasy Essay on the Undead in Film*, revised and expanded edition (Sausalito, CA: Post-Apollo Press, 2003; available for download as a PDF file at: http://www.jalaltoufic.com/downloads.htm), 18.

3

This presents another way in which to understand "Whitman knew how to stay just long enough to leave too early—that is, not too late" (Jalal Toufic, *Distracted*, 2nd ed. [Berkeley, CA: Tuumba Press, 2003; available for download as a PDF file at: http://www.jalaltoufic.com/downloads.htm], 14).

4

"Where are you now" William Burroughs? Didn't Burroughs repeatedly ask a similar question, "Where are we now?" in one of the great American films of the 1960s, Anthony Balch's hypnotic *The Cut-Ups*, made in collaboration with him and Brion Gyson. I suspect that it is not we, the living, who would ask the dead, lost in the labyrinthine realm of undeath, where they are, but the dead who would ask us where we are. I can well envision Hamlet following the ghost to question him about the realm from which he comes only to be asked: "Where are we now?" or better: "Where are you now?" We have the apprehension that the dead would try to hypnotize us. Many believe that they would do it with their stereotypical look in vampire films: eyes wide open and staring deeply into one's eyes (isn't such a vacant concentration that of one who is not distracted by his image since he has none in the mirror?). But lo and behold, what hypnotizes us is rather this seemingly straightforward question: "Where are we now?"

5

This expression appears in Nietzsche's letter of January 5, 1889, to Jacob Burckhardt. In the introduction to his *Ecce Homo*, 1888, one of the greatest philosophico-literary portraits, Nietzsche writes: "Under these circumstances I have a duty against which my habits, even more the pride of my instincts, revolt at bottom—namely, to say: *Hear me! For I am such and such a person. Above all, do not mistake me for someone else*." The addressees of that plea are not only the potential readers of his books, but also himself: with a foreboding of what is to befall him, he is telling *himself* not to mistake himself for someone else. Around a year after finishing writing his book *The Anti-Christ*, he will sign a January 4, 1889, letter to his friend Georg Brandes with "The Crucified"; and he will write in a January 5, 1889 letter to Jacob Burckhardt: "I am Prado, I am also Prado's father, I venture to say that I am also Lesseps.... I am also Chambige.... Every name in history is I."

6
Some fly their B-52 warplanes and drop bombs on an enemy whose radars were rendered inoperative, killing a large number of people without feeling the least ethical qualms; having died before dying, some discover how many people since the initiation of mortality they—under different names yet not through transmigration of souls—have killed.

7
Autobiography of a Schizophrenic Girl, with an analytical interpretation by Marguerite Sechehaye (New York: Grune & Stratton, 1979), 49. Many times have I heard people who were adults during the Lebanese civil war assert, whether in books, plays, films, or conversation, "We're all guilty." Yet these people do not consider themselves mortals in my sense, that is, dead while (physically) alive, but view themselves as solely alive! It is not as living people during the civil war that we, mortals, were all guilty—I and many others were not guilty of the horrors that were taking place at that time—but as already dead then.

8
Ibid., 47–48.

9
Jalal Toufic, *(Vampires): An Uneasy Essay on the Undead in Film*, revised and expanded edition, 254. Daniel Paul

Schreber, who, according to the medical expert's report to the court, "thought he was dead," wrote: "Very early on there predominated in recurrent nightly visions the notion of an approaching *end of the world*, as a consequence of the indissoluble connection between God and myself. Bad news came in from all sides that even this or that star or this or that group of stars had to be 'given up'; at one time it was said that even Venus had to be 'flooded,' at another that the whole solar system would now have to be 'disconnected,' that the Cassiopeia (the whole group of stars) had had to be drawn together into a single sun, that perhaps only the Pleiades could still be saved, etc., etc." (Daniel Paul Schreber, *Memoirs of My Nervous Illness*, introduction by Rosemary Dinnage; translated and edited by Ida Macalpine and Richard A. Hunter [New York: New York Review Books, 2000], 75 and 328).

10
See the section "Counterfeiting" in the revised and expanded edition of my book *(Vampires): An Uneasy Essay on the Undead in Film*.

11
Death and the Labyrinth is the title of Michel Foucault's book on Raymond Roussel.

12
See section "Counterfeiting" in the revised and expanded edition of my book *(Vampires): An Uneasy Essay on the Undead in Film*.

13
Foreman placed a glass wall between the audience and the stage for his play *What Did He See?*

14
These curtains irrupt on stage in a modality that has nothing to do with a return of the repressed; moreover, through similarities in form and material to the ones in Lynch's films and Magritte's paintings, they look external to the theater.
While I would find it legitimate were the holder of the copyright to the Munīr Bashīr music piece that is listed in the credits of my *Credits Included: A Video in Red and Green*

(1995) but is not part of its sound track, since it was withdrawn as a result of a surpassing disaster, to demand a fee, I think that neither artists and writers attempting to resurrect artistic and literary works withdrawn past a surpassing disaster, for example, Borges's fictional character Menard; nor artists and writers who create radical closures, in which what looks like paintings or texts by other artists or writers may irrupt fully formed (for example, in Robbe-Grillet's *La Belle Captive*, the ahistorical Magritte-like images), should pay for images and texts that appear to be identical to works by other writers and artists and that, respectively, become resurrected or irrupt in their works.

15
In this appendix to the play, the front curtain itself has somewhat the modality of something that irrupted in a radical closure, and thus cannot solely be viewed as the conventional one that one expects at the end of a play. Because of this modality, it signals conjointly the end of the play and its continuation, thus effecting an overdetermination of the temporal as well as of the spatial boundary of the work.

16
Hiroshima mon amour, text by Marguerite Duras for the film by Alain Resnais, translated by Richard Seaver; picture editor: Robert Hughes (New York: Grove Press, 1961), 15–18.

17
Ludwig Wittgenstein, *On Certainty*, ed. G. E. M. Anscombe and G. H. von Wright; trans. Denis Paul and G. E. M. Anscombe (Oxford: Basil Blackwell, 1979), #125.

18
Daniel Paul Schreber, *Memoirs of My Nervous Illness*, 144–145. From the quote, it looks like Schreber, who, according to Dr. Guido Weber's report of 1899, "thought he was dead" (ibid., 328) and believed that "he is called to redeem the world" (ibid., 333), intuitively attempted to actualize what Antonin Artaud would demand years later: placing man "again, for the last time, on the autopsy table to remake his anatomy.... / Man is sick because he is badly constructed.... / There is nothing more useless than an organ. / When you will

have made him a body without organs, / then you will have delivered him from all his automatic reactions ..." ("To Have Done with the Judgment of God," in Antonin Artaud, *Selected Writings*, edited, and with an introduction, by Susan Sontag; translated from the French by Helen Weaver; notes by Susan Sontag and Don Eric Levine [Berkeley: University of California Press, 1988], 570–571).

19
Kathleen Brumm, Matthew Walenski, Frank Haist, Shira L. Robbins, David B. Granet, and Tracy Love, "Functional MRI of a Child with Alice in Wonderland Syndrome During an Episode of Micropsia," *Journal of AAPOS* 14, no. 4 (August 2010): 317–322, http://www.ncbi.nlm.nih.gov/pmc/articles/PMC2928409/.

20
"Pratyahara," *Encyclopædia Britannica Online*, http://www.britannica.com/EBchecked/topic/474079/pratyahara.

21
Virginia Woolf, *Mrs. Dalloway*, foreword by Maureen Howard (San Diego: Harcourt, 1981), 86–87.

22
Spinoza, *Complete Works*, translations by Samuel Shirley; edited, with introduction and notes, by Michael L. Morgan (Indianapolis, IN: Hackett, 2002), 267 and 373.

23
Moon in a Dewdrop: Writings of Zen Master Dōgen, ed. Kazuaki Tanahashi; trans. Robert Aitken [et al.] (San Francisco: North Point Press, 1985), 136 and 138.

24
Daniel Paul Schreber, *Memoirs of My Nervous Illness*, 99.

25
Ibid., 128. While through its incorporation of noise, chance procedures, and screaming, fine experimental music often liberates inhuman forces and sides of the human listener, it is still addressed to a human audience. Orpheus's music

was not merely human not only because it liberated inhuman forces and sides of the human listener but also and mainly because it was addressed not only to human ears (in whom it produced a hushing of the interior monologue), but also to animal ears ("and it so came to pass that not from fear / or craftiness were they [animals] so quite then / but to be listening" [Rilke, *Sonnets to Orpheus*]), and even to objects ("Another [of the female Bacchanals], for a weapon, hurls a stone, / Which, by the sound subdu'd as soon as thrown, / Falls at his feet ..." [Ovid's *Metamorphoses*]—"to be listening"). Even more impressive than the hushed silence of the objects was that of *the voices*, which proved sensitive to Orpheus's music. While Orpheus played his music in the underworld, the undead were relieved of the voices that tormented them.

26
Ibid., 145.

27
Ibid., 95.

28
William S. Burroughs, *Naked Lunch: The Restored Text*, ed. James Grauerholz and Barry Miles (New York: Grove Press, 2001), 208.

29
Friedrich Nietzsche, *Thus Spoke Zarathustra: A Book for Everyone and No One*, translated with an introduction by R. J. Hollingdale (Baltimore, MD: Penguin Books, 1961), 201.

30
It is still unclear to me why it was that this apprehension of dying of laughter was triggered in this case and not, say, in response to the news that following the massacre on February 25, 1994, by Baruch Goldstein, a Jewish extremist, of tens of praying Palestinians in the Ibrahim Mosque in Hebron (aka, al-Khalīl) in the West Bank, a curfew was imposed on the city's Palestinian population of 130,000 rather than on the 450 Israeli Jewish settlers in their midst (arguably to guard against potential reprisals by the Palestinians); or on

coming across an article in the *Baltimore Sun* of September 3, 1996, titled, "Saddam Hussein Again Iraq's Machinations: Invasion of Kurdish Zone Must Be Met with U.S. Response," and a September 28, 1996, article in *Slate* magazine, "The Kurds," that starts with: "Early this month, the United States bombed Iraq in retaliation for Saddam Hussein's invasion of the Kurdish city Irbil" (http://www.slate.com/articles/news_and_politics/the_gist/1996/09/the_kurds.html)—as far as I know Erbil was then and still is one of the cities of Iraq.

31
Nietzsche, *Thus Spoke Zarathustra: A Book for Everyone and No One*, 94.

32
See Aristotle's influential definition of man as a rational animal.

33
"For others too can see, or sleep, / But only human eyes can weep" (Andrew Marvell, "Eyes and Tears").

34
Here's a dialogue from *Sylvie and Bruno*, a book written by an author who could have answered the seemingly rhetorical question, "Have we not dimensions?" with a no, at least during one of his migraine episodes ("Migraine is a well-known cause of visual hallucinations.... Patients who have migraines may experience every variety of hallucinatory image from simple unformed lines and spots to highly complex, formed scenes. Visual distortions, including macropsia and micropsia, may also occur. Such sensory distortions have been called the 'Alice-in-Wonderland' syndrome, after the tale by Lewis Carroll who called on his own migraine experiences to describe Alice's dramatic changes in size" [Jeffrey L. Cummings and Bruce L. Miller, "Visual Hallucinations: Clinical Occurrence and Use in Differential Diagnosis," *Western Journal of Medicine* 146, no. 1 (January 1987): 47–48, http://www.ncbi.nlm.nih.gov/pmc/articles/PMC1307180/]): "'What *are* you doing there, Bruno?' I said. 'Spoiling Sylvie's garden.... The nasty cross thing—wouldn't let me go and play this morning—said I must finish my lessons first.... I'll vex her finely,

though!' 'Oh, Bruno, you shouldn't do that!' I cried. 'Don't you know that's revenge? And revenge is a wicked, cruel, dangerous thing!' 'River-edge?' said Bruno.... 'No, not river-edge,' I explained: 'revenge.... Come! Try to pronounce it, Bruno!' ... But Bruno ... said he couldn't; that his mouth wasn't the right shape for words of that kind.... 'Well, never mind, my little man! ... I'll teach you quite a splendid kind of revenge! ... First, we'll get up all the weeds in her garden. See, there are a good many at this end—quite hiding the flowers.' 'But *that* won't vex her!' said Bruno. 'After that,' I said, without noticing the remark, 'we'll water this highest bed—up here. You see it's getting quite dry and dusty.... Then after that ... the walks want sweeping a bit; and I think you might cut down that tall nettle—it's so close to the garden that it's quite in the way—' 'What *is* oo talking about? ... All that won't vex her a bit!' 'Won't it?' I said, innocently. 'Then, after that, suppose we put in some of those coloured pebbles—just to mark the divisions between the different kinds of flowers, you know. That'll have a very pretty effect.' Bruno turned round and had another good stare at me. At last there came an odd little twinkle into his eyes, and he said, with quite a new meaning in his voice, 'That'll do nicely....' '... and then—what kind of flowers does Sylvie like best?' ... 'Violets' ... 'There's a beautiful bed of violets down by the brook—' 'Oh, let's fetch 'em!' ..." *The Complete Illustrated Lewis Carroll*, with an introduction by Alexander Woollcott; illustrations by John Tenniel et al. (Ware, Hertfordshire, England: Wordsworth Editions, 2008), 352–353.

35
Heeding the chapter's title, "Bruno's Revenge," and the symptomatic "At last there came an odd little twinkle into his eyes, and he said, with quite a new meaning in his voice, 'That'll do nicely....'" in response to his interlocutor's "my little man! ... I'll teach you quite a splendid kind of revenge! ... First, we'll get up all the weeds in her garden ..." should the quote from *Sylvie and Bruno* be placed here, as an example of a novel kind of revenge, rather than in the previous footnote as an example of an experiment in evading or undoing the generalized revengefulness around (the latter interpretation is supported by: "'Revenge.... Come! Try to pronounce it, Bruno!' ... But Bruno ... said he couldn't; that his mouth wasn't the right shape for words of that kind")?

36
See "Voice-over-witness" in the second edition of my book *Over-Sensitivity* (Forthcoming Books, 2009; available for download as a PDF file at: http://www.jalaltoufic.com/downloads.htm).

37
One can appreciate the intense tone of withdrawal in Twelver Shi'ism if one remembers that in that branch of Islam one reaches the esoteric through the imām rather than through unmediated experience, and then notes that since the tenth century the imām has been occulted in Twelver Shi'ism.

38
Quoted in Louis Massignon, *The Passion of al-Hallāj: Mystic and Martyr of Islam*, vol. 3, trans. Herbert Mason (Princeton: Princeton University Press, 1982), 139–140. See also Muḥammad b. Aḥmad Abū'l-Ḥusayn Malaṭī (d. 987), *Kitāb al-tanbīh wa'l-radd 'alā ahl al-ahwā' wa'l-bida'* (Baghdad: Maktabat al-Muthannā/Beirut: Maktabat al-Ma'ārif, 1968), 25.

39
On page 76 of *Archive Fever: A Freudian Impression* (trans. Eric Prenowitz [Chicago; London: University of Chicago Press], 1996), having quoted Yosef Yerushalmi's statement in his *Zakhor*, "Only in Israel and nowhere else is the injunction to remember felt as a religious imperative to an entire people," Jacques Derrida asks: "How can one not tremble in front of such a statement?" Why and how does Derrida presume that Yerushalmi did not tremble while writing such a statement? I have trembled while writing many an idea in my books, for example, the exigency of the slaughter of the pilgrims by Abū Ṭāhir al-Jannābī's Qarmaṭīs. I have enough respect for Derrida to know that he must have trembled while writing a number of his statements. Even more disturbing is trembling Derrida's response to that statement: "Unless, in the logic of this election, one were to call by the *unique* name of Israel all the places and all the peoples who would be ready to recognize themselves in this anticipation and in this injunction ..." (77). What a disconcerting solution from Derrida in a book that invokes Yerushalmi, the author of *From Spanish Court to*

Italian Ghetto; Isaac Cardoso: A Study in Seventeenth-Century Marranism and Jewish Apologetics (New York: Columbia University Press, 1971), a book that dwells on the forced mass conversion of the Jews of Portugal! Such a response does not make me tremble—the deaths of over 576,000 Iraqi children as a result of the US-imposed UN sanctions does. But this rhetorical and quasi-performative conversion forced on some other presently existing, or yet to exist peoples certainly induces in me the queasy sense of a threat (my qualification of the performativity of that Derridean gesture is due to the circumstance that the question of who has the right to convert was at the time Derrida wrote those words quite a contentious issue for Jewry, many Orthodox and ultra-Orthodox Jews vehemently contesting the legitimacy of conversions performed by Conservative and Reform rabbis, indeed demanding that the then Israeli government of Netanyahu enact this illegitimacy and promulgate it). Unfortunately, such a kind of statement is not exceptional among a number of otherwise admirable French philosophers of the second half of the twentieth century. In his book *Heidegger and the "jews"*, Lyotard writes that he is using "jews" to indicate that he is writing not only about the Jews but also about those hostage to an unconscious affection. I could respond: why not use "shi'ites"—except the logic and structure of these quotation marks, of designating by the unique name of one people other peoples, is loathsome to me even when it does not, as is virtually always the case, quickly degenerate, despite qualifications and disclaimers, into either a restriction of the ones who are designated with the quotation marks to solely those who are usually designated without such marks (when Lyotard lists three pairs of "jews" and Christians, all the former turn out to be Jews: Kafka, Benjamin, Celan), or some sort of conversion.

40
W. Gunther Plaut, *The Man Who Would Be Messiah*, foreword by Elie Wiesel (Oakville, Ontario: Mosaic Press, 1988).

41
Gershom Scholem, *Sabbatai Sevi: The Mystical Messiah, 1626–1676*, trans. R. J. Zwi Werblowsky (Princeton: Princeton University Press, 1973), 278.

42

Is enlightenment communal as in messianism (the Nizārī communities during the Great Resurrection, etc.), or individual as in Sufism? I feel it is neither, but universal, affecting not only all humans but also all sentient beings, as in Mahāyāna (Great Vehicle) Buddhism.

43

Gershom Scholem, *The Messianic Idea in Judaism and Other Essays on Jewish Spirituality* (New York: Schoken Books, 1995), 121–123.

44

See "The Configuration of the Temple of the Ka'bah as the Secret of the Spiritual Life," in Henry Corbin, *Temple and Contemplation*, trans. Philip Sherrard, with the assistance of Liadain Sherrard (London: Kegan Paul International, 1986).

45

Ḥallāj was accused of being a Qarmaṭī, or at least of having Qarmaṭī affinities. If such an accusation was legitimate, then his view that to perform the pilgrimage incumbent upon Muslims one did not have to actually travel to Mecca but could do so in the locale in which one happened to be would be not a consequence of an internalization and spiritualization of the exoteric pilgrimage, whereby the Kaaba would now be in the heart of the believer, but a response to the withdrawal, implied by its sacking by the Qarmaṭīs, of the holiness of the Kaaba past a surpassing disaster.

46

Anyone who has not protested vehemently against the barbaric sanctions imposed on Iraq, the land where three great Semitic civilizations have flourished (the Assyrian, the Babylonian, and the Arabic), and who either fails to protest, condones, or even encourages the injustice inflicted on the Palestinians, who are Arabs, and therefore Semitic, brandishing the accusation of anti-Semitism only when Jews are being unjustly attacked, is a hypocrite. If one does not protest the former acts of injustice as anti-Semitic but only the latter, one should by now, over half a century after the Shoah, use the term *anti-Jewish*. The Anti-Defamation League, the self-proclaimed "world's leading organization fighting anti-Semitism through programs and services that counteract hatred, prejudice and bigotry," is actually one of its loci since it never considers that there is an anti-Semitic attack when Arabs are slandered and discriminated against in the US, France, or Israel. Indeed since one of the main loci of anti-Arab bigotry is Israel, the latter is one of the major anti-Semitic countries.

47
See Tom Segev, *The Seventh Million: The Israelis and the Holocaust*, trans. Haim Watzman (New York: Hill and Wang, 1993).

48
The ushering in of the Greater Occultation at that time cannot be fully explained just by the sociological, historical, political, and economic conditions at that point, ones that made the continuation of the Lesser Occultation quite problematic: conflicts were beginning to arise among the various claimants to the deputyship, partly over disposing of the fifth of the Shi'ite's earnings due to the imām; seventy-five years had passed since the purported birth of the imam (the average human life span was then significantly shorter) ...

49
Friedrich Nietzsche: "*This, too, is worthy of a hero*.—Here is a hero who has done nothing but shake the tree as soon as the fruit was ripe. Do you think this too little? Then take a look at the tree he shook" (*Human, All Too Human*, translated by R. J. Hollingdale, with an introduction by Richard Schacht [Cambridge; New York: Cambridge University Press, 1996], 393).

50
See Gershom Scholem, *Sabbatai Sevi*, 41 and 53.

51
See "Cyclical Time in Mazdaism and Ismailism," in Henry Corbin, *Cyclical Time and Ismaili Gnosis* (London: Kegan Paul International, 1983).

52

See *Against Silence: The Voice and Vision of Elie Wiesel*, selected and edited by Irving Abrahamson (New York: Holocaust Library, 1985), vol. 2, 171–218, and vol. 3, 139–143; Elie Wiesel, *A Jew Today*, trans. Marion Wiesel (New York: Random House, 1978), 33–39 and 101–113; Elie Wiesel and Philippe-Michael de Saint-Cheron, *Evil and Exile*, trans. Jon Rothschild (Notre Dame, IN: University of Notre Dame Press, 1990), 137–150. My apology to the reader for exposing him or her to such poisonous material, and my apology to my book for dirtying it with such references. Does anyone who has even the barest clue as to what a brutal, unjust phenomenon any war quickly becomes have to get acquainted with the disclosures about massacres perpetuated by Israeli soldiers on Egyptian and Syrian war prisoners (See Ronal Fisher, "Mass Murder in the 1956 Sinai War," *Maariv*, August 8, 1995; and Gabby Bron, "Egyptian POWs Ordered to Dig Graves, Then Shot by Israeli Army," *Yedi'ot Aharonot*, August 17, 1995. Both pieces were translated in the October 1995 edition of Israel Shahak's *From the Hebrew Press* and reprinted in *Journal of Palestine Studies* 99 [Spring 1996]: 148–155) to feel incredible revulsion at lines such as these: "During the Six-Day War the Jewish fighters did not become cruel [how does Wiesel, who moreover was living then in the USA, know that? But one should not be surprised by such a statement from someone who assumes the role of the emissary of the dead, talking in their name(s)]. They became sad.... And if I feel something towards them, the child-soldiers in Israel, it is profound respect" (*Against Silence*, 195)? I hold the one who said these words, a Nobel Peace Laureate (!), to be ethically an accomplice in any crimes perpetrated by Israeli soldiers during the 1967 Arab-Israeli War (including in the following atrocity if it is confirmed: "National Infrastructures Minister Binyamin Ben-Eliezer of Labor may be joining the long list of political officials currently under investigation, following a claim that the reconnaissance unit he commanded during the Six Day War killed 250 prisoners of war.... Last week, Channel 1 aired *Ruah Shaked* [The Spirit of Shaked], a documentary compiled by journalist Ran Edilist. It claimed that Ben-Eliezer's unit killed 250 unarmed Egyptian prisoners of war in the Sinai desert after the fighting had stopped.... Former education minister Yossi Sarid told Egypt's *Al-Ahram* that

… he had not seen the documentary, but that he was aware that Israeli forces had committed such acts" ["Egypt Wants Probe into 'IDF massacre,'" *Jerusalem Post*, March 3, 2007]). "Do you think that there is a single Israeli soldier who enjoys what he's doing? I am ready to swear on the Torah that not a single soldier is acting with joy or pleasure. But that is forgotten" (quoted on page 145 of *Evil and Exile* from an address by Wiesel to the Rashi Center, Paris)—no, what is "forgotten" by Wiesel is that no war, at least no modern war, has not tainted at least some soldiers, certainly among the victors, with *jouissance*. Had the aforementioned words come from a decent Frankist or Dönme adherent, people who have sensed and acknowledged the withdrawal of the Torah (of *beriah*), I would appreciate their irony. In any case, I infinitely prefer the attitude of detachment of the Samurais and of the sword masters of Japan, and the karma-yoga, the yoga of action, that lord Krishna teaches his disciple Arjuna (*Bhagavad-Gita*), to sadness.

53
See pages 58–61 of the present book.

54
Elie Wiesel, *From the Kingdom of Memory: Reminiscences* (New York: Summit Books, 1990), 16.

55
Ibid.

56
Elie Wiesel, *The Fifth Son*, trans. Marion Wiesel (New York: Summit Books, 1985), 142.

57
Unless this monument acknowledging and presenting the withdrawal due to the surpassing disaster has resurrected and made available again such information, it was a mistake on the part of Gerz to have accepted the publication of a book that makes available the names chiseled on the underside of the stones: *2146 Steine Mahnmal Gegen Rassismus Saarbrücken* (Stuttgart: Gerd Hatje, 1993).

58

The one who reportedly resurrected a man in such a thorough manner that no one ever felt that the latter was, in the process, surreptitiously replaced by a double in all probability underwent a withdrawal and was discredited in the eyes of some of his followers as one of the "false messiahs and false prophets [who] will appear and perform great signs and wonders to deceive, if possible, even the elect" (Matthew 24:24) when, following his crucifixion, his prophecy that there would then be "great distress, unequaled from the beginning of the world until now—and never to be equaled again.... [And] immediately after the distress ... 'the sun will be darkened, / and the moon will not give its light; the stars will fall from the sky, / and the heavenly bodies will be shaken.' Then will appear the sign of the Son of Man in heaven. Truly I tell you, this generation will certainly not pass away until all these things have happened" (Matthew 24:21–34), ostensibly failed to materialize.

59

I have the feeling that although in all likelihood they despised horror films, Duras (the author of *Hiroshima mon amour* and the filmmaker of *Le camion*, etc.) as well as the Tarkovsky of *The Sacrifice* would have nonetheless been impressed by the absence of the undead from the mirror in front of which he or she happens to stand.

60

The library's design dates from 1975.

61

András Riedlmayer, "Erasing the Past: The Destruction of Libraries and Archives in Bosnia-Herzegovina," *Middle East Studies Association Bulletin*, July 1995: "On 25 August 1992, Bosnia's National and University Library ... was shelled and burned. Before the fire, the library held 1.5 million volumes, including over 155,000 rare books and manuscripts.... Bombarded with incendiary grenades from Serbian nationalist positions across the river, the library burned for three days; it was reduced to ashes with most of its contents.... Aida Buturovi, a librarian in the National Library's exchanges section, was shot to death by a sniper while attempting to rescue books from the flames. Three months earlier Sarajevo's Oriental Institute, home to the largest collection of Islamic and Jewish manuscript texts and Ottoman documents in Southeastern Europe, was shelled with phosphorus grenades and burned. Losses included 5,263 bound manuscripts in Arabic, Persian, Hebrew, and Aljamiado (Bosnian Slavic written in Arabic script) ... and 200,000 other documents of the Ottoman era.... In each case, the library alone was targeted; adjacent buildings stand intact to this day."

62
In the first edition of *Over-Sensitivity*, I used the term *eruption* to describe the sudden appearance of unworldly entities in radical closures. I now prefer and use the term *irruption* since eruption, if considered not in the sense I wanted, as an indicator of tone, namely the breaking out of a rash on the world, but as a violent or sudden release of some pressure, could easily be misunderstood in terms of a return of the repressed.

63
Lynn Gumpert, *Christian Boltanski* (Paris: Flammarion, 1994), 103.

64
Certainly in the voluminous work of Boltanski, the out-of-focus in some other instances (for example, some of the photographs of his *Detective*, 1972–73, which were cut from a specialized review of crime stories and which are of assassins and victims) reproduces a stereotypical image of the dead as revenants; and in yet other instances, it is simply formal.

65
Does the "You have seen nothing in Hiroshima" automatically include the non-Japanese film spectator? No.

66
When I wrote these words in the first edition of the book (2000), I was, through the term *negotiating*, referring to the plethora of 1990s books, mostly anthologies, with the title *Negotiating* ——. Most, if not all of these books have, deservedly, been forgotten by now, 2013.

67
Sigmund Freud, *The Standard Edition of the Complete Psychological Works of Sigmund Freud*, vol. 14, *On the History of the Psycho-analytic Movement, Papers on Metapsychology, and Other Works (1914–1916)*, translated from the German under the general editorship of James Strachey, in collaboration with Anna Freud; assisted by Alix Strachey and Alan Tyson (London: The Hogarth Press and the Institute of Psycho-analysis, 1957), 296.

68
Sigmund Freud, *The Standard Edition of the Complete Psychological Works of Sigmund Freud*, vol. 4 (1900), *The Interpretation of Dreams*, 1st part (London: The Hogarth Press, 1953), 318.

69
These words appear, neither quoted nor attributed, in Godard's *New Wave*; they are from Jacques Chardonne's *L'amour c'est beaucoup plus que l'amour* (*Œuvres complètes*, vol. 3 [Paris: Albin Michel, 1931]: "Une femme ne peut pas beaucoup nuire à un homme. Il porte en lui-même toute sa tragédie. Elle peut le gêner, l'agacer. Elle peut le tuer. C'est tout"). Some women might feel oversensitive to and wary of such formulation. I have no patience for a reflex reversal, or any abstract reaction; what I would appreciate would be some (comic?) rigorous reformulation, for example by Alenka Zupančič, the author of *The Odd One In: On Comedy* (Cambridge, MA: MIT Press, 2008).

70
This is clear also in the case of a radical closure and the structural eventual irruption of fully formed ahistorical entities in it: the radical closure is all, but, as is made manifest by the irruption of unworldly entities in it, that all is not all.

71
Past some surpassing disaster that caused the withdrawal of *Don Quixote*, it was not the ninth and the thirty-eighth chapters of part 1 of *Don Quixote* written by the Menard of Borges's "Pierre Menard, Author of *Don Quixote*" that were counterfeit, but rather, pending its resurrection,

Cervantes's book. I would think that by the time Menard finished chapter 22 of part 1 of *Don Quixote*, Cervantes's book was resurrected.

72
Answering the question as to whether animals can will would involve discovering whether they are capable of nostalgia and of noticing identical recurrence.

73
See "The Mysterious Record of Immovable Wisdom," in Takuan Soho, *The Unfettered Mind: Writings of the Zen Master to the Sword Master*, trans. William Scott Wilson (New York: Kodansha International, 1986). "In the practice of Buddhism, there are said to be fifty-two stages, and within these fifty-two, the place where the mind stops at one thing is called the *abiding place*. Abiding signifies stopping, and *stopping* means the mind is being detained by some matter.... If ten men, each with a sword, come at you with swords slashing, if you parry each sword without stopping the mind at each action, and go from one to the next, you will not be lacking in a proper action for every one of the ten.... But if the mind stops before one of these men, though you parry his striking sword, when the next man comes, the right action will have slipped away. Considering that the Thousand-Armed Kannon has one thousand arms on its one body, if the mind stops at the one holding a bow, the other nine hundred and ninety-nine will be useless. It is because the mind is not detained at one place that all the arms are useful" (19–22). It is misleading to characterize the interior monologue only or even mainly by fluidity (as Sergei Eisenstein does), for its "free associations" are, as psychoanalysis has shown, often determined by and sucked into the strange attractors that are the traumas, etc., and its circulation is, as Zen master Takuan Soho indicated in his letter to the sword master, constantly impeded by attachments and the stopping of the mind at the matter requiring its attention.

74
Søren Kierkegaard, *Fear and Trembling* & *Repetition*, edited and translated with introduction and notes by Howard V. Hong and Edna H. Hong (Princeton: Princeton University Press, 1983), 131.

75

From an entry in the projected preface, dated November 1887–March 1888, to *The Will to Power*. See Friedrich Nietzsche, *The Will to Power*, trans. Walter Kaufmann and R. J. Hollingdale (New York: Random House, 1968), 3.

76

I am using "distracted" here in its common sense, and not in the different sense developed in my book *Distracted*.

77

Cf. Jalal Toufic, *Distracted*, 2nd ed., 10: "The hotel manager shows him around his room. A few days later, he moves to a different floor. The manager shows him around his new room: a replica of the other one. The manager drops a piece of information about the presence of an item that was also in the first room but wasn't mentioned during the earlier presentation. A hotel room cannot be known by scrutiny, but by a lateral movement from one room to another, from one account to another."

78

The italicized words are a borrowing from Michel Foucault. On "the death of man" in Foucault, see "Appendix: On the Death of Man and Superman," in Gilles Deleuze, *Foucault*, trans. Seán Hand (Minneapolis: University of Minnesota Press, 1988).

79

"The Contemporary Is Still Forthcoming," *e-flux journal*, no. 28 (October 2011), http://www.e-flux.com/journal/the-contemporary-is-still-forthcoming/; http://worker01.e-flux.com/pdf/article_255.pdf.

80

"However gratefully we might approach the *objective* spirit ... nevertheless, in the end we even have to be cautious of our gratitude.... The objective man ... , the *ideal* scholar who expresses the scientific instinct as it finally blossoms and blooms all the way (after things have gone partly or wholly wrong a thousand times over)—he is certainly one of the most expensive tools there is: but he belongs in the hands of someone more powerful. He is only a tool, we will say: he is a *mirror*, ... he is used to subordinating himself in front of anything that wants to be known, without any other pleasure than that of knowing, of 'mirroring forth.' ... His mirror-like soul ... does not know how to affirm or negate any more. He does not command; and neither does he destroy. '*Je ne méprise presque rien*' [I despise almost nothing], he says with Leibniz: that *presque* [almost] should not be overlooked or underestimated! ... In general, he puts himself at too great a distance to have any basis for choosing between good or evil.... He is a tool, a piece of slave (although, without a doubt, the most sublime type of slave) but nothing in himself,—*presque rien* [almost nothing]!" Friedrich Nietzsche, *Beyond Good and Evil: Prelude to a Philosophy of the Future*, ed. Rolf-Peter Horstmann and Judith Norman; trans. Judith Norman (Cambridge; New York: Cambridge University Press, 2002), 97–99.

81
"'Good and Evil' and 'Good and Bad,'" in Friedrich Nietzsche, *On the Genealogy of Morals*, trans. Walter Kaufmann and R. J. Hollingdale (New York: Vintage, 1967), 36 and 39–40.

82
Genesis 2:16–17 (King James Version).

83
Lee Smolin: "Why do things fall? ... A big clue is Galileo's discovery that everything falls with a constant acceleration. What did Newton do with this clue? Newton posited a universal force that pulls on every object proportionally to its mass. But 'mass' is defined, more fundamentally, as the ratio of force to acceleration ($F = ma$), so the more massive a body, the less acceleration it receives from a given force. If the force increases proportionally to the mass but the acceleration decreases proportionally to that mass, then the acceleration with which a body falls doesn't depend on its mass. Nor does it appear to depend on anything else. This, however, makes the fact that all bodies fall with the same acceleration into a kind of coincidence. But Einstein didn't believe in coincidences—at least not in the laws of nature. Einstein ...

posited that falling is the natural state.... Falling is not what requires explanation.... But standing (say) does. If standing is unnatural, it requires a force, and indeed we do feel a force when we are standing—the force pulling us to the ground.... The only time we don't feel a force is when we're falling. *We feel gravity because we are not falling.* What we feel is not the force of gravity, it is the force of the floor or the chair pushing up on us, keeping us from falling" (http://timereborn.com/wp/wp-content/uploads/2013/04/Relativity-appendix-2.pdf).

84
Oxford Dictionary of English, 3rd edition, 2010.

85
The Unbearable Lightness of Being is the title of a novel by Milan Kundera, which appropriately begins with musings on Nietzsche's eternal recurrence (these inane musings are unworthy of being read twice [and therefore once], let alone of being willed to be read eternally). It is disappointing that this novel does not come close to exemplifying its title. Richard Foreman's *No-Body*, 1997, exemplifies a bearable, "paradisiacal" unbearable lightness of being, one that, as long as the will has not been achieved, "could only happen in Poetry City."

86
The gap between desiring to be with those one admires and loves, and the aversion to be with those one despises and loathes is smaller than the chasm between the former and willing the eternal recurrence of the events one desires.

87
Proper names, insinuated with the introduction of mortality, would disappear as a consequence of the abolishing of death with the achievement of the will; the *overman* (as well as *al-Mahdī* and *the Messiah*) is not the common name of someone with a proper name.

88
It would be quite inappropriate to call the operation to realize the will Operation Dracula, for while the vampire (especially since his or her capacity to be affected is reduced to a

few parameters, for example, proximity of blood and changes in the atmosphere announcing the ominous coming of daylight) compulsively repeats similar dark events nightly, beginning with the compulsive resorting to hypnosis to subdue and control yet another indifferent victim (a hypnosis working not by willpower but through the absence of his image in the mirror: "The vampire is not visible in the mirror, but his presence can be detected by the attraction such a hypnotic absence of an image exerts on the look of the other, reflected person" [Jalal Toufic, *(Vampires)*, revised and expanded edition, 115]), he can never will these events to recur eternally. Is there a repetition of evil that is not compulsive but willed? If there is, then the Antichrist would be the figure who wills the eternal recurrence of evil. I rather think that evil is inextricably associated with a compulsion to repeat, and thus a displeasure at being forced to repeat, and therefore cannot be willed to recur eternally. Hell is the endless compulsion to repeat what one cannot *ever* will to recur eternally.

89

It appears that the epoch to which Zeus, Hades, and Sisyphus belonged ceased before Sisyphus could end up willing the eternal recurrence of the events of his repetitive ordeal.

90

Demanding *amor fati* before the will has been established is, exceptionally, not an injunction to nihilism in case it is in relation to the incorporeal events rather than to the states of things. See Gilles Deleuze, *The Logic of Sense*, trans. Mark Lester with Charles Stivale, ed. Constantin V. Boundas (New York: Columbia University Press, 1990).

91

"The Ultimate Free Lunch," in Alan H. Guth, *The Inflationary Universe: The Quest for a New Theory of Cosmic Origins*, with a foreword by Alan Lightman (Reading, MA: Addison-Wesley, 1997). The quote is from pages 12–13.

92

Were these values to be deducible from some future theory, then that the universe is the outcome of a "dice throw" is going to be indicated by other, still undiscovered aspects.

93

In Robert Heinlein's short story "All You Zombies—" (1959) "a young man (later revealed to be intersex) [is] taken back in time and tricked into impregnating his younger, female self (before he underwent a sex change); he thus turns out to be the offspring of that union, with the paradoxical result that he is his own mother and father" (*Wikipedia*'s "All You Zombies [short story]" entry). While the protagonist of Heinlein's "All You Zombies—" could have said, "I ... am my son, my father, my mother, and myself," his statement would be radically different from Artaud's seemingly identical one in "Here Lies."

94

David Deutsch, *The Fabric of Reality: The Science of Parallel Universes—and Its Implications* (New York: Allen Lane, 1997), especially chapter 12, "Time Travel"; and David Deutsch, "Quantum Mechanics Near Closed Timelike Lines," *Physical Review D* 44, no. 10 (November 15, 1991): 3197–3217, particularly page 3201: "The difficulty is illustrated by the following history: A time traveler goes into the past and reveals the proof of an important theorem to the mathematician who had later been recognized as the first to prove it. The mathematician goes on to publish the proof, which is then read by the time traveler before setting out. Who thought of the proof? No one, since each of the two participants obtained that valuable information from the other.

"It is a fundamental principle of the philosophy of science that the solutions of problems do not spring fully formed into the Universe, i.e., as initial data, but emerge only through evolutionary or rational processes. In adopting this evolutionary principle we reject such antirational doctrines as creationism, and more generally we reject all explanations of complex regularity in the observed universe that attribute it to complex regularity in the initial data." I agree with Deutsch's evolutionary principle only if it is limited to relative closures: the mathematical proof mentioned in his story is one of the ahistorical things that may irrupt fully formed in a radical closure.

95

See Frank J. Tipler, *The Physics of Immortality: Modern Cosmology, God and the Resurrection of the Dead* (New York: Doubleday, 1994), 225.

96
Ibid., 31. Tipler bases himself here on Jacob Bekenstein, who "showed that quantum systems—and, according to physics, everything in sight is a quantum system—have only a finite number of states" (ibid.). Regarding the numbers he advanced for a human being, he continues: "These numbers are of course enormous, and as a matter of fact I'm sure that the actual numbers of states and changes are much less than these bounds. But these bounds are nevertheless finite, and firmly based on the central laws of quantum mechanics. They thus prove that a human being is a finite state machine, and *nothing but* a finite state machine" (ibid.).

97
Friedrich Nietzsche, *Thus Spoke Zarathustra: A Book for Everyone and Nobody*, translated with an introduction and notes by Graham Parkes (New York: Oxford University Press, 2005), 192.

98
Frank J. Tipler, *The Physics of Immortality*, 1.

99
As for the confirmation of Nietzsche's "All-too-small the greatest!" one would have to bear in mind that as *good* is to be understood differently when set against the *bad* for the noble or the *evil* for slaves ("how different these words 'bad' and 'evil' are, although they are both apparently the opposite of the same concept 'good.' But it is *not* the same concept 'good'" [Nietzsche]), *small* is to be understood differently when said of the great and the greatest. In the absence of the will, while one can be great without encountering—and extinguishing?—(Lacan's) object small a (aka *objet petit a* and *object a*, the "object-cause of desire"), one cannot be the greatest without doing so (for Charles Lutwidge Dodgson, better known by his pen name, Lewis Carroll, the *object a*, the greatest as far as his desire was concerned, was the little girl, who as the eponymous idol of *Alice's Adventures in Wonderland* at times shrinks and becomes too small, all the while giving the impression that she could go on dwindling until she vanished into thin air ["She was now only ten inches high, and her face brightened up at the thought that she was

now the right size for going through the little door into that lovely garden. First, however, she waited for a few minutes to see if she was going to shrink any further: she felt a little nervous about this; 'for it might end, you know,' said Alice to herself, 'in my going out altogether, like a candle. I wonder what I should be like then?' And she tried to fancy what the flame of a candle looks like after the candle is blown out...."]—all rigorous people who have encountered and extinguished *object small a* have fancied some variant of the following paradox: What is the *object small a* like after it has dwindled into thin air [without, like *Alice's Adventures in Wonderland*'s Cheshire Cat, leaving even a grin]?).

100
Friedrich Nietzsche, *Ecce Homo*, trans. Walter Kaufmann (New York: Random House, 1967), II 9, 255.

101
In Bill Viola's installation *Room for St. John of the Cross*, 1983, through an opening in a black cubicle one can see a tiny monitor showing what appears to be a static shot of a mountain, while outside, on a big screen, one sees what seems to be jerky handheld shots of a mountain range. I would think that the jerkiness of the latter shots is not caused by any camera movement but is rather that of the mountains themselves. Dōgen wrote: "Preceptor Kai of Mt. Dayang addressed the assembly, saying, 'The blue mountains are constantly walking....' Although the walking of the blue mountains is faster than 'swift as the wind,' those in the mountains do not sense this, do not know it" ("Mountains and Waters Sutra" [*Sansui kyō*], in *Treasury of the Eye of the True Dharma*, trans. Carl Bielefeldt); and "Junayd's answer to the enthusiastic Nūrī, who objected to his sitting quietly while the Sufis performed their whirling dance, is famous: 'You see the mountains—you think them firm, yet they move like clouds' (Qur'ān 27:90)" (Annemarie Schimmel, *Mystical Dimensions of Islam* [Chapel Hill: University of North Carolina Press, 1975], 181). Unlike in Islam and Zen Buddhism, it seems that in Christianity mountains do not move on their own and that they can be moved only by faith: "Truly I [Jesus] tell you, if you have faith as small as a mustard seed, you can say to this mountain, 'Move from here to there,' and it will move"

(Matthew 17:20). On his way to be crucified, Jesus Christ warned that there would come a terrible day when people would "say to the mountains, 'Fall on us!' and to the hills, 'Cover us!'" (Luke 23:30). When Jesus's words came to pass, an incarcerated saint (the author of *Ascent of Mount Carmel* and *Dark Night of the Soul*?) made, through his faith, the mountains obey their plea; he did this out of Christian love: "If I have a faith that can move mountains, but do not have love, I am nothing" (1 Corinthians 13:2).

102

Quoted in Giorgio Agamben, *The Coming Community*, trans. Michael Hardt (Minneapolis: University of Minnesota Press, 1993), 53.

103

While, like so many others, I've written on some films after their release, I have also written on others before they were made! For instance the text on *Lost Highway* (1997) in the first edition of *Forthcoming* (2000) that this footnote comments (and which was left unaltered in this edition) turned out to be a description of Lynch's subsequent film, *Mulholland Dr.* (2001).

104

For (the revised version of) the initial, more elaborate essay on my concept *radical closure*, see "Radical Closure" in the second edition of my book *Over-Sensitivity* (Forthcoming Books, 2009; available for download as a PDF file at: http://www.jalaltoufic.com/downloads.htm), 105–154.

105

There is a radical difference between a blank that shows the potentiality from which the rest of the painting issued and a blank that functions as the border of a radical closure, allowing entities to irrupt in the painting even after it is finished. All five of Toba Khedoori's paintings shown at Los Angeles's Museum of Contemporary Art in 1997 were *untitled* (the indication of the models appearing only within parentheses). Unless the radical-closure painter subscribes to a disjunctive relation between the image and the title, his or her paintings are either to be left untitled, since at any time fully formed entities may still irrupt in them, or he or she, while still alive, or a representative of him or her, following his or her death, has to keep revising the title to take into consideration whatever may irrupt in the painting. Aware of the unknowability of what may *yet* irrupt in his or her ostensibly finished radical-closure paintings, the artist may prepare the spectator for such an eventuality by training him to accept the disjunction between title and model/subject matter (which is the case in at least some of Magritte's paintings); leave it untitled (Khedoori); or distance himself from the title by explicitly leaving it to the gallery to add it, thus making it at bottom illegitimate (Francis Bacon).

106

I also suggest that the owners of the following two painting by Francis Bacon, a radical-closure painter, *Figure in Movement* (1976) and *Oedipus and the Sphinx after Ingres* (1983), take out insurance against the eventuality of the disappearance of the bird-like figures from these paintings.

107

My mixed-media work *Radical-Closure Artist with Bandaged Sense Organ* (1997) includes a loop of reedited shots from Hitchcock's *The Birds* (1963): the credits sequence showing the electronic birds flying in an indeterminate plane and accompanied by electronic sounds is cut on movement to shots from the scene of the birds' irruption from behind the school building and their subsequent attack on the school children, the attacking birds thus appearing to come from the credits sequence.

108

Here are Signac's words as quoted in Gustave Cocquiot's *Vincent Van Gogh* (1923), page 194: "Toute la journée il me parla peinture, littérature, socialisme. Le soir il était un peu fatigué. Il faisait un coup de mistral effroyable qui a pu l'énerver. Il voulut boire à même un litre d'essence de térébenthine qui se trouvait sur la table de la chambre. Il était temps de rentrer à l'hospice" (All day long he talked to me of painting, literature, socialism. In the evening he was a little tired. A fearsome mistral was blowing, which may have made him irritable. He tried to gulp down a liter of turpentine that was on his bedroom table. It was time to go back to the hospital), http://vangoghletters.org/vg/letters/let752/letter.html#n-1.

109
Le grand registre de l'asile de Saint-Rémy, Arles, France, May 1889. See http://vangoghletters.org/vg/documentation.html#id8May1889.

110
Were there crows in the painting we presently know as *Wheatfield with Crows* (who gave the painting this title?) by the time Van Gogh died? Did they rather irrupt in it sometime between the death of Van Gogh and the first time someone else saw it?

111
Pierre Cabanne, *Dialogues with Marcel Duchamp* (New York; London: Da Capo, 1987), 43.

112
The italicized words are a borrowing from Francis Bacon.

113
Le grand registre de l'asile de Saint-Rémy, Arles, France, May 9, 1889. See http://vangoghletters.org/vg/documentation.html#id8May1889.

114
The Complete Letters of Vincent van Gogh, with Reproductions of All the Drawings in the Correspondence, vol. 3 (Greenwich, CT: New York Graphic Society, 1959), 123–124.

115
Chris Rodley, "David Lynch," *Icon*, no. 1 (April 1997): 67.

116
Isn't the experience that decided the painter David Lynch to start filmmaking one that is recurrently encountered in Alain Robbe-Grillet's novels: the animation of what was presented initially as an illustration in a newspaper, or a frieze, or a series of sculptures? The change from an inanimate image to film is

present within one of Lynch's films, his sixth feature, *Twin Peaks: Fire Walk with Me* (1992), this time because the radical closure presented by the film allowed the irruption of animated figures into the photograph that Laura Palmer places on the wall.

117

The Frank of David Lynch's *Blue Velvet* kidnaps a man and cuts off his ear; then he has intercourse with the hostage's wife, whose blue velvet dress functioned as a curtain indicating the end of the world when the film's opening credits were overlaid on it (that a certain type of curtain functions as a radical border of the world is even clearer in the case of the red curtain in Lynch's later film, *Twin Peaks: Fire Walk with Me*); then he places in his hostage's mouth a piece of that blue velvet robe and says, "Do it for Van Gogh!" Frank certainly knows more about the two Van Gogh self-portraits with bandaged ear than Kurosawa, who makes the Van Gogh character in his film *Dreams* explain that he cut off his ear because it was jarring the composition of a self-portrait he was painting. Had Frank not cut off his hostage's ear for him, it is likely that the kidnapped man would have ended up doing so himself, in a desperate attempt to stop the kind of unworldly sounds audible when the camera zooms into the ear as it lies in the grass.

118

The quoted words are a borrowing from the title of one of Antonin Artaud's texts, "Van Gogh, the Man Suicided by Society" (1947)—Antonin Nalpas (it was under this name that some of the letters ascribed to Artaud were signed: "As for the name of Nalpas, it is ... the maiden name of my mother.... But that's not why I spoke of it, and *I am greatly surprised that I did*. Because this name has, on the other hand, Legendary, Mystic and sacred origins ...") could have given his letter to Dr. Ferdière dated February 12, 1943, the title, "Antonin Artaud, the Man Suicided by Society": "Antonin Artaud est mort à la peine et de douleur à Ville-Évrard au mois d'Août 1939 et son cadavre a été sorti de Ville-Évrard pendant la durée d'une nuit blanche comme celles dont parle Dostoïevsky et qui occupent l'espace de plusieurs journées intercalaires mais non comprises dans le calendrier de ce monde-ci—quoi[que] vraies comme le jour d'ici" (Antonin Artaud died to trouble and of pain in Ville-Évrard in the month of August 1939 and his cadaver was removed from Ville-Évrard during a sleepless night like those Dostoevsky talks about and that occupy the span of several intercalary days that are not included in the calendar of this world—though they are true as the day from here) (*Nouveaux Écrits de Rodez : Lettres au docteur Ferdière (1943–1946) et autres textes inédits, suivis de Six lettres à Marie Dubuc (1935–1937)* [1977]).

119
Near the end of the "Crows" section in Kurosawa's *Dreams*, Van Gogh is presented as continuing his walk through the field beyond the point where in his painting *Wheatfield with Crows* the path radically ends in a line parallel to the horizon! This continuation beyond the gateless gate is a faux pas on Kurosawa's part since it is impossible and since it undercuts the radical closure of space that allowed the irruption of the unworldly (electronic and shadowless) crows over the field.

120
The italicized words are a borrowing of the title of a collection of Zen koans.

121
Did she then actually leave her radically-closed apartment?

122
An Ash'arite theologian or an Ibn al-Arabi disciple, who believed in the ever-renewed creation of a world that is not self-sufficient, could, indeed might have, said the same words through which, for different reasons, the woman of Duras's film *Le Camion* avers the end of the ostensibly continuing world: "Look at the end of the world, all the time, at every second, everywhere."

123
Discontinuity, whether stylistic or thematic, is encountered throughout my books. In *Distracted*, it basically takes the form of aphorisms separated by blanks. In *(Vampires): An Uneasy Essay on the Undead in Film*, it is encountered in the manner of the (quantum) tunneling of the undead and

teleportation, as well as the "counterintuitive" side effect of these, motionlessness in the absence of any discernable barrier ("One of the tolls for tunneling or teleportation, by means of which one moves through [or finds oneself to the other side of] perceptible barriers, is that unexpected, invisible obstacles will spring up everywhere, resulting in motionlessness where there is no discernable barrier. Many of these barriers will be objects that for no apparent reason cannot be removed, objects that put one in a trance, depriving one of one's motor ability"); over-turns; and the empty space-time zones of the labyrinth, which produce lapses not merely of consciousness but also, more radically, of being. In *Over-Sensitivity*, it is encountered in the guise of the ahistorical fully formed unworldly entities that irrupt in radical closures, and the empty space-time zones in the realm of altered movement, body, silence, music, space, and time into which dance projects a subtle version of the dancer. And here, it is encountered mainly in the mode of the atomic temporality of Islam according to the theology of the Ash'arites and the sufism of Ibn al-'Arabī.

124
Robert S. Fisher, Walter van Emde Boas, Warren Blume, Christian Elger, Pierre Genton, Phillip Lee, and Jerome Engel, Jr., "Epileptic Seizures and Epilepsy: Definitions Proposed by the International League Against Epilepsy (ILAE) and the International Bureau for Epilepsy (IBE)," *Epilepsia* 46, no. 4 (2005): 470–472.

125
Martin Heidegger, *The Fundamental Concepts of Metaphysics: World, Finitude, Solitude*, trans. William McNeill and Nicholas Walker (Bloomington: Indiana University Press, 1995), 242–247: "It has been observed that if its [the bee's] abdomen is carefully cut away while it is sucking, a bee will simply carry on regardless even while the honey runs out of the bee from behind.... The bee is simply taken [*hingenommen*] by its food.... When the bee flies out of the hive to find food it registers the direction in which it stands in relation to the sun.... If we ... take the box in which the bee has been imprisoned back to the hive and place it some distance behind the hive, then the newly freed bee

flies in the direction in which it would have to fly in order to find the hive from the feeding place, even though the hive is relatively nearby, and it does so for the appropriate distance once again.... [The bee] flies back in a pre-established direction over a pre-established distance without regard to the position of the hive. It does not strike out in a given direction prescribed for it by the place in which it has found itself. Rather it is absorbed by a direction, is driven to produce this direction out of itself—without regard to the destination. The bee does not at all comport itself toward particular things, like the hive, the feeding place and so on. The bee is *simply given over* to the sun and to the period of its flight *without being able to grasp either of these as such*.... The animal ... is taken [*hingenommen*], taken and captivated [*benommen*] by things."

126
Zen master Hakuin Zenji: "What is the sound of one hand clapping?"

127
In Ash'arite atomism, atoms revert back to nothingness because the accident of duration (*baqā'*) imparted to them by God does not subsist for longer than an instant.

128
While for Bergson, the philosopher of duration, an atom, like whatever "is not a center of indetermination," is subject to a necessity "which obliges it to act through every one of its points upon all the points of all other images, to transmit the whole of what it receives, to oppose to every action an equal and contrary reaction, to be, in short, merely a road by which pass, in every direction, the modifications propagated throughout the immensity of the universe" (Henri Bergson, *Matter and Memory*, trans. Nancy Margaret Paul and William Scott Palmer [New York: Zone Books, 1988], 36), in a conception of recurrent appearance, disappearance, then appearance of entities, including atoms, the atom recurrently faces away from the linear "action" toward nothingness/the Being who recurrently creates it.

129

According to quantum physics, the indivisible unit of time should be reached at the Planck time, $(Gh/c^5)^{1/2}$ = 5.391 06(32) x 10^{-44} s.

130

Revenants: creatures who have the presumption to themselves settle an outstanding symbolic debt, not leaving it to (the exoteric) God to do that on the Day of Judgment.

131

Why is it that nowhere in the New Testament is there an incident where Christ—who heals the possessed and resurrects the dead—meets a revenant and commands him or her either to come back fully to life or to die until the Day of Judgment?

132

T. E. Lawrence, *Seven Pillars of Wisdom*, with an introduction by Angus Calder (London: Wordsworth Editions, 1997), 22–23.

133

In some other Muslim miniatures, what may appear, color-wise, to be an unrealistic depiction of an earthly body is actually either a realistic presentation of an Imaginal World (*'ālam al-khayāl*) embodied spirit or Intelligence, or a realistic depiction of an earthly body tinged by the various colored photisms that Sufis perceive in a suprasensuous manner as they progress along the spiritual path (to the state in which they perceive the *black light* [*nūr-e siyāh*]).

134

The separation and independence of dance, music, and design, but also of the dance phrases performed by the different dancers or groups of dancers, that is, of what would traditionally be viewed as the components of an organic artwork of dance, in the collaborative work of Cage and Cunningham; as well as the separation and independence of words and images in the work of a number of avant-garde filmmakers and theater artists, for instance in Robert Wilson's theater production of *Hamletmachine* and in Duras's film *Agatha*, should in principle not be difficult to appreciate for someone who has an affinity with or subscribes to the occasionalist standpoint of the Ash'arites or indeed of the *mutakallimīn* in general, where the different accidents that adhere to the bodies and atoms are independent of each other and of the latter.

135

Here's a suggested question to some future interviewer: "If so, Jalal, why are at least some Muslim filmmakers to explore and experiment with this mode of temporality and linkage that is akin to the medium of cinema at the level of the basic apparatus, if the occasionalism connected to this temporality and mode of linking, with its denial of a nature in favor of a custom of God, is alien to reflexivity?"

136

The differentiation between the Kūfic script, which with its rectilinear and angular forms and its monumentality was up to the twelfth century the only script utilized in epigraphic decoration, and the cursive Naskhī script, especially the thuluth variant, which, except for certain titles, replaced Kūfic almost completely from the eleventh and twelfth centuries, shows that Muslim artists were at one level quite sensitive to the different characteristics and properties of various styles, media, and materials. But this discernment of the difference of the various styles, media, and materials—and who could possibly be more sensitive than artists to the difference of styles and materials?—had to yield to their implicit more basic view of the lack of proper nature and characteristics of entities.

137

"The moment of its [the Queen of Sheba's throne's] disappearance from its place is the same as its presence with Solomon, by virtue of the renewal of creation.... Therefore do not say 'then,' which implies a lapse of time, for the word *thumma* in Arabic implies a process of cause and effect in specific situations, as the poet says, 'Like the quivering of the spear, then it shook.' Now the time of its quivering is the same as that of its shaking. He says 'then,' although there is no lapse of time. Similarly with the renewal of creation ... the moment of the nonexistence of a thing is the very moment of the existence of its like ..." Ibn Al 'Arabi, *The Bezels of Wisdom*, translated and introduced by R. W. Austin, preface by Titus Burckhardt (New York: Paulist Press, 1980), 193.

138
In Robbe-Grillet's *L'Immortelle*, whose events take place in Turkey, there is a resonance between two sorts of appearances out of nothing: one in the set radical closure, that of Lale; and one implied by the arabesques, that of ever-renewed creation.

139
François Cheng, *Empty and Full: The Language of Chinese Painting*, trans. Michael H. Kohn (Boston: Shambhala, 1994), 76–77.

140
"The imaginal faculty (*al-quwwat al-mutakhayyila*) and the World of Imagination ... is the closest thing to a denotation (*dalāla*) of the Real. For the Real is 'the First and the Last, the Manifest and the Nonmanifest' (Koran 57:3). Abū Sa'īd al-Kharrāz was asked, 'Through what have you known God?' He answered, 'Through the fact that He brings opposites together.' Then he recited this Koranic verse." William C. Chittick, *The Sufi Path of Knowledge: Ibn al-'Arabi's Metaphysics of Imagination* (Albany: State University of New York Press, 1989), 115.

141
Qur'ān 27:90: "You see the mountains—you think them firm, yet they move like clouds."

142
Or was it really Khadir, or else the angel Gabriel assuming the form of Āṣif b. Barkhayā?

143
Ibn Al 'Arabi, *The Bezels of Wisdom*, 193.

144
Roman Jakobson, *Language in Literature*, ed. Krystyna Pomorska and Stephen Rudy (Cambridge, MA: Harvard University Press, 1987), 71.

145

Can one say: is unique what can be replaced only by itself? One should go further: is unique, and thus irreplaceable, that which cannot be replaced even by himself/herself.

146

What is itself can afford associations away from itself, for example, metaphors; but what is ontologically not itself but only like itself cannot afford such associations, since its singularity consists in this: that the creatural association it induces is first and foremost to itself.

147

Sohrab Shahid Saless's *Still Life* (1974) is another film that should not, for other reasons, be viewed as a capitulation of the cinematic to painting. It is rather, along with Paradjanov's *Sayat Nova*, one of the greatest films of the Middle East and Transcaucasia; one could give it an alternate, cinematic title derived from Beckett: *Stirrings Still—Life*.

148

Cf. Sergei Eisenstein: "It is a weird and wonderful feat to have written a pamphlet on something that in reality does not exist. There is, for example, no such thing as a cinema without cinematography. And yet the author [Naum Kaufman] of the pamphlet [*Japanese Cinema* (Moscow, 1929)] preceding this essay has contrived to write a book about the *cinema* of a country that has no *cinematography*. About the cinema of a country that has, in its culture, an infinite number of cinematographic traits, strewn everywhere with the sole exception of—its cinema. This essay is on the cinematographic traits of Japanese culture that lie outside the Japanese cinema.... Cinematography is, first and foremost, montage.... The Japanese cinema is completely unaware of montage. Nevertheless the principle of montage can be identified as the basic element of Japanese representational culture." *Film Form and The Film Sense*, ed. and trans. Jay Leyda (New York: Meridian Books, 1957), 28.

149

Al-Azhar University objected to Youssef Chahine's first version of the script of *The Emigrant* because the protagonist was ostensibly modeled on and represented the prophet Joseph. When Chahine filmed an apparently insufficiently revised version and screened it in Egypt, he was soon taken to court and his film was pulled from theaters pending the court's decision. The film was subsequently rereleased after Chahine won his appeal (given the widespread degeneracy in Egyptian culture around the time of the release of the film, I was not that surprised that the uproar in certain Egyptian circles was all about the possible transgression of the prohibition of the representation of a Qur'ānic prophet, in other words, that none of it was over the crassness with which ancient Egypt was shown).

150
In this bigoted age of religious and ethnic civil wars, whether in Transcaucasia, between Armenia and Azerbaijan, or elsewhere, it is salutary to have the example of Paradjanov, this Armenian born in Tbilisi, Georgia, who, from *Sayat Nova* onward, created the films to which (many) Muslim filmmakers, including Azerbaijani ones, feel most affined.

151
Ibn Al 'Arabi, *The Bezels of Wisdom*, 100–101.

152
While in Christianity his incarnation allows for Christ's representation, in Islam it is his episodic replacement by another ("They slew him [the Messiah, Jesus son of Mary, Allah's messenger] not nor crucified him, but it appeared so unto them [*shubbiha lahum*]" [Qur'ān 4:157; in his translation of the Qur'ān, John Medows Rodwell, a clergyman, avers that *shubbiha lahum* literally means "one was made to appear to them like (Jesus)"]) that would seem to allow for his representation, if only during the crucifixion.

153
To the question, "Is it permissible to film or direct a scene in which the prophet Muhammad (Peace and blessings of God upon him), or the preceding prophets, or the infallible imams (may God be pleased with them all), or holy historic figures and symbols appear on a film or TV screen, or at the theater?" the answer of Grand Ayatollah Ali al-Husayni al-Sistani, a

marja' taqlīd (source to emulate/follow) was: "If it observes the requirements of veneration and reverence and does not include any offense to their holy images in the spectators' souls, there is no objection." To the question, "Some directors make a historical film about the Prophet and his family (Peace be upon him and his family) or the imams (Peace be upon them). 1) Is it permissible for an actor to impersonate the character of the Holy Prophet (Peace be upon him and his family), appearing before the public as the Prophet (Peace be upon him and his family)—and does the same apply in the case of the imams (Peace be upon them)? 2) If the answer is that it is permissible, is it required that that actor be a believer?" Sistani's answer was: "It is permissible to represent through acting their characters (Peace be upon them), but only if that does not give offense—even in the future—with regard to their honorable statuses and holy images in souls—it may be that the qualities and particularities of the actors who play their roles (Peace be upon them) have some influence in this matter" (http://www.sistani.org/index.php?p=525390&id=291).

154
In comparison to Buñuel, how slow and prone to the defense mechanism of dissociation is Cecil B. DeMille, the filmmaker of two versions of *The Ten Commandments*, in which the mature Moses is played by two different actors: in the 1923 version, Theodore Roberts; in the 1956 version, Charlton Heston.

155
Only in the case of the prophet Muḥammad is there no reason to inquire in what guise he appeared in the dream: he appeared in the same form as in waking life.

156
Cf. Genesis 42:8: "And Joseph recognized his brothers but they did not recognize him."

157
We are told in Genesis that years later Jacob asked Joseph to bury him in Canaan in the same spot where he had buried Leah (49:30–31). Since at no point are we told that old

Jacob visited Canaan during his stay in Egypt, the implication is that he must have buried her before he headed to meet his son in Egypt, i.e., that she was already dead during the scene of Joseph's raising of his parents on a dais and their prostrating themselves before him. Was then the woman who prostrated to Joseph as his mother in Egypt in life-as-a-*dream* Rachel's maidservant (and half-sister?) Bilhah, who was chosen by Rachel to be a surrogate mother for her while she was still sterile and who gave birth to two sons that Rachel named and raised (Dan and Naphtali)?

158
The expression "dream within a dream" (the Arabic expression is *manām fī manām*) appears in "The Wisdom of Light in the Word of Joseph" in Ibn Al 'Arabi's *The Bezels of Wisdom* (121).

159
When in an October 1965 interview in *Cahiers du cinéma*, the interviewer observed, "There is a good deal of blood in *Pierrot* [*le fou*]," Godard retorted: "Not blood, red"—try saying this to a hysteric, for example, to the eponymous heroine of Hitchcock's *Marnie*!

160
If one wants to remain strictly within the Islamic context, then on dying the prophet Joseph, the dreamer, awakened (the prophet Muhammad said in a tradition frequently quoted by Sufi authors: "Men are asleep; they awaken at their death").

161
Plate XXI, Chapter XV, in E. A. Wallis Budge, *The Book of the Dead: The Papyrus of Ani* (New York: Dover Publications, 1967), 326.

162
See Chapter CXXXIII, in Budge, *The Book of the Dead*, 328. "Osiris Ani" has here been replaced by "Osiris Zaphenath-Paneah."

163

See Chapter CXXIV, in Budge, *The Book of the Dead*, 331. Alternatively, what the lector priest could have recited on behalf of Zaphenath-Paneah, aka Joseph (to whom the pharaoh had said: "Thou shalt be over my house, and according unto thy word shall all my people be ruled: only in the throne will I be greater than thou" [Genesis 41:40]), are the following extracts from the pyramid of Pepi I: "Isis speaketh unto thee, Nephthys holdeth converse with thee, and the shining ones come unto thee bowing down even to the ground in adoration at thy feet, by reason of the writing thou hast" (Budge, *The Book of the Dead*, lxxvii).

164

The Standard Edition of the Complete Psychological Works of Sigmund Freud, vol. 4 (1900), *The Interpretation of Dreams*, 1st part, 163.

165

The following are two unsettling sorts of looks of the undead: that of the ancient Egyptian statue, which disregards you even as you stand in front of it; and that of the vampire/undead, who has no mirror image and thus gazes at you across media (in a film, the vampire facing the mirror in which he has no image and to the other side of whose empty frame the camera is placed is specifically looking at each individual film spectator).

166

Is it surprising to encounter in a tale titled *The Sphinx* (Poe) someone who considers a creature sixteenth of an inch in length "to be far larger than any ship of the line in existence ... [its] proboscis some sixty or seventy feet in length, and about as thick as the body of an ordinary elephant"?

167

It is therefore quite on the mark for Poe's *The Sphinx* to revolve around a mistake with regards to distance and location, the narrator confusing the insect of the genus *Sphinx*, of the family *Crepuscularia*, on the spider web at the window just sixteenth of an inch from him with a giant winged monster at the landslide section of a remote hill.

168
Is it possible that only a few die? To be dead, in other words, to be an undead, is already a form of courage: owing to over-turns in the undeath realm, even turning back is forging ahead. (Un)death is not for cowards. Cowardice applies only in situations from which one can escape; there is no cowardice past the point of no return. A coward can enter or find himself or herself neither in a labyrinth, nor in undeath, nor in the mainstream Christian or Muslim hell—he or she can find himself or herself in the hell concocted by mind-projections in the bardo of becoming, since he or she can escape from the latter by rebirth. The courage of the dead, whose bodies, like that of Daniel Paul Schreber during his dying before (physically) dying, which was "for a long time without a stomach, without intestines, ... without a bladder," are gut-less, is tainted with a stain of cowardice not because virtually all of them attempt—unsuccessfully—to turn back, but because of the meaning, informal, of the word "gutless": "lacking courage or determination."

In terms of a gradation of courage, one descends from:
— One who is a mortal, that is, dead while (physically) alive, and who is aware of that and who nonetheless, incredibly, risks his life for recognition in life and the world. "The Master is the man who went all the way in a Fight for prestige, who risked his *life* in order to be *recognized* in his absolute superiority by *another* man.... Thus, he 'brought to light,' proved (*bewährt*), realized, and revealed his *superiority* over biological existence, over *his* biological existence, over the natural World in general and over everything that knows itself and that he knows to be *bound* to this World, in particular, over the Slave" (Alexandre Kojève, *Introduction to the Reading of Hegel: Lectures on the Phenomenology of Spirit*, assembled by Raymond Queneau; edited by Allan Bloom; translated from the French by James H. Nichols, Jr. [New York: Basic Books, 1969], 45). I would qualify (Kojève's exegesis of) Hegel: what would indicate one's going beyond given, natural being is not only the willingness to risk one's life, but also that one subsequently become an undead, rather than merely biologically cease. The mortal master should not be defined solely by his willingness to risk his life for recognition: only the living master should be so defined. What fully defines the master is rising above the natural world—at any price, even dying and

thus being misrecognized by everyone, including (the voices and) himself. While his courage in life brought him the recognition of other living humans, the over-turns he underwent in the (un)death realm, which resulted in his forging ahead despite his terror, and thus in his projection of courage, led not only to his lack of recognition by the other dead, but also to his misrecognition by them since, failing repeatedly to answer their calls, they ended up coming to the conclusion that they mistook another for him.

— One who is a mortal, that is, dead while (physically) alive, and who is aware of that and who consequently fails to risk his life for recognition, ending up a slave. The mortal slave is someone who did not go all the way in the "life and death" struggle for recognition with another mortal or not mortal living man, revealing thus that he is, as living, bound to the natural world; but later "finds" "himself" in undeath, thus freed from the natural world. Such a slave is doubly unrecognizable in the realm of death: he, so cowardly while alive, continued to advance, ostensibly not turning back (his turn was repeatedly overturned by over-turns) notwithstanding the terror ahead (while the courage of the living is psychological, that of the dead is not) and the calls of others.

— One who is a mortal, that is, dead while (physically) alive, but who is unaware of that and thus more disposed to risk his life for recognition, becoming, in case he does not die in the duel for recognition, a master. Some slaves' contempt for some masters is therefore not to be ascribed to resentment—at least not fully—but is warranted: in the "life and death" fight, the future Hegelian master proved to be more courageous than the mortal slave merely because he was unaware of the undeath realm.

— One who is not really a mortal, that is, not dead while (physically) alive, since, like (most other) animals, he is merely going to physically die in the future, and who risks his life for recognition. In case the other man in the duel to death for recognition yields, we have the Hegelian master, who fully risks his life for recognition and is thus freed from the natural world, but later merely ceases to live rather than becoming an undead thus revealing that he is still bound, as a corpse surrounded by mourners then buried under a tombstone indicating some variant of "Here Lies —— [his name while alive]," to the natural world. He had won so many fights to the death for

pure prestige that he began not only to feel but also to brag: "I cannot die." The others grew to believe him. But one day, to the surprise of everybody, he unexpectedly expired—and yet he, not really a mortal, did not die *for* [the] *real*.
— One who is not really a mortal, that is, who is not dead while (physically) alive, since, like (most other) animals, he is merely going to physically die in the future, and who, afraid, fails to unreservedly risk his life for recognition. Such a man is fully a slave since he is doubly bound to the natural world: he does not go all the way in the Hegelian "life and death" struggle for recognition, and he does not later become an undead, but merely ceases to live, thus continues to belong then, as a corpse, to the natural world.

If we rather discover that we all die, that is, become undead, then that would mean that we are all fundamentally courageous.

169

In humanist Cairo, there is a suffocating mixing of persons, but frequently a sort of dissociation from the buildings: an acquaintance who worked at the Lebanese embassy told me that when a person inquired of the sentry there about the whereabouts of the Yemeni embassy, he indicated the embassy he was guarding.

170

With over thirty films to his name, he remains the filmmaker of only one superb film, *The Earth* (*al-Arḍ*), 1968, and two fine ones, *Alexandria ... Why?*, 1978, and *Cairo as Told by Youssef Chahine* (*al-Qāhira minawwara bi-Ahlaha*), 1991.

171

An undead, he was in touch with and penetrated by the earth not when he lay, frozen, on dirt in his coffin during the daylight, but when he emerged at night from his frozen state and, like psychotics, was penetrated by everything, including the earth he was ostensibly no longer in touch with.

172

This was not the first instance of one or more scientists calculating an age of the universe that would make it younger than one of its ostensible parts: "[Edwin] Hubble was able to compare his observations of the distance of these spiral galaxies ... with [Vesto] Slipher's measurements of the velocities by which they were moving away. In 1929, with the help of a Mount Wilson [Observatory] staff member, Milton Humason, ... he announced the discovery of a remarkable empirical relationship, now called Hubble's law: There is a linear relationship between recessional velocity and galaxy distance.... They ... also gave a quantitative estimate of the expansion rate itself.... From this estimate ... the Big Bang happened approximately 1.5 billion years ago. Even in 1929, however, the evidence was already clear ... that the Earth was older than 3 billion years. Now, it is embarrassing for scientists to find that the Earth is older than the universe." Lawrence M. Krauss, *A Universe from Nothing: Why There Is Something Rather Than Nothing*, with an afterword by Richard Dawkins (London: Simon & Schuster, 2012), 11–16.

173
John Noble Wilford, "Astronomers Debate Conflicting Data on Age of the Universe," *New York Times*, December 27, 1994, http://www.nytimes.com/1994/12/27/science/astronomers-debate-conflicting-answers-for-the-age-of-the-universe.html?pagewanted=all&src=pm.

174
Dr. Allan R. Sandage, "who learned his astronomy under the great Edwin P. Hubble," is "the foremost defender of a low Hubble constant and so of a much more slowly expanding and older universe of perhaps 15 billion to 20 billion years" (ibid.). Such a universe is older than the estimated age of its oldest stars.

175
Antonin Artaud, *Selected Writings*, 499.

176
The fourth entry in Malte's notebooks begins with: "I am learning to see." And the following entry begins with, "Have I said it before? I am learning to see," and continues with, "For example, it never occurred to me before how many faces there are. There are multitudes of people, but there are many more faces, because each person has several of them.

There are people who wear the same face for years; naturally it wears out, gets dirty, splits at the seams, stretches like gloves worn during a long journey. They are thrifty, uncomplicated people; they never change it, never even have it cleaned.... Of course, since they have several faces, you might wonder what they do with the other ones. They keep them in storage. Their children will wear them. But sometimes it also happens that their dogs go out wearing them....

"Other people change faces incredibly fast ... and wear them out. At first, they think they have an unlimited supply; but when they are barely forty years old they come to their last one. There is, to be sure, something tragic about this. They are not accustomed to taking care of faces; their last one is worn through in a week, has holes in it, is in many places as thin as paper, and then, little by little, the lining shows through, the non-face, and they walk around with that on" (Rainer Maria Rilke, *The Notebooks of Malte Laurids Brigge*, trans. Stephen Mitchell [New York: Random House, 1983], 5–7).

177

Similarly, when one turns one's head backward near the exit of the church of the Santissima Trinità dei Monti, Rome, the previously dissimulated figure of Saint Francis kneeling in prayer in Emmanuel Maignan's fresco *Saint Francis of Paola as a Hermit*, 1642, looks at one not with its eyes, closed in prayer, but with its whole body, including the dress.

178

Robert Graves, *The Greek Myths*, vol. 1 (London: Penguin, 1960), 286–287.

179

Were the interior monologue, which includes one's voiceless call of oneself (which is inaudible to anyone other than the image in the mirror), to stop, then the mirror image would only face one when one utters an express call of oneself in front of it.

180

The child's anticipation of motor control through the mirror image includes the ability to turn around to answer a call neither in Lacan's oral presentation "The Looking-Glass Phase" in 1936, nor, more disappointedly, in "The Mirror Stage as Formative of the Function of the I," published in 1949—twelve years after Magritte painted *Reproduction Prohibited*.

181
Althusser writes in "Ideology and Ideological State Apparatuses (Notes towards an Investigation)": "Ideology 'acts' or 'functions' in such a way that it 'recruits' subjects among the individuals (it recruits them all), or 'transforms' the individuals into subjects (it transforms them all) by that very precise operation which I have called *interpellation* or hailing, and which can be imagined along the lines of the most commonplace everyday police (or other) hailing: 'Hey, you there!' Assuming that the theoretical scene I have imagined takes place in the street, the hailed individual will turn round. By this mere one-hundred-and-eighty-degree physical conversion, he becomes a *subject*. Why? Because he has recognized that the hail was 'really' addressed to him, and that 'it was *really him* who was hailed' (and not someone else)" (Louis Althusser, *On Ideology* [London; New York: Verso, 2008], 48).

182
"We shall give the name of *diffuse animism* to the general tendency of children to confuse the living and the inert.... All external movement is regarded as necessarily purposive.... All activity is regarded as necessarily conscious.... Diffuse animism is ... a primary datum in the child's consciousness." Jean Piaget, *The Child's Conception of the World*, trans. Joan and Andrew Tomlinson (Lanham, MD: Rowman and Littlefield, 2007), 236–237.

183
Joan Copjec, *Read My Desire: Lacan against the Historicists* (Cambridge, MA: MIT Press), 32.

184
Is anyone who has the potential to undergo an over-turn ever in the Rilkean Open? Is it legitimate to advance that one day the human child in the mirror turned toward himself, and was no longer in the Rilkean Open?

185
The Selected Poetry of Rainer Maria Rilke, ed. and trans. Stephen Mitchell; with an introduction by Robert Hass (New York: Random House, 1982), 193.

186
The King James translation of the Bible is flawed when it translates the Hebrew *'āḏām* as Adam, a proper name, already when the man is told to give names to animals, prior to dying before physically dying upon partaking of the tree of the knowledge of good and evil; the New International Version does not make the same mistake, translating *'āḏām* as a common name, "man," at that point.

187
See Gordon Gallup, Jr., "Can Animals Empathize? Yes," *Scientific American Presents* 9, no. 4 (Winter 1998).

188
Gilles Deleuze and Félix Guattari, *A Thousand Plateaus: Capitalism and Schizophrenia*, translation and foreword by Brian Massumi (Minneapolis: University of Minnesota Press, 1987).

189
Chapter 6 of Gilles Deleuze's *Cinema 1: The Movement-Image*, trans. Hugh Tomlinson and Barbara Habberjam (Minneapolis: University of Minnesota Press, 1986).

190
Pascal Bonitzer, "Bobines ou: le labyrinthe et la question du visage," in *Le Champ aveugle: Essais sur le réalisme au cinéma* (Paris: Cahiers du Cinéma/Gallimard, 1982).

191
Magritte provides a variant rationale for the apparent discrepancy in the painting: "The famous pipe. How people reproached me for it! And yet, could you stuff my pipe? No, it's just a representation, is it not? So if I had written on my picture 'This is a pipe,' I'd have been lying!" Harry Torczyner, *Magritte: Ideas and Images*, trans. Richard Miller (New York: H. N. Abrams, 1977), 118.

192

Jean-Luc Godard, *Jean-Luc Godard: Interviews*, ed. David Sterritt (Jackson: University Press of Mississippi, 1998), 129–130. There is an oscillation on Godard's part regarding the goal of reaching this pre-name condition: whether to have the opportunity of naming anew, or to dispense altogether with the name. In *King Lear*, the character played by Godard asserts: "I am not interested in names," and then, over a shot of a so-called flower, asks: "Do I need a name to see thy beauty?" My answer to this question is: "No." Does one need a name to resurrect that so-called flower? No; no name is invoked during the resurrection of that so-called flower in Godard's aforementioned film: its petals are simply reattached to it in backward motion. One also does not need a name to resurrect even a so-and-so animal. "Who are they who need a name to exist?" Ancient Egyptians who died physically needed a name so they could be resurrected: "Arise.... Thou shalt not perish. Thou hast been called by name. Thou hast been resurrected" (*Egyptian Book of the Dead*); physically dead mortals who are to be resurrected physically (and otherwise) need a name: "Lazarus, come out!" (John 11:43); and those who though then still among the living were as mortals, that is, as dead while physically alive, to be resurrected by Jesus Christ, the life (John 11:25), into humans who were solely and fully alive needed a name (Joseph of Arimathea?). Had Godard's film tried to resurrect neither a flower nor a theater play that became withdrawn following a surpassing disaster, but a human, then the inadequacy of this dismissal of the name would have become manifest to its director.

193

Philippe Nemo: "In *Totality and Infinity* you speak at great length of the face. It is one of your frequent themes. What does this phenomenology of the face, that is, this analysis of what happens when I look at the Other face to face, consist in and what is its purpose?" Emmanuel Levinas: "I do not know if one can speak of a 'phenomenology' of the face, since phenomenology describes what appears. So, too, I wonder if one can speak of a look turned toward the face, for the look is knowledge, perception. I think rather that access to the face is straightaway ethical." Emmanuel Levinas,

Ethics and Infinity: Conversations with Philippe Nemo, trans. Richard A. Cohen (Pittsburgh: Duquesne University Press, 1985), 85.

194
Emmanuel Levinas, *Totality and Infinity: An Essay on Exteriority*, trans. Alphonso Lingis (Pittsburgh: Duquesne University Press, 1969), 202.

195
The over-turn is a paradoxical turn since it is not gradual but discrete, a turn without turning, a turn that is not experienced as a turn, indeed that is not experienced *tout court*. My hyphenation of "over-turn" is to evoke, through association with another hyphenated "over," "voice-over," and thus cinema. It is as if during a film shoot, after the actor playing the dead or mad (that is, dead before dying) character turned in accordance with the director's prior instructions, the director said, "Cut," then commanded the actor to turn in the opposite direction, then, after the latter did, said, "Action": while the actor experienced the second, non-diegetic turn, the character he is playing, a dead or mad person, did not experience the reversal of his or her turn. Or it is as if the film camera, not shooting in master shots, crossed the *imaginary line*, this resulting in the reversal of the character's turn in the edited film. Given that the undead turned in response to being called and that he did not experience any turn in the opposite direction, he assumed that he must be moving toward the caller. "He had gone only two steps when his legs, of their own volition, refused to carry him farther. His body comprehended what his mind refused to accept" (Philip K. Dick, *Eye in the Sky*): his back still to the caller, he was moving away from her.

196
Louis Althusser, "Ideology and Ideological State Apparatuses (Notes towards an Investigation)," in *On Ideology*, 48.

197
For (the revised version of) my initial, more elaborate essay on dance, see "The Subtle Dancer" in the second

edition of my book *Over-Sensitivity* (Forthcoming Books, 2009), 79–105.

198

Similarly, even though I had collaborated in an untimely manner with David Lynch through the section on radical closure in the first edition of my book *Over-Sensitivity*, 1996, when I first watched his *Lost Highway*, 1997, I felt anxiety on seeing how closely the film matched what I had written.

199

Monochromatic intense colors facilitate suction into dance's realm of altered movement, space, and time; once encountered in that realm, they, as backdrops, maintain, through bringing to mind cinematic mattes, the impression that the dancer before them is not fully in the space—which moreover has a fractional dimension—where he or she ostensibly is.

200

In *Eureka* (1974), a film in which Ernie Gehr used archival footage taken from a streetcar in San Francisco in 1905, the boy in the back of the car that precedes the streetcar and that gradually recedes in the distance is by the same movement disappearing in the future in relation to the streetcar but also into the past from which the film detached him.

201

The auto-mobility of objects in dance's realm of altered movement, which is made possible by the immobilization of the dancers, is exemplified by that of the dancer's shoes (Powell and Pressburger's *The Red Shoes*) and the ground. *The Red Shoes* fails to show or imply that although unable to stop these auto-mobile slippers, the dancer can enter the freezing state, which would affect the shoes themselves with immobility.

202

In Busby Berkeley's films, the frequent flattening of the picture plane through the placement of the camera straight above the performers intimates their inability to create space. The figures of Berkeley are not real dancers and therefore do not cross into mirrors or other flat surfaces, but remain at their border. The dancer crosses the mirror, which has a dimension of two, to dance's fractional space, and moves in the latter by creating space at the pace of his or her movement (thus this space creation is rarely noticed).

203
When in *The Red Shoes* the other dancers go ahead with the performance despite the unexpected death of the principal ballerina moments before the parting of the curtain, the state of the dancer who hands the inexistent ballerina the red shoes, as well as of the other dancers, and of the audience must be the fetishistic one of disavowal: "I know very well, but all the same ...," more specifically: "I know very well that she is not here with the other dancers, but all the same I act as if she is." But since what this scene in *The Red Shoes* shows is the case whenever dancers are projected as subtle bodies in separate branches of dance's realm of altered body, movement, space, and time, a modicum of fetishistic disavowal is required for any dance of this kind in which more than one dancer participates.

204
Gilles Deleuze, *Cinema 1: The Movement-Image*, 4.

205
Ibid., 6.

206
Once the audience has had a chance to witness an obvious manifestation of the auto-mobility of objects in dance, perceiving it to be a facet of dance's realm of altered movement, body, silence, music, space, and time, the director can then show such auto-mobility in more subtle manners. In Charles Walters's *The Belle of New York*, the medium shot of Astaire and his partner dancing in the moving carriage, although ostensibly not showing auto-mobility (since in earlier shots we saw and in later shots we are going to see the horse pulling the carriage), hints at auto-mobility by not showing the horse. When dancing together in the streetcar, Astaire and his partner are doing so across the two separate branches of the realm of altered body, movement, space, and time into which

dance projected subtle versions of them, all the while, as a consequence of the auto-mobility of the carriage allowed by the dance, being detached from the horse that is ostensibly pulling the carriage. The auto-movement of objects allowed by dance provides an occasion for a manneristic motion of the one ostensibly pulling or pushing these objects.

207

This letter was sent to Christy Turlington, care of Ford Modeling Agency, 142 Green Street, New York, NY 10012.

208

Dancers did not have to wait for digital telepresence to be able to directly link non-contiguous spaces-times.

209

If someone could have said to a woman, "This is what you're going to look like in heaven," it was Aleksandr Sokurov to Isolda Dychauk, the actress who played the role of Margarete in his film *Faust* (2011). Having been told by someone that Faust is the one who killed her brother, Margarete hastens to visit him. But then, at his place, she proves reluctant to ask him, with whom she is becoming infatuated, whether he is the one who killed her brother; stammering, she asks him instead questions about various objects in his house. Is she embarrassed of appearing credulous to such a learned man? Or is it that she intuits that she should give both of them a chance—to have grace? And lo, these irrelevant questions are followed by a luminous shot of her face, a shot that shows her in heaven. This vision of Margarete as she is in heaven functions somewhat like the experience of "the Radiance of the Clear Light of Pure Reality" in the bardo of the moment of death (*chikhai bardo*). According to the *Bardo Thodol*, if while experiencing the Radiance of the Clear Light of Pure Reality the dead man recognizes it and that his "present intellect, in real nature void, not formed into anything as regards characteristics or colour, ... is the very Reality, ... the All-good Buddha," this "will cause the naked consciousness to be recognized as the Clear Light; and, ... recognizing one's own self [thus], one becometh permanently united with the Dharma-Kāya and Liberation will be certain." According to the *Bardo Thodol*, if the dead man fails to be liberated during this stage and the related following one of the *chikhai bardo*, during which he experiences the secondary Clear Light, then he will undergo the *chönyid bardo*, when the karmic apparitions appear. In Sokurov's film, Faust fails to respond felicitously to the vision of Margarete as she is in heaven, and so the next shot is back to both of them as they were before this rapture and she now asks him: "Was it you who killed my brother?" And he answers, "Yes, I killed him."

210

In Terence Fisher's *Horror of Dracula* (1958), Doctor Van Helsing warns Arthur Holmwood: "This is not Lucy, the sister you loved. It's only her shell, possessed and corrupted by the evil of Dracula."

211

In my book *Over-Sensitivity*, I proposed that Francis Bacon would have been a fitting artist to direct a remake of *Invasion of the Body Snatchers*, for both his work and that novel deal with radical closure and the irruption of unworldly entities in the latter. The three figures in Bacon's triptychs of portraits and self-portraits present the following three different modes: one figure is the model compacted to a concentrate that would "come across directly onto the nervous system," short-circuiting illustration; the second figure is Bacon's illustration of the model's portrait made by the universe at the radical closure's event horizon; and the third figure is in some cases Bacon's illustration of the becoming similar to the worldly model of the unworldly imposter who irrupted in the radical closure, and in other cases what irrupted fully formed, outside of any direct action of Bacon, in the radical closure he constructed through painting, and in other cases still Bacon's illustration of the model in the radical closure as an alien since he or she is no longer a monad and hence no longer enfolds everyone else and everything in the world. Therefore, a model who not only cannot recognize herself in one of the figures of a Bacon triptych, but even feels repulsion toward it, is not to be automatically criticized as of limited aesthetic judgment.

212
David Sylvester, *The Brutality of Fact: Interviews with Francis Bacon*, 3rd ed. (New York: Thames and Hudson, 1987), 146.

213
Paul Gauguin writes in his journals: "The idea occurred to me to do his [Van Gogh's] portrait while he was painting the still-life he loved so much—some ploughs. When the portrait [*Van Gogh Painting Sunflowers*] was finished, he said to me: 'It is certainly I, but it's I gone mad'" (*The Intimate Journals of Paul Gauguin* [London: KPI, 1985], 12). I would think that Van Gogh, who cut off his ear the next day, painted *Self-Portrait with Bandaged Ear and Pipe* and/or *Self-Portrait with Bandaged Ear* as a defense against Gauguin's valid portrait, which could not be countered simply by invoking some asylum doctor's diagnosis that Van Gogh's "condition has greatly improved" (the quoted words are from Dr. Urpar's certificate of May 7, 1889, http://www.vangoghletters.org/vg/documentation.html).

214
Auguste Rodin, *Rodin on Art*, translated from the French of Paul Gsell by Romilly Fedden (New York: Horizon, 1971), 75–76.

215
Leonard Susskind, "Black Holes and the Information Paradox," *Scientific American* 276, no. 4 (April 1997): 55. On gravitational time dilation, see also Kip S. Thorne, *Black Holes and Time Warps: Einstein's Outrageous Legacy* (New York: W. W. Norton, 1994): "Near a black hole gravitational time dilation is enormous: If the hole weighs 10 times as much as the Sun, then time will flow 6 million times more slowly at 1 centimeter height above the hole's horizon than far from its horizon; and right at the horizon, the flow of time will be completely stopped" (100).

216
"Albert Einstein ... wrote to a friend, 'The past, present and future are only illusions, even if stubborn ones.' Einstein's startling conclusion stems directly from his special theory of relativity, which denies any absolute, universal significance

to the present moment. According to the theory, simultaneity is relative. Two events that occur at the same moment if observed from one reference frame may occur at different moments if viewed from another. Such mismatches make a mockery of any attempt to confer special status on the present moment, for whose 'now' does that moment refer to? If you and I were in relative motion, an event that I might judge to be in the as yet undecided future might for you already exist in the fixed past. The most straightforward conclusion is that both past and future are fixed. For this reason, physicists prefer to think of time as laid out in its entirety—a timescape, analogous to a landscape—with all past and future events located there together. It is a notion sometimes referred to as block time. Completely absent from this description of nature is anything that singles out a privileged special moment as the present or any process that would systematically turn future events into present, then past, events. In short, the time of the physicist does not pass or flow" (Paul Davies, "That Mysterious Flow," *Scientific American* 287, no. 3 [September 2002]: 41–42).

217
Dōgen: "An ancient Buddha said: 'For the time being stand on top of the highest peak.... / For the time being three heads and eight arms. / For the time being an eight- or sixteen-foot body....' 'For the time being' here means time itself is being, and all being is time. A golden sixteen-foot body is time.... 'Three heads and eight arms' is time.... Yet an ordinary person who does not understand buddha-dharma may hear the words *the time-being* this way: 'For a while I was three heads and eight arms.... Even though the mountains and rivers still exist, I have already passed them.... Those mountains and rivers are as distant from me as heaven is from earth.' It is not that simple. At the time the mountains were climbed and the rivers crossed, you were present. Time is not separate from you, and as you are present, time does not go away" ("The Time-Being" [*Uji*], in *Moon in a Dewdrop: Writings of Zen Master Dōgen*, 76–77).

218
Alain Robbe-Grillet, *Project for a Revolution in New York: A Novel* (New York, Grove Press, 1972), 1–3.

219

If one considers a black hole as a radical closure, then there are two sorts of possible photographs that are specific to it: the freezing and flattening at its *gateless gate*, the event horizon; and the photographs, shot by no one and no camera, that irrupt "in" it (by *objective chance* the unworldly photograph, taken by no camera, that irrupts inside the black hole may show the same image as the "photograph," also taken by no camera, of the astronaut frozen and flattened at the black hole's event horizon).

220

And there is a sort of video that is specific to a radical closure: the video that irrupts in it without being shot by anyone within it. In David Lynch's *Lost Highway*, the circumstance that Fred Madison and his wife twice omitted setting the alarm system on the day preceding their reception of the anonymous videotape showing shots of the interior of their house leaves open the possibility that they are dealing with an unlawful entry through the door or window by someone who then took these shots with a camera. The two detectives who come to investigate the case ask Fred to thenceforth activate his alarm system. Therefore we can assume that (unlike in the script, where he again fails to activate the alarm) he did so, and, moreover, since he does not hear the alarm sound, that no unlawful entry took place through any of the entrances of the house, and, consequently, that no camera served to take the new video shots of the inside of the house—the videotape, unworldly, shot by no one, irrupted in the radical closure. Similarly, it is quite possible that the tracking shot of the highway at night, with the yellow broken lines illuminated by the headlights of a moving car, which is first seen in *Blue Velvet*, 1986, and which accompanies the opening credits sequence and the ending of *Lost Highway*, 1997, was not filmed for the latter film but irrupted in it from the earlier one. Since the highway of *Lost Highway* is a cinematic shot from an earlier film rather than a road, it cannot be used to flee somewhere else—unless the person flees his pursuers not farther along the highway but through (his double's?) irruption into the shot of the highway (that is why, while being unsettled, I am not surprised that when the Mystery Man, standing next to Fred Madison, hands the wounded man on the desert sand a portable pocket television, that monitor shows the Mystery Man handing a portable pocket television while standing next to Madison, that is, as an image).

221
For example, David Lynch's "Paintings and Drawings," Touko Museum of Contemporary Art, Tokyo, January 12–27, 1991; and *David Lynch: Sala Parpalló – Palau dels Scala, Mayo–Junio 1992, Diputación Provincial de Valencia* (Valencia; Sala Parpalló: Edicions Alfons el Magnànim, Institució Valenciana d'Estudis i Investigació).

222
Here are two examples of the artist as producer: Warhol, who simply turned on the camera and let it shoot what was in front of it until the end of the film roll, or else assigned others to make the films or the silkscreens; and Robbe-Grillet, who produced radical closures in which images that are ostensibly those of others (Magritte, Rauschenberg, etc.) irrupted (in the process introducing singularly unfamiliar elements amid his recurrent imagery).

223
One did not have to wait for digital technology (with the absence of generation loss it makes possible) to question the veracity and historicity of photographs, their indexical function.

224
In Francis Bacon's work, painting foregrounds or at least addresses its being a two-dimensional medium not so much in a self-reflexive manner but through dealing with the flattening of the figure (from the reference frame of an outside observer) at the border of the radical closures he establishes.

225
Paintings such as *Triptych March 1974*, where the figure is shown holding a camera next to its face, presumably in the act of taking a photograph, are exceptional in Francis Bacon's work.

226

While the figure that is seemingly divided into two at the juncture of the panel in Francis Bacon's *Study from the Human Body*, 1981, is not actually dislocated but just represented and viewed from two reference frames, when painting it the painter had to mentally place himself and when looking at it the spectator finds himself paradoxically in two reference frames simultaneously: outside the radical closure, from which he would see the two-dimensional figure, but also inside the radical closure, where he would see the three-dimensional figure.

227

Henri Bergson, *Matter and Memory*, 134.

228

Kip S. Thorne, *Black Holes and Time Warps: Einstein's Outrageous Legacy*, 52.

229

Henri Bergson, *Matter and Memory*, 88, and, more generally, "The Two Forms of Memory." Cf.: "There are, we have said, two memories which are profoundly distinct: the one, fixed in the organism, is nothing else but the complete set of intelligently constructed mechanisms which ensure the appropriate reply to the various possible demands. This memory enables us to adapt ourselves to the present situation; through it the actions to which we are subject prolong themselves into reactions that are sometimes accomplished, sometimes merely nascent, but always more or less appropriate. Habit rather than memory, it acts our past experience but does not call up its image. The other is the true memory.... It retains and ranges alongside of each other all our states in the order in which they occur, leaving to each fact its place and, consequently, marking its date, truly moving in the past and not, like the first, in an ever renewed present" (ibid., 150–151).

230

Ibid., 152.

231

Ibid.

232

Henri Bergson: "A human being who should dream his life instead of living it would no doubt thus keep before his eyes at each moment the infinite multitude of the details of his past history. And, conversely, the man who should repudiate this memory with all that it begets would be continually acting his life instead of truly representing it to himself: a conscious *automaton*, he would follow the lead of useful habits which prolong into an appropriate reaction the stimulation received" (ibid., 155; my italics).

233

Gilles Deleuze, *Cinema 2: The Time-Image*, trans. Hugh Tomlinson and Robert Galeta (London: Continuum, 2005), 76.

234

Henri Bergson: "Our duration is not merely one instant replacing another; if it were, there would never be anything but the present.... Duration is the continuous progress of the past which gnaws into the future and which swells as it advances. And as the past grows without ceasing, so also there is no limit to its preservation. Memory, as we have tried to prove [*Matter and Memory*, chapters 2 and 3], is not a faculty of putting away recollections in a drawer, or of inscribing them in a register. There is no register, no drawer; there is not even, properly speaking, a faculty, for a faculty works intermittently, when it will or when it can, whilst the piling up of the past upon the past goes on without relaxation. In reality, the past is preserved by itself, automatically. In its entirety, probably, it follows us at every instant.... The cerebral mechanism is arranged just so as to drive back into the unconscious almost the whole of this past, and to admit beyond the threshold only that which can cast light on the present situation or further the action now being prepared—in short, only that which can give *useful* work" (*Creative Evolution*, authorized translation by Arthur Mitchell [New York: H. Holt and Company, 1911], 4–5).

235

Since "signals and other causal influences cannot travel faster than light, ... for a given event E, the set of events that lie on or inside the past light cone of E would also be the set of all events that could send a signal that would have time to reach E and influence it in some way.... Likewise, the set of events that lie on or inside the *future* light cone of E would also be the set of events that could receive a signal sent out from the position and time of E, so the future light cone contains all the events that could potentially be causally influenced by E. Events which lie neither in the past or future light cone of E cannot influence or be influenced by E in relativity" (*Wikipedia*'s "Light Cone" entry).

236
"When British physicist Stephen Hawking ... studied the quantum theory of electromagnetism near black holes, he found that black holes actually emit radiation.... How can black holes emit radiation? ... The answer lies in quantum uncertainty. All over spacetime the quantum electromagnetic field is undergoing ... little negative-energy quantum fluctuations. Normally ... the negative-energy photons disappear as quickly as they form. But near the horizon of a black hole, it is possible for such a photon to form outside the hole and cross into it. Once inside, it is actually viable: it is possible to find trajectories for photons inside the horizon that have negative total energy. So such a photon can just stay inside, and that leaves its positive-energy partner outside on its own. It ... becomes one of the photons of the Hawking radiation. In this picture, *nothing actually crosses the horizon from inside to out*. Instead, the negative-energy photon falls in, freeing the positive-energy photon. The net result of this is that the hole loses mass: the negative-energy photon makes a negative contribution to the mass of the hole when it goes in." Bernard F. Schutz, *Gravity from the Ground Up* (Cambridge; New York: Cambridge University Press, 2003), 304 (my italics).

237
This is the case if we consider the black hole part of the universe.

238
Jorge Luis Borges, *Collected Fictions*, trans. Andrew Hurley (New York: Viking, 1998), 327.

239
Leibniz, *Monadology* § 66–68.

240
Kip S. Thorne, *Black Holes and Time Warps: Einstein's Outrageous Legacy*, 33.

241
Cf. "Composites" in the revised and expanded edition of my book *(Vampires): An Uneasy Essay on the Undead in Film*: "The living person is a composite that dissociates in death-as-undeath or during some states of altered consciousness first into separate subunits that are themselves composites, most of them uglier than the original one, then into elements, becoming alien. Each of us is common, not alien, both because each of us is a composite of all the others, even of those who lived erstwhile and who are long dead, and because each of us is part of the composite that constitutes the others. That is why we do not find others or for that matter ourselves alien, and that is why they too do not find us alien. In certain states of altered consciousness, though, we see the dead, people who have become not merely uglier, but alien, and that is because they are no longer composites (the withdrawal of the cathexis of the world).... The double is not the other, but I divested of all others. That is why whenever I encounter him, even in a crowded public place, I feel I am alone with him, *alone with the alone*; he embodies the divestment from the world. That is why encountering the double is such a desolate experience, and is a premonition of death with its bereavement from others and the rest of the world" (173–174).

242
In Bacon's triptych *Two Figures Lying on a Bed with Attendants*, 1968, the gazes of the left panel's seated human figure looking right, of the center panel's recumbent couple, and of the right panel's seated human figure looking left, although sharply separated by the panels' frames, are aligned, suggesting that the figures perceive each other or at least are aware of each other. Triptychs or diptychs with figures (other than dancers) whose gazes or gestures are aligned across the various panels suggest a monadic ontology (triptychs and diptychs have in monadic ontology a raison

d'être). In the aforementioned Bacon triptych, the left panel's human figure does not at all perceive the bird-like creature visible to us in the same panel, for the latter is an unworldly entity, thus incompossible with the world expressed by the monad, though allowed by that expressed world's radical closure. There is intra-action among the monadic figures that enfold the same world; there is no relation between the monadic figure and the unworldly entity that irrupts in a radical closure; and there is interaction between the unworldly entities that irrupt in a radical closure.

243
Friedrich Nietzsche, *The Gay Science: With a Prelude in German Rhymes and an Appendix of Songs*, ed. Bernard Williams; trans. Josefine Nauckhoff; poems trans. Adrian Del Caro (Cambridge; New York: Cambridge University Press, 2001), no. 166, 135.

244
Jean-François Lyotard, *The Differend: Phrases in Dispute*, trans. Georges Van Den Abbeele (Minneapolis: University of Minnesota Press, 1988), no. 100, 65–66: "The conjunction *and* (*and so forth*, *and so on*) ... signals a simple addition, the apposition of one term with the other, nothing more. [Erich] Auerbach [in *Mimesis*] turns this into a characteristic of 'modern' style, paratax, as opposed to classical syntax. Conjoined by *and*, phrases or events follow each other, but their succession does not obey a categorial order (*because*; *if, then*; *in order to*; *although* ...). Paratax ... connotes the abyss of Not-Being which opens between phrases.... Instead of *and*, and assuring the same paratactic function, there can be a comma, or nothing."

245
This is not an issue in the Qur'ān since "They killed him [Christ, Jesus the son of Mary, the Apostle of God] not, nor crucified him, but so it was made to appear to them" (4:157) and since "God raised him up unto Himself" (4:158).

246
Rainer Maria Rilke, *The Notebooks of Malte Laurids Brigge*, 8–9.

247
Ibid., 9.

248
Ibid., 10.

249
Ibid., 13–15.

Jalal Toufic is a thinker and a mortal to death. He was born in 1962 in Beirut or Baghdad and died before dying in 1989 in Evanston, Illinois. Many of his books, most of which were published by Forthcoming Books, are available for download as PDF files from his website: http://www.jalaltoufic.com. He was most recently a participant in the Sharjah Biennial 11, the 9th Shanghai Biennale, Documenta 13, "Art in the Auditorium III" (Whitechapel Gallery ...) and "Six Lines of Flight" (San Francisco Museum of Modern Art); and he was a guest in 2011 of the Artists-in-Berlin Program of the DAAD.

Jalal Toufic
Forthcoming
Second edition

First edition published in 2000 by Atelos.

ISBN 978-3-95679-055-3

Publisher
Sternberg Press

Series editors
Julieta Aranda, Brian Kuan Wood, Anton Vidokle

Managing editors
Kaye Cain-Nielsen, Mariana Silva

Copyediting and proofreading
Max Bach, Kaye Cain-Nielsen, Rachel Ichniowski

Design
Kloepfer-Ramsey-Kwon

For further information, contact journal@e-flux.com.
www.e-flux.com/journal

Sternberg Press
Caroline Schneider
Karl-Marx-Allee 78
D-10243 Berlin
www.sternberg-press.com

This book is available for download free of charge (as a PDF) from the author's website: www.jalaltoufic.com.